IGNORANCE, CONFIDENCE,

AND

FILTHY RICH FRIENDS

IGNORANCE, CONFIDENCE,

AND

FILTHY RICH FRIENDS

THE BUSINESS ADVENTURES OF MARK TWAIN, CHRONIC SPECULATOR AND ENTREPRENEUR

PETER KRASS

John Wiley & Sons, Inc.

Published by John Wiley & Sons, Inc., Hoboken, New Jersey.
Published simultaneously in Canada.

Wiley Bicentennial Logo: Richard J. Pacifico

For general information on our other products and services or for technical support, please
contact our Customer Care Department within the United States at (800) 762-2974,
outside the United States at (317) 572-3993 or fax (317) 572-4002.

Wiley also publishes its books in a variety of electronic formats. Some content that appears in
print may not be available in electronic books. For more information about Wiley products,
visit our web site at www.wiley.com.

Library of Congress Cataloging-in-Publication Data:

Krass, Peter.
    Ignorance, confidence, and filthy rich friends : the business adventures of
 Mark Twain, chronic speculator and entrepreneur / Peter Krass.
       p.   cm.
    ISBN 978-0-471-93337-3 (cloth)
    1. Twain, Mark, 1835–1910—Knowledge—Commerce.   2. Authors, American—19th
century—Biography.   3. United States—Commerce—History—19th century.   I.
Title.
PS1342.C65K73   2007
818'.409—dc22   2006030738

Printed in the United States of America

10 9 8 7 6 5 4 3 2 1

For Diana

CONTENTS

*All you need in this life is ignorance
and confidence, and then Success is sure.*

—Mark Twain, 1887

chapter one

EARLY HARD KNOCKS ON THE ROAD TO RICHES AND FAME

"To me, merit is everything—in fact, the only thing."

In his youth, Sam Clemens's views on business began to take shape as his family struggled to fight off poverty born of his father's business mistakes and the United States' tumultuous business cycles that resulted in frequent financial panics. From 1848 to 1850, Clemens (a.k.a. Mark Twain) was apprenticed to the irascible publisher of the Hannibal Courier *newspaper, which gave him a bird's-eye view of local industry and served as his business education. He then took a series of typesetting jobs that allowed him to travel to St. Louis, New York, and Philadelphia, before returning homeward in 1855. In this formative period—the first 20 years of his life—Clemens became intolerant of haphazard business methods and was keenly focused on his own skills and production.*

The world knows Mark Twain as a renowned author who churned out such classics as *The Adventures of Huckleberry Finn*, *Life on the Mississippi*, and *The Prince and the Pauper*; however, in addition to being a writer, Twain considered himself a hard-nosed, visionary businessman. In fact, more than half of his life was consumed by moneymaking pursuits, which often resulted in book projects being neglected. Not so surprisingly, his roller-coaster business dealings are quite illuminating and entertaining, inspired many a character in his books, and breathe a human quality into the legendary Twain himself.

Born Samuel Langhorne Clemens (the name he always used in personal and business correspondence and which will be used here), before the age of 30 Clemens was a printer's apprentice, a typesetter, a riverboat pilot, a precious metals miner, and a speculator. After he laid his literary golden egg in midlife and took the pseudonym Mark Twain, Clemens pursued his own inventions that included gadgets for everyday use. He was also a venture capitalist who supported other inventors; a Wall Street investor who made a fortune more than once; a media mogul who founded his own publishing firm; and a pioneer in salesmanship. Clemens certainly was not lacking when it came to business and investment opportunities. Having been born on November 30, 1835, he came of age during the Industrial Revolution; he witnessed and experienced the excesses, pitfalls, and successes of the epic, freewheeling, economic boom of the time. And, embracing the capitalist spirit, he took advantage of the plethora of opportunities this period in history presented.

But before examining his rollicking business career—which was wrought with daring adventure, blind ambition, and insightful instruction—one particular point needs to be made about how important the business of business was to Clemens: He actually set aside writing *Huckleberry Finn* to focus on his investments and inventions. It took him from 1876 to 1883 to write what would become a definitive classic for all eternity.

So what would propel Clemens to neglect his writing? What critical events and circumstances shaped his Robber Baronesque perspective on money and business? Well, he has already been psychoanalyzed to the nth degree by overzealous literary critics, namely because the dueling alternate personalities of Samuel L. Clemens and Mark Twain are ripe for analysis. Certainly, he was a complex man who was almost schizophrenic in the way he could be outrageously funny one moment and stern-faced gloomy the next, and in how he was torn between being an enlightened man of letters and a materialistic capital-ist. However, here's what his primal drive boils down to: He was motivated by a relentless desire to accumulate great wealth. The source of his sometimes unhealthy compulsion is easily traced to his boyhood, when he justifiably developed an irra-tional fear of poverty.

His Father's Dream of Being a Land Baron Curses the Clemens Family

There is a maxim about learning at the "school of hard knocks," which conveniently either justifies what appear to be unjust early experiences one goes through before becom-ing successful, or is a gentle way of explaining that someone was an idiot but finally smartened up. The former applies to young Clemens, only it was his own father knocking him and the family down with a *financial* brick. This vignette begins in the backwoods and backwaters of north central Tennessee, not far from Jamestown, where self-educated lawyer turned modest farmer John Marshall Clemens envisioned himself a land baron.

Even though he had a growing family to support—his wife Jane Lampton and three children at that time—every penny he earned he put into land, and he eventually purchased over 70,000 acres for more than $400, a princely sum circa 1830.[1] An earnest, preacher-looking man, the studious Marshall fig-ured the land to be rich in natural resources. "He had always said that the land would not become valuable in his time but that it would be a commodious provision for his children some day," Clemens wrote in his autobiography. "It contained coal, copper, iron and timber, and he said that in the course of time railways would pierce to that region and then the property would be property in fact as well as in name."

Suffering from visions of grandeur, Marshall was convinced his children would inherit great wealth. "My father's dying charge was, 'Cling to the land and wait; let nothing beguile it away from you,'" Clemens recalled. "My mother's favorite cousin, James Lampton, who figures in *The Gilded Age* as Colonel Sellers, always said of that land—and said it with blazing enthusiasm too—'There's millions in it—millions!' It is true that he always said that about everything—and was always mistaken too, but this time he was right; which shows that a man who goes around with a prophecy-gun ought never to get discouraged. If he will keep up his heart and fire at everything he sees he is bound to hit something by and by."[2] Decades later, according to Clemens, some oil was discovered on the land, but this was long after it would do the family any good. Such was cruel fate.

Because the family had high expectations for the land, Clemens concluded it was, ironically speaking, a curse: "Thus with the very kindest intentions in the world toward us he laid the heavy curse of prospective wealth upon our shoulders. He went to his grave in the full belief that he had done us a kindness. It was a woeful mistake but fortunately he never knew it."[3] He never knew it because he mercifully died in 1847. This land debacle affected Clemens to such a degree that decades later, in his autobiography, he went on a prolonged tirade that covered several pages:

> I shall have occasion to mention this land again now and then, as I go along, for it influenced our life in one way or another during more than a generation. Whenever things grew dark it rose and put out its hopeful Sellers hand and cheered us up and said, "Do not be afraid—trust in me—wait." It kept us hoping and hoping during forty years and forsook us at last. It put our energies to sleep and made visionaries of us—dreamers and indolent. We were always going to be rich next year—no occasion to work. It is good to begin life poor; it is good to begin life rich—these are wholesome; but to begin it poor and prospectively rich! The man who has not experienced it cannot imagine the curse of it.[4]

The land would haunt the family in a perversely funny way. At one point, the Clemens children were offered $200,000 for their Tennessee property by a prospective buyer whose plan was to turn it into a "wine-growing" district. After signing the papers, Clemens forwarded them to his older brother Orion, who had unfortunately gotten religion: "I sent the contracts and things to Orion for his signature, he being one of the three heirs. But they arrived at a bad time—in a doubly bad time, in fact. The temperance virtue was temporarily upon him in strong force and he wrote and said that he would not be a party to debauching the country with wine."[5] Of course, the other Clemens children now felt like debauching themselves with wine, thanks to Orion's blind righteousness.

Clemens Learns How to Turn Failure into Profit by Having Fun with It

Desperate to find the silver lining, Clemens later realized that he had, at the very least, through his father's failures, discovered some colorful characters to include in his 1873 novel, *The Gilded Age*, co-written with Charles Dudley Warner. "If any penny of cash ever came out of my father's wise investment but that [the book], I have no recollection of it," he wrote. "No, I am overlooking a detail. It furnished me a field for Sellers [a flamboyant character in *The Gilded Age*] and a book. Out of my half of the book I got $15,000 or $20,000; out of the play I got $75,000 or $80,000—just about a dollar an acre. It is curious; I was not alive when my father made the investment, therefore he was not intending any partiality; yet I was the only member of the family that ever profited by it."[6]

Marshall Clemens's investment in land that would yield no return was merely the first misstep in a series of financial blunders that would drive the family into poverty. In the early 1830s Marshall tried his hand at owning a general store, farming, and working as a postmaster, until, facing failure, in 1834 he moved the family to Florida, Missouri, a village 30 miles west of the mighty Mississippi River. Here Samuel L. Clemens was born on November 30, 1835, two months premature, a sickly infant, but a fighter. And here his sadly optimistic father bought a half-share in another general store—it was merely another opportunity to fail. Land was cheap, too—$1.25 an acre if bought in bulk—as the government sold off the Louisiana Purchase, which presented yet another chance for Marshall to mercilessly overextend himself. Betting little Florida would eventually host a railroad depot, he bought hundreds of surrounding acres. Unfortunately, the railroad was built through Paris, Missouri, 10 miles away. Ah, location, location, location.

It Becomes Clear That Incurring Too Much Debt is Totally Destructive

Short on credit and long on debt, late in 1839 Marshall moved his family to Hannibal, Missouri, on the Mississippi River, a hundred miles north of St. Louis. At the time, Clemens was one of five surviving children, the family having lost two. There was Orion, born in 1825; Pamela Ann, born in 1827; Benjamin, born in 1832, but who would die in 1842; Sam; and his one younger sibling, Henry, born in 1838. Often confined to his bed the first three years of his life, here on the Mississippi Clemens would bloom. Thin, red-haired, and prone to moodiness and vicious nightmares, young Sam was viewed as high-strung and aloof. However, he did enjoy a good prank, which included putting snakes and bats in his mother's sewing basket. In turn, she told him brutal tales of Indian massacres. Growing up with a dour, austere father, he relished her stories and those told by the black slaves. He became fascinated with their language, songs, and spirituality. A dreamy kid, his imagination was also tantalized by the expanse of the prairie, the powerful river, and even the way the moonlight played across the landscape.

By the 1840s the river was teeming with life, which brought adventure and tales from afar. The first steamboat on the Mississippi River was the *New Orleans*, which was built in Pittsburgh in 1811. Three years later only 21 steamboats passed through New Orleans itself, a major trading port, but in1833 the number ballooned to 1,200, as the steamboat age arrived on the Mississippi. Convinced that Hannibal, a bustling yet modest town of 1,000 residents, would boom thanks to the steamboat, Marshall, who had sold his Florida, Missouri property, bought a 9,000-square-foot city block for a mere $7,000. He established yet another general store, investing $2,000 in goods. Despite the prospects offered by the town, he was now so deep in debt—and saddled with a wife and five children—that financially he would never see the light of day.

It didn't help that credit was tight due to the United States' banking system being in complete disarray, which resulted in disruptive financial panics and economic downturns. The blame for that chaos has been pinned on President Andrew Jackson's economic policies, which contributed to the inflationary boom of the mid-1830s, to the commercial and financial panic of 1837, and (according to various conspiracy theories) may have had a role in plunging the United States into a prolonged depression lasting from 1839 to 1843. During this tumultuous economic period, only state-chartered banks existed in what is called the Free Banking Era (circa 1837–1862), apparently "free" because the banks freely went under—their average lifespan only five years—and about a third of them couldn't redeem their notes. With money extremely tight, Marshall was faced with bankruptcy in 1846 and creditors seized the family home.

Fortunately, Marshall had built a reputation as an honest man. He became Justice of the Peace and then was appointed clerk of the Surrogate Court, a well-paying job. It was perversely fitting that soon after he started collecting a decent paycheck, on March 24, 1847, he died from pneumonia, which he contracted because he had earnestly insisted on going out in bad weather to conduct business. "Thus our splendid new fortune was snatched from us and we were in the depths of poverty again," Clemens reflected ruefully.[7]

It also meant that the boy's formal education was over. In 1840 he had attended a dame school, which was simply women teaching classes from their home. The next year, he attended a "Select School" which was held in a church basement. Hardly inspirational, the curriculum involved the typical Puritan method of learning by rote; however, Clemens did learn to read, which opened up the whole world to him and sparked his desire to educate himself. Throughout his life he would be a voracious reader, absorbing everything he could about history, culture, language, and business.

With the family now destitute, his older sister Pamela gave piano lessons to keep food in the pantry, but it was not enough. At age 11, Sam Clemens was about to be thrown into the working world.

Clemens Determines That It's Best to Trust No One and to Form Your Own Opinion through Investigation

One positive result of his father's failures: Clemens trusted no one, especially when it came to business partnerships, and was determined to rely on himself. His cagey attitude was more than apparent nine years after his father's death, when, in the summer of 1856, while working as a typesetter, he dreamed of going to Brazil. Specifically, the 21-year-old wanted to investigate an Amazon vegetable rumored to have amazing healing powers that he had read about and was now interested in importing. This wondrous vegetable would be none other than coca leaves, the rather key ingredient for cocaine, which certainly brought many an unscrupulous man riches.

Initially, he considered letting his potential business partner, a Mr. Ward, go alone, but soon thought better of it. "My confidence in human nature does not extend quite that far," Clemens wrote to his younger brother Henry. "I won't depend upon Ward's judgment, or anybody's else—I want to see with my own eyes, and form my own opinion. . . . Ma knows my determination . . ."[8] He was determined to rely on himself, one of his maxims being "To me, merit is everything—in fact, the only thing. All else is dross." (Going to the dictionary here, *dross* is defined as trivial.) In other words, he was determined to succeed on his own personal merit; there would be no underhanded wheeling and dealing, no ass-kissing the powers that be, no buying success. In this case, however, the adventure never came to pass.

As for a negative consequence of his family's absolute destitution, there was Clemens's phobic fear of poverty, which would, in turn, cause him to stumble financially in his own manic pursuit of wealth as he attempted to compensate for his father's failure. Yes, it would be a vicious, repetitive cycle as he made some of the same mistakes his father had. But in 10 years he would have a taste of the good life, which would further whet his appetite for the finer things. To fund his high living, he would occasionally find himself in debt; however, thanks to his father's bungling, he hated being in debt to anyone for any amount and would immediately pay it off. When the catastrophic financial hammer eventually fell on him during the great depression of the 1890s, he would refuse to declare bankruptcy as his father had, and would resurrect himself. But that's a story yet to come.

Sickened by His Father's Haphazard Ways, Clemens Becomes a Perfectionist at Work

Properly cursed by his father, Clemens could now make his way in the world. To help support the family, in 1847 and 1848 he worked at a grocery store, a bookstore, an apothecary shop, and a blacksmith shop, and was quite successful at each—successful at getting himself fired. Apathy, an uncontrollable sweet tooth, and helping himself to his employers' goods did not help. In June 1848, his exasperated mother apprenticed him to Joseph P. Ament, publisher of the Hannibal *Courier* and, according to young Clemens, "a diminutive chunk of human meat."[9] Clearly, he was not endeared to the man, but the apprenticeship saved his mother the expense of feeding a growing teenager. At first, Clemens was a mere errand boy charged with sweeping the shop floor, but then he learned to set type, a marketable skill he would soon peddle to pay for an adventurous journey to the east coast.

At the age of 13—already sporting his signature unruly tuft of reddish-brown hair, furrowed brow, and piercing gray eyes—Clemens was fortunate enough to find himself at one of the major crossroads of commerce: the newspaper. Almost 300 years prior, in 1451, Johannes Gutenberg had used a press to print a classic German poem, and in 1690 the first newspaper appeared in the United States, *Publick Occurrences Both Foreign and Domestick*, published in Boston, but not until the 1800s would eco-demographic dynamics create an environment in which the U.S. newspaper industry could flourish. Throughout the 1800s the country witnessed a rise of both urban centers and the middle class, along with increased literacy; democracy, capitalism, and the accompanying need for information became strongly rooted. Beginning in the late 1840s, the telegraph disseminated information instantly, and technology had advanced to a degree that allowed for the cheap, mass production of printed products.

As a typesetter, Clemens was perfectly positioned to absorb not only the usual blood-and-guts news items, but the various micro and macro forces behind the business of business. Always hungry for knowledge, he learned who was manufacturing what, who imported, who exported, which industries were in decline, and which were booming. At the same time, as he took

For this daguerreotype made in 1851 or 1852, Clemens already had his signature bushy hair and critical eye. (COURTESY OF THE MARK TWAIN HOUSE & MUSEUM, HARTFORD, CT)

in the big picture, the nature of typesetting molded the boy into an exacting—you might say anal—perfectionist who paid attention to details such as grammar, punctuation, and font styles. To be able to grasp the big picture as well as the minutiae would benefit both his writing and his aspirations of winning fortune.

A Disciplined Use of Personal Journals Yields a Number of Benefits

As a young man, Clemens's attention to detail immediately manifested itself in the personal journals he kept. In his first, from 1855, he jotted down his clothing laundry list—nothing special there, except that the exacting young man who was a stickler for good writing used semicolons. In the same journal, he also noted everything from his personal to-do lists to how many dogs were killed in town, from his personal observations of people's characteristics—a turned-up pug nose "denotes vanity"—to real estate transactions.[10] These journals packed with information were key to his success as he used them to manage his daily life and as a reference tool for his writing and business.

Clemens escaped the irascible Mr. Ament in September 1850, when his brother Orion—who resembled a stern Abraham Lincoln, yet moderately more handsome—bought the Hannibal *Journal*, the *Courier's* competitor, and immediately stole away his younger brother. Orion hired Clemens to set type and dabble in reporting, but the arrangement would quickly test the ridiculously idealistic notion of brotherly love, resembling more closely the relationship between Cain and Abel. Somehow the adventurous, impetuous Clemens lasted with the exceedingly righteous, prudent, and otherwise boring Orion for over two years. "I was educated not only in the common school at Hannibal but also in my brother Orion's newspaper office," he reflected, "where I served in all capacities, including staff work. My literature attracted the town's attention 'but not its admiration' (my brother's testimony)."[11]

Although Orion's righteousness was grating at times, Clemens respected his character: "I will also remark that his sincerity was never doubted; his truthfulness was never doubted; and in matters of business and money his honesty was never questioned. Notwithstanding his for-ever-recurring caprices and changes, his principles were high, always high, and absolutely unshakable." Character was everything to Clemens.

Orion's practical business acumen was another matter. After he bought the newspaper for $500, which he borrowed at 10 percent interest, Orion then "reduced the subscription price of the paper from two dollars to one dollar. He reduced the rates for advertising in about the same proportion and thus he created one absolute and unassailable certainty—to wit: that the business would never pay him a single cent of profit."[12] With the newspaper struggling, by the spring of 1853 Clemens was ready to abandon stagnant Hannibal and see the world.

Clemens Is Acutely Self-Aware of His Strengths and Weaknesses and Is Not Afraid to Admit Them

The first stop was a real romantic humdinger: St. Louis, where, in June, Clemens took a job setting type for a weekly newspaper. He lived with his sister Pamela, who had married William Moffett, a prominent resident of the city. After two months, it was to New York City, where he arrived on the morning of August 24. To get there, he had to take a steamboat, a train, a stagecoach, two more trains, then a steamer across Lake Erie, and another train to Albany, where he took a steamer down the Hudson River to New York City. At the time, the city boasted a population of over 500,000 and was a true melting pot— within a couple years more than a half of the population would originate from outside the U.S.[13] The explosive growth gave rise to the vicious slums of Five Points, labor unrest, and political corruption. There were so many homeless people that over a six-month period in 1853, some 25,000 people sought shelter in police department precincts.[14]

In spite of widespread unemployment, Clemens immediately found a job setting type at a job-printing house on Cliff Street. Regardless of the grueling nature of the job and criminally low wages, he took pride in his work, writing his mother that "out of all the proofs I saw, without boasting, I can say mine was by far the cleanest. . . . I do believe I set a clean proof."[15] Clemens's genuine interest in all aspects of publishing, including his burgeoning interest to be a contributing writer, and his self-awareness concerning personal production are evident in an 1853 letter to Orion, who, along with his family and mother, Jane, had moved to Muscatine, Iowa, where he became publisher of the Muscatine *Journal*:

> How many subscribers has the Journal got? What does the job-work pay? and what does the whole concern pay? . . .
>
> I will try to write for the paper occasionally, but I fear my letters will be very uninteresting, for this incessant night-work dulls one's ideas amazingly.
>
> From some cause, I cannot set type nearly so fast as when I was at home. Sunday is a long day, and while others set 12 and 15,000, yesterday, I only set 10,000. However, I will shake this laziness off, soon, I reckon. . . ."[16]

Clemens continued his vagabond journey, arriving in Philadelphia in mid-October 1853, where he played tourist, visiting the Liberty Bell, the Old State House where the Declaration of Independence was signed, and Benjamin Franklin's grave. He also took a job setting type for the *Inquirer*. Increasingly worried that his meticulous typesetting work was hurting his eyes, Clemens was anxious to return westward to begin a new, as yet undetermined career.[17] Before doing so, he bounced south to Washington, D.C., for some sightseeing in February 1854, and then journeyed to St. Louis, after which he continued on to Keokuk, Missouri, located north of Hannibal, where Orion, who had moved yet again, was now trying his hand as a printer. In helping Orion manage his business, Clemens was very focused, conscious of production and efficiency. When his obsessive need to control was disrupted, he was not happy, which is exemplified in a letter to his mother:

> The Directory [his current project] is coming on finely. I have to work on it occasionally, which I don't like a particle. I don't like to work at too many things at once. They take Henry and Dick away from me too. Before we commenced the Directory, I could tell before breakfast just how much work could be done during the day, and manage accordingly—but now, they throw all my plans into disorder by taking my hands away from their work.
>
> . . . I am not getting along well with the job work. I can't work blindly—without system. I gave Dick a job yesterday, which I calculated he would set in two hours and I could work off in three, and therefore just finish it by supper time, but he was transferred to the Directory, and the job, promised this morning, remains untouched. Through all the great pressure of job-work lately, I never before failed in a promise of the kind.[18]

Fed up with Orion's haphazard business methods, which resulted in the letter of complaint to his mother, and dreadfully underpaid, before 1855 was over Clemens quit and took a typesetting job in Warsaw, Illinois. A glutton for punishment, not long after, he returned to work for his brother in Keokuk. Inadvertently, here a series of events would (thankfully for us) lead him to his next career: riverboat pilot. For every bit of dreariness in setting type, the job of riverboat pilot was filled with grandeur and adventure. It would end with tragedy.

QUIRKY HABITS AND BRAZEN PHILOSOPHY

How to Outwit Your Superiors

"Revenge is wicked, & unchristian & in every way unbecoming, & I am not the man to countenance it or show it any favor. (But it is powerful sweet, anyway.)"

Due to his hardscrabble youth, Clemens clung to a somewhat cynical view of authority—whether it be parents or bosses—which is apparent in a speech he made to a young men's club. He was supposed to say "something suitable to youth—something didactic, instructive, or something in the nature of good advice." However, he couldn't help but let his humor supersede earnestness—for which his audience was no doubt thankful. Nevertheless, in this edited version of the speech there are some juicy tidbits for the young and old alike, especially when it comes to outwitting your superiors—or exacting revenge.

Advice to Youth

Always obey your parents, when they are present. This is the best policy in the long run, because if you don't, they will make you. Most parents think they know better than you do, and you can generally make more by humoring that superstition than you can by acting on your own better judgment.

Be respectful to your superiors, if you have any, also to strangers, and sometimes to others. If a person offend you, and you are in doubt as to whether it was intentional or not, do not resort to extreme measures; simply watch your chance and hit him with a brick. That will be sufficient. If you shall find that he had not intended any offense, come out frankly and confess yourself in the wrong when you struck him; acknowledge it like a man and say you didn't mean to. Yes, always avoid violence; in this age of charity and kindliness, the time has gone by for such things. Leave dynamite to the low and unrefined.

Go to bed early, get up early—this is wise. Some authorities say get up with the sun; some say get up with one thing, others with another. But a lark is really the best thing to get up with. It gives you a splendid reputation with everybody to know that you get up with the lark; and if you get the right kind of lark, and work at him right, you can easily train him to get up at half past nine, every time—it's no trick at all.

Now as to the matter of lying. You want to be very careful about lying; otherwise you are nearly sure to get caught. Once caught, you can never again be in the eyes to the good and the pure, what you were before. Many a young person has injured himself permanently through a single clumsy and ill finished lie, the result of carelessness born of incomplete training. Some authorities hold that the young ought not to lie at all. That, of course, is putting it rather stronger than necessary; still, while I cannot go quite so far as that, I do maintain, and I believe I am right, that the young ought to be temperate in the use of this great art until practice and experience shall give them that confidence, elegance, and precision which alone can make the accomplishment graceful and profitable. Patience, diligence, painstaking attention to detail—these are requirements; these, in time, will make the student perfect; upon these only may he rely as the sure foundation for future eminence. . . . A feeble, stupid, preposterous lie will not live two years—except it be a slander upon somebody. It is indestructible, then of course, but that is no merit of yours. A final word: begin your practice of this gracious and beautiful art early—begin now. If I had begun earlier, I could have learned how.

(Continued)

How to Outwit Your Superiors (Continued)

Never handle firearms carelessly. The sorrow and suffering that have been caused through the innocent but heedless handling of firearms by the young! Only four days ago, right in the next farm house to the one where I am spending the summer, a grandmother, old and gray and sweet, one of the loveliest spirits in the land, was sitting at her work, when her young grandson crept in and got down an old, battered, rusty gun which had not been touched for many years and was supposed not to be loaded, and pointed it at her, laughing and threatening to shoot. In her fright she ran screaming and pleading toward the door on the other side of the room; but as she passed him he placed the gun almost against her very breast and pulled the trigger! He had supposed it was not loaded. And he was right—it wasn't. So there wasn't any harm done. It is the only case of that kind I ever heard of. . . . A youth who can't hit a cathedral at thirty yards with a Gatling gun in three quarters of an hour, can take up an old empty musket and bag his grandmother every time, at a hundred. . . .

There are many sorts of books; but good ones are the sort for the young to read. Remember that. They are a great, an inestimable, and unspeakable means of improvement. . . .

But I have said enough. I hope you will treasure up the instructions which I have given you, and make them a guide to your feet and a light to your understanding. Build your character thoughtfully and painstakingly upon these precepts, and by and by, when you have got it built, you will be surprised and gratified to see how nicely and sharply it resembles everybody else's.[19]

chapter two

HOW TO QUIT A GOOD JOB AND THEN LOSE A MILLION DOLLARS

"They do say that when a man starts down hill everybody is ready to help him with a kick, and I suppose it is so."

Beginning in 1855 Clemens served under a riverboat pilot on the Mississippi River and in 1859 earned his pilot's license. During this period he learned practical yet often intangible leadership skills, such as making quick decisions, having courage, visualizing a course of action, and improvising when the situation calls for it. In 1861, the outbreak of the Civil War forced him to head west to Nevada Territory, where the silver mining fever was in full swing. Because he encountered every scam imaginable, Clemens soon trusted no one as he sought to strike it rich, and he became a tough negotiator in his own right. He also learned the art of playing the stock market game as stocks in particular mining operations were traded among investors with abandon.

It was the previously mentioned dreams of making a fortune in the coca plant trade that brought Clemens to the Mississippi River. "I had been reading Lieutenant Herndon's account of his explorations of the Amazon and had been mightily attracted by what he said of coca," Clemens recollected. "I made up my mind that I would go to the head-waters of the Amazon and collect coca and trade in it and make a fortune."[1] For centuries coca had been rumored to have magical healing powers: In the

1600s Spanish explorers reported that their doctors used it to heal wounds and strengthen broken bones, and that the indigent people chewed it incessantly for nourishment. It was in 1855 that a German chemist isolated the cocaine alkaloid and brilliantly provided the groundwork for a drug trade that would destroy millions of lives. In reading about Lieutenant William Lewis Herndon, who had been directed by the Navy Department to explore the Amazon River and its tributaries, Clemens knew bigger adventures awaited him. So he once again quit his job with Orion and, in 1856, caught the steamer *Paul Jones* to New Orleans, where he hoped to find passage to the headwaters of the Amazon.

Even though, by his count, he had almost drowned in the river nine times when a youngster, while aboard the *Paul Jones* Clemens's boyhood dreams of glory and adventure on the Mississippi were awakened. "When I was a boy, there was but one permanent ambition among my comrades in our village on the west bank of the Mississippi River," he reflected. "That was, to be a steamboatman."[2] Yes, clowns and pirates came in and out of favor, but a steamboatman was forever. Clemens's niece, Annie Moffett, recalled, "Piloting in those days was a dramatic and well-paid profession, and in a river town it was a great honor to have a pilot in the family."[3] When the daily packet boat arrived from either St. Louis or Keokuk, the town of Hannibal came alive. Clerks, wagon-pulling donkeys, and even the town drunkard stumbled to their feet. Alongside the river, Clemens witnessed the steamboats, the barges, the coal-fleets, and the massive timber rafts that were an acre large with a crew of two dozen men or more. He and his friends would swim out to these rafts and hitch a ride, observe "the rude ways," and listen to "the tremendous talk" of the crew.[4] The ebb and flow of the river business seeped into his consciousness, knowledge he would later put to use in both his writing and capitalist ventures.

But back to Clemens's grand plans to trade coca. He overlooked one important point before leaving: to investigate whether commercial ships were even going to the Amazon.

"When I got to New Orleans I inquired about ships leaving for Para and discovered that there weren't any and learned that there probably wouldn't be any during that century," he recalled with chagrin. With no money and no friends in New Orleans, Clemens turned to the pilot of the *Paul Jones*, Horace Bixby, for help "and asked him to make a pilot out of me."[5] Over several days he argued his case, and his persistence paid off, but it cost him $500. Bixby agreed to teach him for $500, with $100 down, the rest to be paid when he started earning wages. With his family financially strapped, Clemens borrowed the down payment from his generous and civic-minded brother-in-law William Moffett.

It Is Possible to Overcome a Memory Filled with Blank Cartridges and Use Visualization to Enhance Your Performance

Clemens quickly discovered that what appears to be and can be a glorious, fun-filled job often requires intense training. "If I had really known what I was about to require of my faculties," he reflected, "I should not have had the courage to begin."[6] It would be a grueling 18 months before Clemens would become a full-fledged pilot. In the interim, Bixby, graced with an imposing Roman nose but otherwise apish face with a jutting jaw, pushed him mercilessly. Initially, convinced that young Clemens was a "dunderhead," Bixby told him, " 'My boy, you must get a little memorandum-book, and every time I tell you a thing, put it down right away. There's only one way to be a pilot, and that is to get the entire river by heart. You have to know it just like A.B.C.' " The lesson was implicit: You cannot be a good pilot, ergo leader, without knowing your stuff, because anyone can sniff out a blowhard spewing hogwash.

"That was a dismal revelation to me;" Clemens wrote, "for my memory was never loaded with anything but blank cartridges."[7] Bixby demanded perfection, demanded that Clemens know the shape of the river just as precisely as he would the hallways of his home. It was all about visualization, for, as Clemens later explained, "you learn it with such absolute certainty that you can always steer by the shape that's in *your head*, and never mind the one that's before your eyes."[8] When the already anxious young man realized the river looked completely different when going down instead of up, or vice versa—and that he was going to have to learn the river in both directions—he became all the more distraught.

In addition to the directional differences, the river's condition, from currents to sandbars, was constantly changing. You had to learn how to read the water, to know, for example, where it was running over reefs and shoals. A floating log meant the river was rising; a particular look to the sun meant wind the next day; lines and circles in slick water warned of shoaling. "The face of the water, in time, became a wonderful book—a book that was a dead language to the uneducated passenger," Clemens wrote, "but which told its mind to me without reserve, delivering its most cherished secrets as clearly as if it uttered them with a voice. And it was not a book to be read once and thrown aside, for it had a new story to tell every day."[9] So it is in any industry, each with its own language, each filled with cockamamie jargon to decipher.

Clemens also discovered that piloting involved a much different kind of discipline—diametrically opposed, really—than the methodical, repetitive setting of type; now he had to recognize that the world around him was in constant flux and that he had to vigilantly adapt to it. And then there were the intangibles of solid leadership required by pilots: "He must have good and quick judgment and decision, and a cool, calm courage that no peril can shake. . . ." Clemens wrote. "Judgment is a matter of brains, and a man must start with a good stock of that article or he will never succeed as a pilot."[10] To tease out these qualities, when Clemens was at the wheel, mentor Bixby had the crew trick him into thinking they were in trouble, in danger, about to hit a sandbar. The crew started yelling out different commands and warnings, cruelly prompting Clemens to spin the wheel and change direction frantically. The simulation was a good lesson, Clemens admitted ruefully, but rattled his nerves.

As a cub pilot, he certainly took his share of abuse from the seasoned hands. Next, Clemens trained under William Brown, pilot of the *Pennsylvania* and a tyrant who enjoyed calling him a numbskull, among other choice names. Clemens description of Brown was equally unflattering: "He was a middle-aged, long, slim, bony, smooth-shaven, horse-faced, ignorant, stingy, malicious, snarling, fault-hunting, mote-magnifying tyrant." Brown was always looking to find fault, and if he couldn't find fault he invented problems. As a result, Clemens claimed, there were nights when he killed Brown in 17 different ways—in his dreams. "I often wanted to kill Brown, but this would not answer," he wrote. "A cub had to take everything his boss gave, in the way of vigorous comment and criticism. . . ."[11] It wasn't until Brown blamed Clemens's younger brother Henry—for whom Clemens had secured the position of mud-clerk—for one of his own errors and then took a swing at the boy that Clemens finally attacked his object of hate. In a quick, scrappy fight, the cub pilot pummeled his superior. Certain he would be thrown off the ship, Clemens was surprised when Captain John S. Kleinfelter congratulated him because he, too, despised Brown's maliciousness. So there was some justice in the world—but it was short-lived.

After the incident, Kleinfelter transferred Clemens so he could escape the menace Brown; however, Henry Clemens remained aboard the *Pennsylvania*. Shortly thereafter, on June 13, 1858, the ship's boiler exploded, killing Brown instantly. Severely burned, young Henry survived for several agonizing days—enough time for Clemens to visit him on his deathbed. Although there was nothing he could have done to prevent the tragic accident— such explosions occurred at least two or three times every year on the Mississippi alone—he blamed himself for his brother's death, a torment he carried with him his entire life.

There Is Great Satisfaction and Pride in Achieving Independence

Still determined to become a pilot, at age 23 Clemens was finally granted a license on April 9, 1859, which brought with it a hefty $250 monthly salary. More than some unskilled factory workers made in a year, this relatively prodigious income brought Clemens a taste of the good life, beginning with rich Cajun dinners in New Orleans and upgrading his wardrobe with alligator boots. Reveling in newfound wealth aside, the experience of being a pilot itself was rich with satisfaction: "If I have seemed to love my subject, it is no surprising thing, for I loved the profession far better than any I have followed since, and I took measureless pride in it. The reason is plain: a pilot, in those days, was the only unfettered and entirely independent human being that lived in the earth."[12] The pilot took orders from no one—except, on rare occasions, from the captain.

The pilots were a tight-knit group, a brotherhood, who shared information, relying on each other to relay news concerning the ever-changing river. "Your true pilot cares nothing about anything on earth but the river," Clemens wrote, "and his pride in his occupation surpasses the pride of kings."[13] Until the outbreak of the Civil War, in the spring of 1861, he was completely dedicated to his job, even brushing off a request from Orion for publishable travel letters detailing what he witnessed and experienced on the river. Once worried that his memory would fail him in his bid to become a pilot, Clemens concluded, "Astonishing things can be done with the human memory if you will devote it faithfully to one particular line of business."[14] In fact, he became so earnest in his belief that a person's memory could be improved that more than 20 years later, in 1885, he would patent a memory game to help people keep their facts straight.

Another future benefit he realized from his riverboat days

was the cast of colorful characters he met on the river, many of whom he would incorporate into his stories. "I am to this day profiting somewhat by that experience;" he wrote in the 1880s, "for that brief, sharp schooling, I got personally and familiarly acquainted with about all the different types of human nature that are to be found in fiction, biography, or history. . . . My profit is various in kind and degree; but the feature of it which I value most is the zest which that early experience has given to my later reading. When I find a well-drawn character in fiction or biography, I generally take a warm personal interest in him, for the reason that I have known him before—met him on the river."[15]

An ability to read people, to understand their character and motivations, Clemens learned, was as important as reading the river. By being able to read people, he knew whether to handle them aggressively or with gentle persuasion, whether to trust them, and whether to enter into business partnerships with them. Of course, there is always the charismatic, hypnotic scoundrel who can hoodwink even the most cautious, and Clemens would indeed encounter such unsavory characters.

Shortly after being forced to quit the piloting business due to the Civil War, and before eventually vamoosing to the Wild West to escape the hostilities, Clemens did witness one battle— or, rather, was caught in a battle he had never intended to see. The month after Confederate forces seized Fort Sumter in April 1861, he happened to be a passenger aboard the *Nebraska*, steaming north to St. Louis, when, shortly before reaching the city, Federal artillery fired on them. The second shot tore through the pilothouse and killed the pilot. Clemens hit the deck and stayed low.

"Good Lord Almighty! Sam," his friend Zeb Leavenworth said, "what do they mean by that?"

"I guess they want us to wait a minute," the future humorist replied dryly.

Attempting to Avoid the Silver-Mining Craze, Clemens Seeks Profit in an Industry Supporting the Miners

In the summer of 1861, Clemens joined the Confederate army for a brief stint—a *very* brief stint: "In June I joined the Confederates in Ralls County, Missouri, as a second lieutenant under General Tom Harris and came near having the distinction of being captured by Colonel Ulysses S. Grant. I resigned after two weeks' service in the field, explaining that I was 'incapacitated by fatigue' through persistent retreating."[16]

About this time, brother Orion actually had a change of luck for the better and was appointed Secretary of the Territory of Nevada, thanks to an old family friend now serving in Lincoln's administration. Painfully jealous that his 36-year-old brother would "have all kinds of adventures, and maybe get hanged or scalped, and have ever such a fine time, and write home and tell us about it, and be a hero," and would get rich by taking afternoon hikes to pick pails of silver and gold off the hillsides, Clemens seized the opportunity to take the position of secretary to the secretary (at no salary).[17] The two hopped aboard a packet that took them westward on the Missouri River and then booked passage on a stagecoach to Carson City, Nevada Territory.

They traveled over hardscrabble roads haunted by thieves, murderers, and "Injuns." While passing through Nebraska Territory, their driver was murdered at a junction, no small comfort to Clemens, who had brought about $800 in silver coin, all he had managed to save. To protect himself, he was packing "a pitiful little Smith & Wesson's seven-shooter. . . . It appeared to me to be a dangerous weapon," he wrote. "It only had one fault— you could not hit anything with it."[18] At the end of August 1861, 20 days after leaving home, they arrived in Carson City, the capital of Nevada Territory, which had been established by Congress that year. Main Street was all of four blocks long, lined by white frame stores and houses, and there was a central plaza used for auctions, horse trading, and public meetings.

Clemens figured the war would be over in a few months' time and he would then escape this desert hellhole to return to piloting. Little did he know he would be gone six infernal years, during which time he would become both a millionaire and a pauper.

As his brother's secretary, the best advice he gave Orion concerned the location of his office and its décor: "Wherever you go, fit up the office superbly. I don't like Gov. J.'s as well as Harrington's, because the former is not on the principal business street." Clearly, the young man had a head for image and properly impressing people. However, other than that, Clemens had no real interest in politics. Once settled in a Carson City boarding house, his attention was quickly diverted to the various mining ventures, the fabulous wealth of a few lucky ones, and his own chances at striking it rich. In a colorful letter to his mother, Clemens, who was determined not to marry until he could afford servants, made it clear that he and Orion should soon be able to receive her in fine style:

> I hope you will all come out here someday. But I shan't consent to invite you, until we can receive you in style. But I guess we shall be able to do that, one of these days. . . . Well, "Gold Hill" sells at $5,000 per foot, cash down; "Wild cat" isn't worth ten cents. The country is fabulously rich in gold, silver, copper, lead, coal, iron, quick silver, marble, granite, chalk, plaster of Paris (gypsum), thieves, murderers, desperadoes, ladies, children, lawyers, Christians, Indians, Chinamen, Spaniards, gamblers, sharpers, coyotes (pronounced Ki-yo-ties), poets, preachers, and jackass rabbits. I overheard a gentleman say, the other day, that it was 'the d—dest country under the sun.'—and that comprehensive conception I fully subscribe to.[19]

In his first months there, Clemens resisted the temptation to strike out with pickax and pail; instead he tried his hand at one of the many burgeoning industries serving the miners: lumber.

He and a friend, John D. Kinney, made for the spectacular mountains surrounding Lake Bigler (later renamed Tahoe) where 100-foot-tall yellow pines towered, and cut down several to mark their claim—all that was necessary in those days to take possession of land. On the shore of the lake, Clemens lit a campfire, but then, distracted by the surrounding landscape, the tenderfoot left it unattended. In a short time the insanely greedy fire spread rapidly and successfully burned down the mountainside of trees Clemens had hoped to cut himself. Thus ended his timber enterprise.

Leather-Headed Thieves Are Selling Stock Like Hotcakes Even Though Their Company Has Yet to Yield a Profit

Back in Carson City, the chance of striking it rich was just too hard to resist. Stories abounded of ignorant but lucky fools stumbling across veins fairly spitting out silver and gold. Seedy customers who couldn't afford a beer one day were roaring drunk on champagne the next. Stories in the newspaper perpetuated the craze. "By and by I was smitten with the silver fever. . . ." Clemens recalled. "Plainly this was the road to fortune. . . . I would have been more or less than human if I had not gone mad like the rest. Cart-loads of solid silver bricks, as large as pigs of lead, were arriving from the mills every day, and such sights as that gave substance to the wild talk about me. I succumbed and grew as frenzied as the craziest."[20]

By October Clemens was deep into mine speculation, buying feet in various claims (also called shares, not unlike buying stock in a company), and soon owned over 1,600 feet in various shafts, veins, and otherwise nondescript pieces of desert land. When it came to financing such ventures, he knew his limitations and, in a letter to his sister Pamela Clemens Moffet, expressed a desire for their colorful relative James Lampton—their mother's cousin but whom he refers

to as Uncle Jim—an experienced businessman, to venture
westward with ready capital:

> Orion and I have confidence enough in this country to think that
> if the war will let us alone we can make Mr. Moffett rich without
> its ever costing him a cent of money or particle of trouble. We shall
> lay plenty of claims for him, but if they never pay him anything,
> they will never cost him anything, Orion and I are not financiers.
> Therefore, you must persuade Uncle Jim to come out here and
> help us in that line. I have written to him twice to come. . . . I
> would not say anything about our prospects now, if we were nearer
> home. But I suppose at this distance you are more anxious than
> you would be if you saw us every month—and therefore it is
> hardly fair to keep you in the dark. However, keep these matters to
> yourselves, and then if we fail, we'll keep the laugh in the family.[21]

Determined to be discreet, especially as a hedge in case he
failed, Clemens waited quietly and patiently for one of the unproven enterprises he had invested in to make a profitable strike.
In short order, he learned that the Wild West was littered with
blowhards who talked a good game, who promised nuggets but
came up with dirt. He learned to assume that everyone exagger-
ates or outright cheats as he now witnessed every swindle imaginable. He came to understand that there were mining companies
selling stock in their company before they ever started drilling or
making a profit, a modus operandi that echoed almost 150 years
later in the Internet plays of the dot-bomb era.

Of one particular deal touted, Clemens observed of the organization, "They are not partial to any particular mining district. They are going to 'carry on' a general 'gold and silver
mining business'!—the untechnical, leather-headed thieves!
The company 'to be' organized—at some indefinite period in
the future—probably in time for the resurrection." No business
plan, no profit, but selling stock like hotcakes . . . hmm.
Clemens's concern was for the unsuspecting multitude: "Now
this swindle ought to be well ventilated by the newspapers—

not that sound business men will ever be swindled by it, but the unsuspecting multitude, who yearn to grow suddenly rich, will assuredly have their slender purses drained by it. . . ."[22] The swindles and lying he encountered would make Clemens a wary, hard-nosed negotiator, especially in the future when it came to dealing with slick-talking big-city publishers.

Clemens's feet or shares in various mines produced nothing of significance, and come winter he was running out of money and patience. It was time to do a little backbreaking digging of his own. He targeted Humboldt County in Nevada Territory, which was reportedly the richest in precious metal, with one local reporter declaring, "'The intestines of our mountains are gorged with precious ore to plethora.'"[23] In December, Clemens departed for the distant, mirage-like Humboldt, along with three partners: a friend from Keokuk, Billy Clagett; a blacksmith named Combury Tillou; and a lawyer named Gus Oliver (the latter two renamed Ballou and Oliphant in Twain's book *Roughing It*). Interestingly, rather than the lawyer grating on Clemens, it was the blacksmith's use of big words that annoyed the future author: "His one striking peculiarity was his Parkingtonian fashion of loving and using big words *for their own sakes*, and independent of any bearing they might have upon the thought he was purposing to convey. . . . One was always catching himself accepting his stately sentences as meaning something, when they really meant nothing in the world."[24] Through thick and thin, he continued to glean useful insights into human character.

Having Patience and Not Having Fear of Failure Keep Clemens Going

It took them 15 grueling days to travel the 175 miles north, although Clemens claimed they could have gotten there in 10 if they had towed their pathetic horses behind the wagon. When they finally arrived in Unionville, the Humboldt County seat, he "expected to find masses of silver lying all about the ground," so, as soon as the chance came, he slipped away from his partners, hiked to a relatively remote area, and started collecting rocks shining with silver. That night, when he shared them with his partners, the more experienced of the lot scoffed: the rocks were filled with nothing more than glittering mica. "Moralizing, I observed, then," Clemens wrote, "that 'all that glitters is not gold.' "[25]

The men staked a claim, built a cabin, and, in the cold January weather—the average high in the low 40s—toiled away. Clemens learned the art of prospecting, which, much to his chagrin, involved more climbing and searching than throwing chunks of silver into pails. Once they found a vein with potential, they dug and blasted. Ultimately, playing cards and drinking whiskey proved much easier work, so, after two weeks of this backbreaking work, Clemens resigned and returned to Carson City. He resorted back to staking claims, buying shares in unproven claims, and trading claims with others; however, as he noted, even though their claims may one day be worth millions, their credit was no good at the grocers. And he was hungry—sick of subsisting on slabs of bacon, stale bread, and black coffee.

Now looking more objectively at his fellow prospectors "stark mad with excitement," Clemens concluded it was "the strangest phase of life one can imagine."[26] Yet, while a windfall from mining continued to elude him, he refused to quit speculating: "If I have to wait longer than expected," he wrote home, "let it be so—I have no fear of failure." It was brave talk because he certainly feared poverty. However, if nothing less, Clemens understood the value of perseverance. After kicking around Carson City for a couple of months, he lit out for the Esmeralda mines to the south, where he would spend the next five months in relative squalor. He and sundry new partners staked claims and started digging shafts to hold said claims, but it appeared fruitless.

Back in Carson City, the dribble of money Clemens managed to make was handled by Orion, who had very strict orders from Clemens not to fund or lend money to any other speculators or enterprises. In April 1862 Clemens wrote a series of letters to Orion demanding he send $40, $50, or $100 to cover mining expenses and tunnel construction. "Don't buy *anything* while I am here—but save up some money for me," he commanded. "Don't send any money home. I shall have your next quarter's salary spent before you get it, I think. I mean to make or break here with the next two or three months." It was all or nothing for Clemens. In another April letter, he wrote, "No, don't buy any ground, anywhere. The pick and shovel are the only claims I have any confidence in now. My back is sore and my hands blistered with handling them to-day. But something must come, you know."[27]

When Orion did divert funds from the Clemens Company, which the brothers had created for the purposes of staking claims and funding their little operation, Clemens's fierce determination and firm management style were on display in his response:

Yours of 17th, per express, just received. Part of it pleased me exceedingly, and part of it didn't. Concerning the latter, for instance: You have promised me that you would leave all mining matters, and everything involving an outlay of money, in my hands. Now it may be a matter of no consequence at all to you, to keep your word with me, but I assure you I look upon it in a very different light. Indeed I fully expect you to deal as conscientiously with me as you would with any other man. Moreover, you know as well as I do, that the very best course that you and I can pursue will be, to keep on good terms with each other—notwithstanding which fact, we shall certainly split inside of six months if you go on in this way. You see I talk plainly. Because I know what is due me, and

I would not put up with such treatment from anybody but you. . . .

Now, Orion, I have given you a piece of my mind—you have it in full, and you deserved it—for you would be ashamed to acknowledge that you ever broke faith with another man as you have with me. I shall never look upon Ma's face again, or Pamela's, or get married, or revisit the "Banner State," until I am a rich man—so you can easily see that when you stand between me and my fortune (the one which I shall make, as surely as Fate itself,) you stand between me and home, friends, and all that I care for—and by the Lord God! You must clear the track, you know![28]

More convinced than ever that he was close to a strike, Clemens also became increasingly aggressive in the field. When armed men attempted to take over one of their claims, he explained to Orion that he refused to readily capitulate:

Two or three of the old "Salina" company entered our hole on the Monitor yesterday morning, before our men got there, and took possession, armed with revolvers. And according to the d—-d laws of this forever d—-d country, nothing but the District Court (and there ain't any) can touch the matter, unless it assumes the shape of an infernal humbug which they call "forcible entry and detainer," and in order to bring that about, you must compel the jumpers to use personal violence toward you! We went up and demanded possession, and they refused. Said they were in the hole, armed and meant to die for it, if necessary.

I got in with them, and again demanded possession. They said I might stay in it as long as I pleased, and work but they would do the same. I asked one of our company to take my place in the hole, while I went to consult a lawyer. He did so. The lawyer said it was no go. They must offer some "force."

Our boys will try to be there first in the morning—in which case they may get possession and keep it. Now you understand the shooting scrape in which Gebhart was killed the other day. The Clemens Company—all of us—hate to resort to arms in this matter, and it will not be done until it becomes a forced hand—but I think that will be the end of it, never-the-less.[29]

Being a Millionaire for 10 Days Teaches the Uselessness of Self-Upbraidings

Then, after nearly a year of toil and futile hope in Humboldt County, Clemens and his friend Calvin Higbie, a straightforward, muscular young man who wasn't averse to physical work, appeared to stumble across a blind lead in the vicinity of an incredibly rich vein that would indeed make them millionaires. They posted their claim and recorded it at the clerk's office. "No one can be so thoughtless as to suppose that we slept that night," he recalled. "Higbie and I went to bed at midnight, but it was only to lie broad awake and think, dream, scheme."[30] Shortly thereafter Higbie went off to investigate a cement-making operation and Clemens was called away to help with a sick friend. Both left unbeknownst to each other, and neither starting digging their shaft within the required 10-day time frame to hold their claim.

When Clemens finally returned to their cabin, he found Higbie looking violently ill: The claim had been taken over by another party and there was nothing they could do about it. "A minute before, I was rich and brimful of vanity; I was a pauper now, and very meek," Clemens wrote. "We sat still an hour, busy with thought, busy with vain and useless self-upbraidings, busy with 'Why *didn't* I do this, and why *didn't* I do that,' but neither spoke a word."[31] In his 1871 book *Roughing It*, which details and lampoons these misadventures, his dedication was: "To Calvin H. Higbie of California, an honest man, a genial comrade, and a steadfast friend, this book is inscribed by the author in memory of the curious time when we two were millionaires for ten days."

With little money in his pocket, Clemens quit the mining business and found work at a mill. "That is to say," he recalled, "I went to work as a common laborer in a quartz-mill, at ten dollars a week and board."[32] It was dreary, arduous work and a far cry from his glory days of making $250 a month as a pilot. "But this palatial life," he wrote sarcastically, "this gross and luxurious life, had to come to an end and there were two sufficient reasons for it. On my side I could not endure the heavy labor; and on the company's side they did not feel justified in paying me to shovel sand down my back; so I was discharged just at the moment that I was going to resign."[33]

Yet there was always hope on his horizon: "Shortly after this I began to grow crazy, along with the rest of the population, about the mysterious and wonderful 'cement-mine,' and to make preparations to take advantage of any opportunity that might offer to go and help hunt for it."[34] Thankfully, he did not pursue this particular castle in the sky. Instead, Clemens took stock of his own life and considered his next move: "I had gained a livelihood in various vocations, but had not dazzled anybody with my successes; still the list was before me, and the amplest liberty in the matter of choosing, provided I wanted to work—which I did not, after being so wealthy."[35] He had been a grocery clerk, a bookseller, a tolerable typesetter and printer, and a respectable riverboat pilot. Then came the silver mining debacle. There would be no receiving his mother in grand style, which Clemens had so desired; there would be no servants tending to his every need, and no champagne to wash down his food. It was time for a change of scenery and occupation. Amazingly, oft-maligned brother Orion saved the day.

QUIRKY HABITS AND BRAZEN PHILOSOPHY

Even a Crank Knows to Dress for Success

*"Clothes make the man. Naked people
have little or no influence in society."*

Early in his career, Clemens was known for being coarse
in language and dress; he slouched around in lumpy suits
and string ties, and preferred an ordinary sack suit to
proper evening dress. In 1867 one powerful publisher in
New York, who could have propelled Clemens to
greater heights, refused to take him seriously because he
appeared "disreputable." Friends finally forced him to see
a first-class tailor, and by the 1870s he realized that his
backwoods, Wild West image was no longer going to cut
it if he was to be taken seriously as a literary figure.[36]
Once Clemens donned finer clothes, there was no turning back.

Like many business icons and celebrities, Clemens
learned that clothes are more than a mere necessity; they
are about feeling good, about image, about advertising
one's self: "We must put up with our clothes as they are—
they have their reason for existing. They are on us to expose us—to advertise what we wear them to conceal. They
are a sign; a sign of insincerity; a sign of suppressed vanity;
a pretense that we desire gorgeous colors and the graces of
harmony and form; and we put them on to propagate that
lie and back it up."

To Clemens, a group of businessmen in dark suits "looks
like a flock of crows, and is just about as inspiring."[37] En-
dorsing the extreme opposite, to garnish his image and
spiritually enliven himself, he purchased six white suits,

each outfit consisting of a white doubled breasted jacket, white trousers, white waistcoat, an ascot cravat, and white shoes. In an interview with the New York *World*, he jokingly explained that this white suit was "the uniform of the American Association of Purity and Perfection, of which I am president, secretary and treasurer and the only man in the United States eligible to membership." Incidentally, in that same interview, reprinted below, he also alludes to a peek-a-boo waist that presages the more minimalist clothes of our time preferred by those not afraid to show a little skin:

Why don't you ask why I am wearing such apparently unseasonable clothes? I'll tell you. I have found that when a man reaches the advanced age of 71 years as I have, the continual sight of dark clothing is likely to have a depressing effect upon him. Light-colored clothing is more pleasing to the eye and enlivens the spirit. Now, of course, I cannot compel every one to wear such clothing just for my especial benefit, so I do the next best thing and wear it myself.

Of course, before a man reaches my years, the fear of criticism might prevent him from indulging his fancy. I am not afraid of that. I am decidedly for pleasing color combinations in dress. I like to see the women's clothes, say, at the opera. What can be more depressing than the somber black which custom requires men to wear upon state occasions. A group of men in evening clothes looks like a flock of crows, and is just about as inspiring.

After all, what is the purpose of clothing? Are not clothes intended primarily to preserve dignity and also to afford comfort to the wearer? Now I know of nothing more uncomfortable than the present-day clothes of men. The finest clothing made is a person's own skin, but, of course, society demands something more than this.

(Continued)

Even a Crank Knows
to Dress for Success *(Continued)*

The best-dressed man I have ever seen, however, was a native of the Sandwich Islands, who attracted my attention thirty years ago. Now, when that man wanted to don especial dress to honor a public occasion or a holiday, why he occasionally put on a pair of spectacles. Otherwise the clothing with which God had provided him sufficed.

Of course, I have ideas of dress reform. For one thing, why not adopt some of the women's styles? Goodness knows, they adopt enough of ours. Take the peek-a-boo waist, for instance. It has the obvious advantages of being cool and comfortable, and in addition it is almost always made up in pleasing colors which cheer and do not depress."[38]

chapter three

SOMETIMES NECESSITY
IS THE MOTHER OF A CAREER

"We are chameleons, and our partialities and prejudices
change places with an easy and blessed facility, and
we are soon wonted to the change and happy in it."

*I*n *1862, a relatively destitute Clemens came to understand the neces-*
sity of taking chances, including a career change, when he became the
editor of the Virginia City Enterprise. *There he learned to carry himself*
with utter confidence, which greatly enhanced his reputation; to appreciate
the power of information; and to network, which provided him with a
plethora of insider information, allowing him to make more money on
mining stocks than ever before. In 1866 he journeyed to the Hawaiian
Islands, his assignment being to report on the burgeoning sugar industry.
He then lectured about his voyage, but had to overcome stage fright,
which he did by using a number of tricks still applicable today.

Still serving as secretary of Nevada Territory, Orion had a connection at the Virginia City *Territorial Enterprise* and, in the
summer of 1862, secured for his younger brother the position
of staff reporter. It paid $25 a week—again, not quite the $250
a month Clemens had earned as a riverboat pilot, but it was
better than crushing rock. With the job located in Virginia City
and little money in his pocket, he was forced to walk the 120
miles north. Destitute and exhausted, he arrived without coat,
in a blue woolen shirt and pantaloons tucked into his boots,

sporting a slouch hat and a beard that cascaded halfway down his chest. He still carried his useless revolver, which was tucked into his belt, giving him the air of a semi-serious desperado.

Nevertheless, according to Clemens, he was also offered the position of city editor, which he was inclined to turn down because he didn't feel he was fit for the position. "Yet if I refused this place I must presently become dependent upon somebody for my bread," he wrote, "a thing necessarily distasteful to a man who had never experienced such a humiliation since he was thirteen years old. . . . So I was scared into being a city editor. I would have declined, otherwise. Necessity is the mother of 'taking chances.'"[1] Whether it was taking chances or the need for money, it appeared fate was pushing the 28-year-old Clemens toward writing.

One of the first lessons he learned as an editor was to the necessity of carrying oneself and, by extension, one's newspaper with absolute confidence: "Unassailable certainty is the thing that gives a newspaper the firmest and most valuable reputation."[2] However, not quite a devout moralist, while at the *Enterprise*, Clemens was quite open to taking a few feet of mine under the table for reportorial and editorial favors. When wildcatters staked a claim, invariably they came to the newspaper to have a notice published and a few positive words said about the claim in order to boost the market price of the feet the wildcatter would subsequently attempt to sell. In a relatively harmless trade, in return for the newspaper inches, these calculating but not necessarily malicious speculators would give Clemens 40 or 50 feet in their claim.

"Very often it was a good idea to close the transaction instantly," he reflected, "when a man offered a stock present to a friend, for the offer was only good and binding at that moment, and if the price went to a high figure shortly afterward the procrastination was a thing to be regretted."[3] If a particular claim made a stir in the market, Clemens would search through his trunk of "feet" and sell what he had. Or if he needed some money, he'd sell $100 worth of feet. In fact, as a newspaperman, Clemens made more money on wildcat mines by cashing in on these opportunities than he had in his mining days.

Still very much attuned to the ore business, Clemens was a frequent patron of saloons, networking with the wildcatters—and drinking his share of whiskey. (After one particularly vicious bout with the bottle, he was thrown in jail for public drunkenness.) He closely monitored production of the various claims—more than $20 million of ore would be removed from the area's Comstock load—and he reported on the latest scams du jour. One favorite swindle was to "salt" a wildcat claim, which involved the owner buying rich ore from another vein, then dumping a portion of it in his worthless shaft, and keeping some to show as evidence of what he had supposedly mined so far. He'd then find some poor sucker to buy his claim for far more than it was worth—because it was actually worthless.

Hardly a dedicated writer yet, in a February 1863 letter to his mother and sister, Clemens still imagined himself making a killing in silver, a passion he expressed with a humorous twist:

> Well, I have no news to report, unless it will interest you to know that they 'struck it rich' in the 'Burnside' ledge last night. The stock was worth ten dollars a foot this morning. It sells at a hundred tonight. I don't own in it, Madam, though I might have owned several hundred feet of it yesterday, you know, & I assume I would, if I had known they were going to 'strike it.' None of us are prophets, though. However, I take an absorbing delight in the stock market. I love to watch the prices go up. My time will come after a while, & then I'll rob somebody. I pick up a foot or two occasionally for lying about somebody's mine. I shall sell out one of these days, when I catch a susceptible emigrant.[4]

By the summer of 1863, Clemens was making enough money from his salary and mining stock transactions that he could send $20 or so home on occasion and still live the high life. He and a buddy boarded at the ritzy Occidental Hotel and then at the Lick House; they dined at fancy restaurants and drank their way through every saloon; they soaked up the opera; and they were fitted for handmade suits. At the time—a boom period, regardless of what the Northerners would call the Civil War—hotels, saloons, brothels, courts, and jails were overflowing with customers. As Clemens pointed out, "Vice flourished luxuriantly during the heyday of our 'flush times.' . . . A crowded police-court docket is the surest of all signs that trade is brisk and money plenty."[5] (However, vice never did become a leading indicator used by the government to monitor the economy's health.)

Clemens Understands That a Strong Name Is Critical to Creating a Memorable Image

Clemens settled into the writing business with an excess of self-assurance, a cockiness that spilled over into his letters written home. Not impressed, his mother attempted to deflate his ego, but he retorted with the biting, wry, and self-deprecating voice the world would come to appreciate:

> Ma, you have given my vanity a deadly thrust. Behold, I am prone to boast of having the widest reputation, as a local editor, of any man on the Pacific coast, and you gravely come forward and tell me "if I work hard and attend closely to my business, I may aspire to a place on a big San Francisco daily, some day." There's a comment on human vanity for you! Why, blast it, I was under the impression that I could get such a situation as that any time I asked for it. But I don't want it. No paper in the United States can afford to pay me what my place on the "Enterprise" is worth. If I were not naturally a lazy, idle, good-for-nothing vagabond, I could make it pay me $20,000 a year. But I don't suppose I shall ever be any account. I lead an easy life, though, and I don't care a cent whether school keeps or not. Everybody knows me, and I fare like a prince wherever I go, be it on this side of the mountains or the other. And I am proud to say I am the most conceited ass in the Territory.[6]

Whether purposefully or accidentally, he signed this letter "Mark," as in Mark Twain, his outspoken, bon vivant alter ego who was apparently creeping into every aspect of his life. While working for the *Enterprise*, on February 3, 1863, he first used his nom du plume, Mark Twain, a term lifted from his riverboat days. It translates to *mark two*, or a depth of 12 feet, which is safe for navigation.[7] Whatever psychological analysis may be applied to his adoption of a pseudonym, there was a certain marketing brilliance involved. Mark Twain was a strong, vivid name rich in river adventure tradition—it was a name that resonated with people and would not be forgotten. In addition, whenever the writer annoyed or embarrassed others, or otherwise made a jackass of himself, Sam Clemens could always put the blame on Mark Twain. It is also important to note that while the world still refers to this man as Mark Twain, the letter to his mother signed "Mark" was an exception; throughout his life he signed almost all personal correspondence with S. L. Clemens, or S. L. C.

In late May 1864, two circumstances expedited Clemens's departure from the *Enterprise*: He wore out his welcome because he kept inserting satire, which included savage attacks on public figures, into what was supposed to be unbiased reportage; and his good friend Steve Gillis, who weighed just 95 pounds, all of which seemed to be in his fists, almost killed a man in a duel. Together he and Steve hightailed it for San Francisco. "I wanted a change. I wanted variety of some kind," Clemens claimed.

In San Francisco, with less than $50 to his name, he took a reporter position at the San Francisco *Morning Call* for $35 a week. An immediate problem surfaced: The editors at the *Morning Call*—like those at the *Enterprise*—were interested in facts. Again, their seriousness was in conflict with the outrageous tales Clemens preferred to spin about bloody fights over gold and gruesome massacres that echoed the stories his mother once told him about vengeful Indians. He found the work to be "fearful drudgery, soulless drudgery, and almost destitute of interest."[8]

While he found straight journalism dull, it is apparent that the power of the pen excited him, as seen in a September 1864 letter to his mother and sister:

I am taking life easy, now, and I mean to keep it up for awhile. I don't work at night any more. I told the "Call" folks to pay me $25 a week and let me work only in daylight. So I get up at ten every morning, and quit work at five or six in the afternoon. You ask if I work for greenbacks? Hardly. What do you suppose I could do with greenbacks here?

I have engaged to write for the new literary paper—the "Californian"—same pay I used to receive on the "Golden Era"—one article a week, fifty dollars a month. I quit the "Era," long ago. It wasn't high-toned enough. The "Californian" circulates among the highest class of the community, and is the best weekly literary paper in the United States—and I suppose I ought to know.

I work as I always did—by fits and starts. I wrote two articles last night for the Californian, so that lets me out for two weeks. That would be about seventy-five dollars, in greenbacks, wouldn't it? . . .

I have triumphed. They refused me and other reporters some information at a branch of the Coroner's office—Massey's undertaker establishment, a few weeks ago. I published the wickedest article on them I ever wrote in my life, and you can rest assured we got all the information we wanted after that.[9]

It wasn't long before Clemens ushered himself out the door at the *Morning Call.* He had been permitted to hire an assistant, who soon did the job better than he did, so, taking advantage of his earnest lieutenant, he delegated more and worked less. Yes, it was a brilliant hire, except, before 1864 was out, Clemens was either fired because he was lazy or resigned because he was bored, depending on whether you believed management's story or his.

With no immediate job prospect, Clemens finally applied himself: He fervently gambled at cards and on silver stocks, which hardly seemed risky as stocks. Unfortunately, at the very time he returned to speculating, the stock market, which had been moving briskly upward during a bull market, reached its peak. A slow decline began that suddenly accelerated in the spring of 1865 (a parallel to the defeat of the Confederates, who would surrender in April). Clemens reflected on the ecstasy and the agony:

> Stocks went on rising; speculation went mad; bankers, merchants, lawyers, doctors, mechanics, laborers, even the very washerwomen and servant-girls, were putting up their earnings on silver stocks, and every sun that rose in the morning went down on paupers enriched and rich men beggared. What a gambling carnival it was! . . . And then—all of a sudden, out went the bottom and everything and everybody went to ruin and destruction! The wreck was complete. The bubble scarcely left a microscopic moisture behind it. I was an early beggar and a thorough one. My hoarded stocks were not worth the paper they were printed on.[10]

A victim of market forces and his own carefree lifestyle, Clemens found himself without a penny to his name, slinking around, and avoiding acquaintances: "I felt meaner, and lowlier, and more despicable than the worms."[11]

While It Might Not Be the Favored Choice, Sometimes Necessity Dictates That You Choose a Career That Plays to Your Strongest Suit

Desperate and an incorrigible speculator, in December 1864 Clemens left San Francisco for gold prospecting in the California mountains, at a place fittingly called Jackass Hill in Tuolumne County. For three months he searched for nuggets washed out of the ground, but found nothing meaningful and was forced to return to the city. With his credit "about exhausted" and he "too mean and lazy" to find work with a newspaper, the situation appeared hopeless.

However, while holed up in Jackass Hill, Clemens had written a backwoods tale, a twice-told tale, that would change his fortune forever. It was the "The Celebrated Jumping Frog of Calaveras County," a hilarious tale about frog races and brazen cheaters. He sent it to the renowned satirist Artemus Ward, whom he had befriended when Ward was touring the Nevada Territory, and the story eventually made it to *Saturday Press* in New York, which published it on November 18, 1865. The story won him rave reviews, was then widely reprinted around the country, and would open doors of opportunity.

Perhaps more importantly, at the time he was refining the tale for publication, Clemens wisely took stock of his life, as he was prone to do. Having been a relative drifter in recent years, he was sensing it was time to focus his energy. In a letter to Orion, he expressed what amounted to an epiphany:

> I never had but two powerful ambitions in my life. One was to be a pilot, & the other a preacher of the gospel. I accomplished the one & failed in the other, because I could not supply myself with the necessary stock in trade—i.e., religion. . . . But I have had a "call" to literature, of a low order—i.e. humorous. It is nothing to be proud of, but it is my strongest suit, & if I were to listen to that maxim of stern duty which says that to do right you must multiply the . . . talents which the Almighty entrusts to your keeping, I would long ago ceased to meddle with things for which I was by nature unfitted & turned my attention to seriously scribbling to excite the laughter of God's creatures. Poor, pitiful business![12]

So, at the age of 30, it appeared that Mr. Clemens was prepared to relinquish the reins to Mark Twain and embark on a life of writing.

Yet, just months after this epiphany, in January 1866, he was ambivalent about a career in writing and was dreaming of his days on the Mississippi. Clemens wrote to his mother and sister, "I wish I was back there piloting up & down the river again. Verily, all is vanity and little worth—save piloting."[13] In addition, while he certainly enjoyed writing and relished the power of the pen, it was not a career he would pursue unless there was money in it, a fact of life he noted when offered his first book contract in January 1867. As he explained to his mother, "But I had my mind made up to one thing—I wasn't going to touch a book unless there was money in it, and a good deal of it."[14]

Money would always be his primary focus. Throughout his life, while Clemens expressed satisfaction with his writing and tended to crack himself up with his own humor, he measured his success by his personal production and income: how many words and how many pages of manuscript he generated, how many books he sold, and how much revenue was generated. The evidence is plain in the many letters he wrote to his friends and publishers, in which he crowed about his capacity to churn out words and speculated about how many books would sell.

On the heels of his critical success with the "Jumping Frog," Clemens was still unable to settle down and sought new adventure. "I wanted another change," he wrote. "The vagabond instinct was strong upon me. Fortune favored, and I got a new berth and a delightful one. It was to go down to the Sandwich Islands and write some letters for the Sacramento *Union*, an excellent journal and liberal with employees."[15] In March 1866, he boarded the *Ajax* for the Sandwich Islands—now Hawaii—which Captain James Cook had visited in early 1778 and named in honor of his friend and benefactor, John Montague, the 4th Earl of Sandwich. (The name would fall from common use in the early 1900s.)

Sugar cane had been introduced to the islands in the 1830s, and Clemens's mission was to report on the sugar business, which was flourishing but beset with strife. The native people were displeased on a number of fronts: namely, control of the industry was falling into a few powerful hands; an acute labor shortage had resulted in the importation of unwanted Chinese workers; and capitalists in the U.S. government with links to sugar interests in the Caribbean maintained high tariffs on Hawaiian imports, thus severely restricting trade. There for four months, Clemens reported on not only the sugar industry, but whatever else of interest he witnessed. A memorable local custom he naturally felt compelled to study was the hula dance and its various technical aspects. And on one occasion, the rascally humorist came upon "a bevy of nude native young ladies bathing in the sea, and went and sat down on their clothes to keep them from being stolen."[16]

In the fall of 1866 Clemens was back in San Francisco, yet again without work, and yet again necessity would be the mother of his career. "I tortured my brain for a saving scheme of some kind, and at last a public lecture occurred to me!" he wrote of his plan to lecture about the Sandwich Islands. "I sat down and wrote one, in a fever of hopeful anticipation. I showed it to several friends, but they all shook their heads. They said nobody would come to hear me, and I would make a humiliating failure of it."[17]

To Overcome Fear of Public Speaking, Clemens Uses a Variety of Tricks

What Clemens had going for him was a reputation earned from his colorful Sandwich Island letters and a fan of his who knew show business: "Thomas McGuire, proprietor of several theaters, said that now was the time to make my fortune— strike while the iron was hot—break into the lecture field! I did it." Another motivating factor: Clemens had not forgotten Artemus Ward's 1863–1864 tour that had netted the humorist $30,000, so now he wisely modeled himself after the successful Ward, with whom he had become chums.

Clemens had already taken a pseudonym, as had Ward, whose real name was the more staid sounding Charles Farrar Browne. On the surface, their writing styles were very similar, too, as Ward was a satirist who poked fun at his contemporaries in various pieces he wrote for the Cleveland *Plain Dealer*, writing pun-ridden, misspelled, and ungrammatical accounts that made war-weary readers laugh. A deadpan comedian and lecturer of renown, Ward used backwoods characters and local dialect to accentuate his social commentary. Sound familiar? That was Clemens. The two even shared a physical resemblance: They both had bushy, unkempt hair and drooping mustaches, which added to their comedic air.

Bolstered by McGuire's confidence, Clemens rented the largest venue: San Francisco's Academy of Music, which could seat as many as 2,000 people and was owned by Thomas McGuire, of course. It would be the first of many times that he leveraged his connections with those who were rich and higher on the social ladder than he. The McGuire connection also cost him $50 plus half of the receipts for use of the venue. In the weeks before his first performance, he spent $150 on handbills and a newspaper ad. The witty and bold text was pure Twain—er, Clemens:

A SPLENDID ORCHESTRA is in town, but has not been engaged.

A DEN OF FEROCIOUS WILD BEASTS will be on exhibition on the next block.

MAGNIFICENT FIREWORKS were in contemplation for this occasion, but the idea has been abandoned.

A GRAND TORCHLIGHT PROCESSION may be expected; in fact, the public are privileged to expect whatever they please.

"I announced a lecture on the Sandwich Islands," Clemens recalled, "closing the advertisement with the remark: 'Admission one dollar; doors open at half past seven, the trouble begins at eight.' A true prophecy. The trouble certainly did begin at eight, when I found myself in front of the only audience I had ever faced, for the fright which pervaded me from head to foot was paralyzing. It lasted two minutes and was as bitter as death; the memory of it is indestructible but it had its compensations, for it made me immune from timidity before audiences for all time to come."[18]

Throughout the lecture, he kept the audience off balance, shifting smoothly from a dramatic description of a volcano eruption to threatening to demonstrate cannibalism by eating a baby onstage; from a random joke about Horace Greeley, among other "snappers," to dramatic pauses that left the audience on the edge of their seat. To set up a punch line or to emphasize a point, Clemens strongly believed in the power of the pause:

> For one audience the pause will be short, for another a little longer, for another a shade longer still; the performer must vary the length of the pause to suit the shades of difference between audiences. These variations of measurement are so slight, so delicate, that they may almost be compared with the shadings achieved by Pratt and Whitney's ingenious machine which measures the five-millionth part of an inch. An audience is that machine's twin; it can measure a pause down to that vanishing fraction.
>
> I used to play with the pause as other children play with a toy. . . . I had three or four pieces in which the pauses performed an important part, and I used to lengthen them or shorten them

according to the requirements of the case, and I got much pleasure out of the pause when it was accurately measured and a certain discomfort when it wasn't.[19]

The October 2, 1866, lecture, the first of thousands of lectures, grossed $1,200 but Clemens netted only $400 due to expenses. Seeing the potential to pocket far more than he had made as a riverboat pilot, he immediately hired a business manager, Denis E. McCarthy, who knew the business and could assist him in laying out a lecture tour with a more favorable return than permitted by the wily McGuire.[20] The very next week it was off to Sacramento, and then on to other principal towns in California and Nevada, where his Sandwich letters had been reprinted in local papers and there would be a rapt audience. After this western tour, it was time to turn east and conquer the rest of the civilized world. The three-month 1861 "pleasure trip" with Orion to the silver mines of Nevada had lasted almost six years.

Giving Away a Product Can Pay Future Dividends

Before departing for New York City, Clemens wrote a letter to his mother in which he reveled in the social connections he was making with community leaders, albeit mostly clergymen (the humorous irony here being the fact that Clemens would reject organized religion). He had even set his eyes on the renowned minister Henry Ward Beecher, who would later be caught up in a sex scandal, accused of having an inappropriate relationship with another man's wife:

MY DEAR FOLKS,—I have written to Annie and Sammy and Katie some time ago—also, to the balance of you.

I called on Rev. Dr. Wadsworth last night with the City College man, but he wasn't at home. I was sorry, because I wanted to make his acquaintance. I am thick as thieves with the Rev. Stebbings, and I am laying for the Rev. Scudder and the Rev. Dr. Stone. I am running on preachers, now, altogether. I find them gay. Stebbings is a regular brick. I am taking letters of introduction to Henry Ward Beecher, Rev. Dr. Tyng, and other eminent parsons in the east. Whenever anybody offers me a letter to a preacher, now I snaffle it on the spot.[21]

Although Clemens arrived in New York on January 12, 1867, his debut as a lecturer did not occur until that spring, when he was booked for an engagement at the Peter Cooper Institute. It was a high-profile venue that sat 3,000, but he feared an empty house because he wasn't sure New Yorkers knew of him and his Sandwich Islands adventures. Also, there were competing events that night. His new lecture circuit manager, Frank Fuller, said not to worry—he had a plan. He proceeded to hand out bushels of free tickets. Clemens trusted Fuller, whom he had met in 1861 when the charismatic Fuller was secretary of the Utah Territory. Well, the auditorium was indeed packed, but they only took in a measly $35. As Fuller explained to Clemens, it would pay hefty future benefits, and the strategy did indeed succeed:

> He [Fuller] was perfectly delighted, perfectly enchanted. He couldn't keep his mouth shut for several days. "Oh," he said, "the fortune didn't come in—that didn't come in—that's all right. That's coming in later. The fame is already here, Mark. Why, in a week you'll be the best-known man in the United Sates. This is no failure. This is a prodigious success."
>
> That episode must have cost him four or five hundred dollars but he never said a word about that. He was as happy, as satisfied, as proud, as delighted, as if he had laid the fabled golden egg and hatched it.
>
> He was right about the fame. I certainly did get working quantity of fame out of that lecture. The New York newspapers praised

it. The country newspapers copied those praises. The lyceums of the country—it was right in the heyday of the old lyceum lecture system—began to call for me. . . . I went West and lectured every night for six or eight weeks at a hundred dollars a night—and I now considered that the whole of the prophecy was fulfilled. I had acquired fame and also fortune.[22]

At age 32 Clemens was raking in money from his lectures and newspaper articles. He was the toast of the literati, hob-nobbing with the social elite who wished to be entertained, and residing in the opulent Metropolitan Hotel on Broadway and Prince Street. Opened in 1852 and once considered the most magnificent hotel on lower Broadway, the Metropolitan was now surrounded by even more palatial hotels such as the St. Nicholas, as well as fantastic emporiums, theaters, and fine restaurants, most built from marble, brownstone, or decorative cast iron. The six-story Metropolitan, designed in a style reminiscent of Roman palazzos, had all the latest amenities such as gas lighting, steam heat, speaking tubes, and bathrooms on each floor. The lavish decor included rare marble, polished oak banisters, rosewood furniture, silk damask curtains, and stained-glass windows. The hotel also housed retail stores that boasted huge panes of glass for displaying goods.

However, all of this luxury and high living had not come to Clemens overnight. His career had taken a very winding path to date—and would continue to be derailed from time to time—as he evolved as both author and businessman. In the coming years, he would knock heads with slick-talking Elisha Bliss, who would become his publisher, and then, as the 1870s unfolded, he would find himself with enough disposable cash to fancy himself a capitalist in the mold of such tycoons as Cornelius Vanderbilt, albeit more compassionate than the cut-throat commodore.

QUIRKY HABITS AND BRAZEN PHILOSOPHY

Overcoming Stage Fright and Winning the Audience as a Public Speaker

*"When an audience do not complain,
it is a compliment, & when they do,
it is a compliment, too, if unaccompanied by violence."*

Before launching into his sharply crafted lectures, Clemens felt "the necessity of preceding it with something which would break up the house with a laugh and get me on pleasant and friendly terms with it at the start. . . ." During the lecture itself, sometimes he would randomly repeat a well-known, over-used anecdote four or five times in a deadpan manner, which on the third time or so would get a laugh just because he was repeating it. Even when discoursing on serious subjects, Clemens understood that people were there to be entertained, which included humor. If the audience didn't laugh fully a half dozen times over an hour, he felt the talk was a failure.

Clemens believed strongly in practicing his lecture, because any fool knew the "lecturers who were 'new to the business' [and] did not know the value of 'trying it on the dog.' "[23] One of his best strategies for insuring success with the audience, even when delivering a pitiable talk, was to plant friends in the crowd, which the wily Clemens did at his first-ever lecture on October 2, 1866. Nevertheless, the days and the moments leading up to his debut were filled with anxiety, an experience retold in his book *Roughing It*:

In three days I did a hundred and fifty dollars' worth of printing and advertising, and was the most distressed and frightened creature on the Pacific coast. I could not sleep—who could, under such circumstances? For other people there was facetiousness in the last line of my posters, but to me it was plaintive with a pang when I wrote it:

"Doors open at 7 1/2. The trouble will begin at 8."

That line has done good service since. Showmen have borrowed it frequently. I have even seen it appended to a newspaper advertisement reminding school pupils in vacation what time next term would begin. As those three days of suspense dragged by, I grew more and more unhappy. I had sold two hundred tickets among my personal friends, but I feared they might not come. My lecture, which had seemed "humorous" to me, at first, grew steadily more and more dreary, till not a vestige of fun seemed left, and I grieved that I could not bring a coffin on the stage and turn the thing into a funeral. I was so panic-stricken, at last, that I went to three old friends, giants in stature, cordial by nature, and stormy-voiced, and said:

"This thing is going to be a failure; the jokes in it are so dim that nobody will ever see them; I would like to have you sit in the parquette, and help me through."

They said they would. Then I went to the wife of a popular citizen, and said that if she was willing to do me a very great kindness, I would be glad if she and her husband would sit prominently in the left-hand stage-box, where the whole house could see them. I explained that I should need help, and would turn toward her and smile, as a signal, when I had been delivered of an obscure joke—"and then," I added, "don't wait to investigate, but respond!"

She promised. Down the street I met a man I never had seen before. He had been drinking, and was beaming with smiles and good nature. He said:

"My name's Sawyer. You don't know me, but that don't matter. I haven't got a cent, but if you knew how bad I wanted to laugh, you'd give me a ticket. Come, now, what do you say?"

(Continued)

Overcoming Stage Fright and Winning the Audience as a Public Speaker *(Continued)*

"Is your laugh hung on a hair-trigger?—that is, is it critical, or can you get it off easy?"

My drawling infirmity of speech so affected him that he laughed a specimen or two that struck me as being about the article I wanted, and I gave him a ticket, and appointed him to sit in the second circle, in the centre, and be responsible for that division of the house. I gave him minute instructions about how to detect indistinct jokes, and then went away, and left him chuckling placidly over the novelty of the idea.

I ate nothing on the last of the three eventful days—I only suffered. . . . I thought of suicide, pretended illness, flight. I thought of these things in earnest, for I was very miserable and scared. But of course I had to drive them away, and prepare to meet my fate. I could not wait for half-past seven—I wanted to face the horror, and end it—the feeling of many a man doomed to hang, no doubt. I went down back streets at six o'clock, and entered the theatre by the back door. I stumbled my way in the dark among the ranks of canvas scenery, and stood on the stage. The house was gloomy and silent, and its emptiness depressing. I went into the dark among the scenes again, and for an hour and a half gave myself up to the horrors, wholly unconscious of everything else. Then I heard a murmur; it rose higher and higher, and ended in a crash, mingled with cheers. It made my hair raise, it was so close to me, and so loud.

There was a pause, and then another; presently came a third, and before I well knew what I was about, I was in the middle of the stage, staring at a sea of faces, bewildered by the fierce glare of the lights, and quaking in every limb with a terror that seemed like to take my life away. The house was full, aisles and all!

The tumult in my heart and brain and legs continued a full minute before I could gain any command over myself. Then I recognized the charity and the friendliness in the faces before me, and little by little my fright melted away, and I began to talk. Within three or four minutes I was comfortable, and even content. My three chief allies, with three auxiliaries, were on hand, in the parquette, all sitting together, all armed with bludgeons, and all ready to make an onslaught upon the feeblest joke that might show its head. And whenever a joke did fall, their bludgeons came down and their faces seemed to split from ear to ear.

Sawyer, whose hearty countenance was seen looming redly in the centre of the second circle, took it up, and the house was carried handsomely. Inferior jokes never fared so royally before. Presently I delivered a bit of serious matter with impressive unction (it was my pet), and the audience listened with an absorbed hush that gratified me more than any applause; and as I dropped the last word of the clause, I happened to turn and catch Mrs. ——'s intent and waiting eye; my conversation with her flashed upon me, and in spite of all I could do I smiled. She took it for the signal, and promptly delivered a mellow laugh that touched off the whole audience; and the explosion that followed was the triumph of the evening. I thought that that honest man Sawyer would choke himself; and as for the bludgeons, they performed like piledrivers. But my poor little morsel of pathos was ruined. It was taken in good faith as an intentional joke, and the prize one of the entertainment, and I wisely let it go at that.[24]

WELCOME TO CORPORATE AMERICA: HARD-NOSED NEGOTIATING AND PROFIT-DRIVEN MANAGEMENT

"For all the talk you hear about knowledge being such a wonderful thing, instinct is worth forty of it for real unerringness."

*C*lemens entered the often cutthroat book publishing world in 1868, when he signed a book contract with the American Publishing Company, Hartford, Connecticut. Rather than accepting a flat fee, he took a calculated risk by opting for a royalty rate that could bring a greater reward. From 1868 to 1879, Clemens became a seasoned negotiator, demanded accountability from his publisher, and fought to protect his own interests, which included attacking his publisher's board of directors and initiating lawsuits against anyone violating his copyrights. In 1880, Clemens sought a new publisher who offered more lucrative terms, settling on his friend James R. Osgood.

These were heady days as the budding author fielded generous offers from a number of newspapers, but held out for the right opportunity. It would come late in 1867 when a Hartford, Connecticut–based publisher approached him about writing a book. Clemens would seize the offer; however, he would find himself in a circle of cold, calculating businessmen, as opposed to the bon vivant newspaper editors he was accustomed to.

Fortunately, the incisive lessons he had learned during his rag-tag mining days—spotting swindlers, playing hardball, and his bungling of the million-dollar claim—would aid him in his negotiations and subsequent dealings.

Meanwhile, there were too many parties and events to attend as he ingratiated himself with the likes of Henry Ward Beecher, who, at age 54, was 22 years Clemens's senior. A captivating speaker, studious looking but with a slight, playful grin, and long hair that dangled to his collar, he had the brains, wit, and charm Clemens appreciated in a man. A community leader, a man of letters, and the brother of Harriet Beecher Stowe, Beecher also had the connections with New York's elite with whom Clemens so desired to mingle. The Missouri native won invitations to New York's venerable Century Club, whose membership included the influential poet William Cullen Bryant as well as other reputable authors and artists. And—though it had been a long time coming—he visited his mother and sister Pamela, who had moved to St. Louis.

His plodding, more unwittingly incremental than methodically planned writing career took another step forward in May 1867, when his friend Charles Henry Webb, the founder of the *Californian* journal, requested permission and issued *The Celebrated Jumping Frog of Calaveras County, and Other Sketches*. This collection of stories, essays, and travel letters was poorly produced and had anemic sales, but the critics reviewed his work positively, which Clemens was able to use for self-promotion. He also considered pulling together a book of all his Sandwich Island travel letters, but he feared the book market was weak because *Jumping Frog* was not selling strongly. Additionally, the buying public was tentative as the economy was going through its usual upheavals thanks to scoundrels like Cornelius Vanderbilt, Jay Gould, and Daniel Drew, who were battling over the Erie Railroad and dumping worthless stock on the market. So Clemens exercised patience rather than setting himself up for failure.

In a June 7 letter to his mother, Clemens appeared to have

lost interest in New York, as he portrayed a complex, restless side of his nature that would forever distract him from writing. He also provided a brief status report of his career and hinted at adventure to come:

> Corresponding has been a perfect drag ever since I got to the states. If it continues abroad, I don't know what the Tribune and Alta folks will think. I have withdrawn the Sandwich Island book—it would be useless to publish it in these dull publishing times. As for the Frog book, I don't believe that will ever pay anything worth a cent. I published it simply to advertise myself—not with the hope of making anything out of it.
>
> Well, I haven't anything to write, except that I am tired of staying in one place—that I am in a fever to get away. . . .
>
> You observe that under a cheerful exterior I have got a spirit that is angry with me and gives me freely its contempt. I can get away from that at sea, and be tranquil and satisfied—and so, with my parting love and benediction for Orion and all of you, I say goodbye and God bless you all—and welcome the wind that wafts a weary soul to the sunny lands of the Mediterranean![1]

Clemens had succeeded in winning an invitation from Reverend Beecher—a consummate publicity hound—to join an expedition to the Holy Land, as well as to Egypt, Greece, and other points of interest along the Mediterranean shore and on the Continent. Organized for the summer of 1867, it was to be a faith-based media bonanza as these noted pilgrims returned to the land of Jesus. A diligent opportunist, Clemens subsequently negotiated deals with the *Daily Alta Californian* and the New York *Tribune* to send letters for publication. Ergo, the trip would be both spiritual and profitable. Although Beecher couldn't make the journey, the 80 or so pilgrims departed New York on June 9 aboard the paddle steamer *Quaker City* and—almost six months later—returned November 19.

During the voyage, Clemens wrote travel letters that lampooned his fellow travelers more than they reveled in the historical sights. He excelled at annoying his fellow pilgrims with his profanity, card playing, and smoking, and by calling them "old asses" and "enterprising idiots" in his articles—those articles eventually making their way to the ship via mail packages. Although aware of their displeasure, Clemens hardly suppressed himself, and the trip provided fodder for his future book *The Innocents Abroad*. He also roomed with a short, fat man named Dan Slote, who shared his propensity to have fun at everyone else's expense, and who would figure in Clemens's future as a business partner.

Be Certain of the Details and Check References before Inking Any Kind of Deal

Shortly after wayward pilgrim Clemens returned to New York, he received an enticing letter from the smooth-talking Elisha Bliss, secretary of the American Publishing Company:

HARTFORD, CONN, Nov 21, 1867.

SAMUEL L. CLEMENS Esq.
Tribune Office, New York.

DR. SIR,—We take the liberty to address you this, in place of a letter which we had recently written and was about to forward to you, not knowing your arrival home was expected so soon. We are desirous of obtaining from you a work of some kind, perhaps compiled from your letters from the East, &c., with such interesting additions as may be proper. We are the publishers of A. D. Richardson's works, and flatter ourselves that we can give an author as favorable terms and do as full justice to his productions as any other house in the country. We are perhaps the oldest subscription house in the country, and have never failed to give a book an immense circulation. We sold about 100,000 copies of Richardson's F. D. & E. (Field, Dungeon and Escape) and are now printing 41,000, of "Beyond the Mississippi," and large orders ahead. If you have any thought of writing a book, or could be induced to do so, we should be pleased to see you; and will do so. Will you do us the favor to reply at once, at your earliest convenience.

Very truly, &c.,

E. BLISS, Jr.
Secty.[2]

Clemens had already thought of writing a book about his pilgrim voyage, and suggested such in a December 2 reply. However, thanks to his Wild West days that had promised buckets of silver, a seasoned Clemens was wary of the success alluded to by the effusive Bliss, a vigilant-looking stalker of profits who was completely bald across his scalp but had bushy sideburns that ran down along his jaw until linking up with a trimmed mustache. The exacting author wanted to know what specifications Bliss had in mind for a book and what it would pay. He wanted details nailed down. "If you think such a book would suit your purpose," Clemens wrote, "please drop me a line, specifying the size and general style of the volume; when the matter ought to be ready; whether it should have pictures in it or not; and particularly what your terms with me would be, and what amount of money I might possibly make out of it. The latter clause has a degree of importance for me which is almost beyond my own comprehension. But you understand that, of course."

Clemens played it cool with Bliss, too, stating that he knew Richardson, which strongly suggested he could easily learn more about Bliss's treatment of authors, and intimating that there were other lucrative deals in the works: "I have other propositions for a book, but have doubted the propriety of interfering with good newspaper engagements, except my way as an author could be demonstrated to be plain before me. But I know Richardson, and learned from him some months ago, something of an idea of the subscription plan of publishing. If that is your plan invariably, it looks safe."[3]

Clemens Refuses to Compromise Himself and Takes a Calculated Risk on His First Book Deal

Negotiations with Bliss continued into January 1868, but Clemens was tiring of Bliss's haggling. The author couldn't tolerate being nickel-and-dimed. Whenever he felt slighted, he became notoriously fiery. As a prime example, such was the case in November 1867 when the *Herald* newspaper inadvertently forgot to include his byline on an article. "I had a fine row with the Herald people this morning because they left out my signature—" he wrote home, "however I went to dinner with the whole editorial corps and they explained and we settled it without bloodshed. It looked shabby to me, but the foreman was innocently to blame in the matter, not the editors."[4]

Bliss would also soon learn that any attempt to place parameters or restraint on Clemens's writing would be fruitless. Consider the author's forthright response to an offer by the New York *Herald*: "I stopped in the Herald office as I came through New York," he explained to his mother and sister that January, "to see the boys on the staff, and young James Gordon Bennett asked me to write twice a week, impersonally, for the Herald, and said if I would I might have full swing, and (write) about anybody and everybody I wanted to. I said I must have the very fullest possible swing, and he said 'all right.' I said 'It's a contract—' and that settled that matter."[5]

Clemens also updated his mother on the Bliss negotiations, which had an all-or-nothing tone to them: "But the best thing that has happened was here. This great American Publishing Company kept on trying to bargain with me for a book till I thought I would cut the matter short by coming up for a talk." He understood that a face-to-face would quickly clear up any loose ends and result in an advantageous contract. Wisely, he still sought advice from Reverend Beecher, who perhaps shared a sliver of God's omniscience:

> I met Rev. Henry Ward Beecher in Brooklyn, and with his usual whole-souled way of dropping his own work to give other people a lift when he gets a chance, he said, "Now, here, you are one of the talented men of the age—nobody is going to deny that—but in matters of business, I don't suppose you know more than enough to come in when it rains. I'll tell you what to do, and how to do it." And he did.
>
> And I listened well, and then came up here and made a splendid contract for a Quaker City book of 5 or 600 large pages, with illustrations, the manuscript to be placed in the publishers' hands by the middle of July. My percentage is to be a fifth more than they have ever paid any author, except Horace Greeley. Beecher will be surprised, I guess, when he hears this.
>
> But I had my mind made up to one thing—I wasn't going to touch a book unless there was money in it, and a good deal of it. I told them so. I had the misfortune to "bust out" one author of standing. They had his manuscript, with the understanding that they would publish his book if they could not get a book from me, (they only publish two books at a time, and so my book and Richardson's Life of Grant will fill the bill for next fall and winter)—so that manuscript was sent back to its author today."[6]

As for the almighty dollar, Bliss now offered two options to Clemens: "In lieu of the royalty I was offered the alternative of ten thousand dollars cash upon delivery of the manuscript. I consulted A.D. Richardson and he said, 'Take the royalty.' I followed his advice and closed with Bliss."[7] Clemens negotiated for a 5 percent royalty, a full point higher than what Richardson was being paid. While there was greater risk in not taking the $10,000—a very sizable sum in 1868—there was the potential of a much greater reward. Clemens was not only putting faith in his ability to produce a successful book, but was counting on Bliss's sales force.

A Willingness to Listen to Others—As Painful As It Is— Yields Benefits

Having quit the grueling lecture circuit, publishing few news-paper pieces, and being distracted by love, Clemens would need all the money he could get from a book deal. "In twelve months (or rather I believe it is fourteen,)" he wrote home in June, "I have earned just eighty dollars by my pen—two little magazine squibs and one newspaper letter—altogether the idlest, laziest 14 months I ever spent in my life. And in that time my absolute and necessary expenses have been scorchingly heavy—for I have now less than three thousand six hundred dollars in bank out of the eight or nine thousand I have made during those months, lecturing. My expenses were something frightful during the winter. I feel ashamed of my idleness, and yet I have had really no inclination to do anything but court Livy. I haven't any other inclination yet."[8]

He was courting one Olivia "Livy" Langdon, whom he had met through her brother, Charley, a shipmate and drinking part-ner from Beecher's pilgrim ship. Ten years Clemens's junior, the 22-year-old Livy had pure ivory skin that was a stark contrast to her dark hair, dreamy eyes, and ears that protruded ever so slightly but added to her attractiveness. She lived in Elmira, New York, and was the daughter of a successful, self-made capitalist, which further enticed Clemens. Jervis Langdon was everything Clemens's father had not been, which boiled down to being rich, having made a fortune in coal, among other ventures. Livy would become his wife and lifelong editor.

While Clemens was uncompromising in some respects, he was broad-minded enough to seek input when it came to his writing. "In the beginning of our engagement the proofs of my first book, *The Innocents Abroad*, began to arrive and she read them with me," Clemens recounted of his relationship with Livy as he began the painful process of writing his first book. "She also edited them. She was my faithful, judicious and painstaking editor from that day forth until within three or four months of her death—a stretch of more than a third of a century."[9]

While inviting her into his author's world was a suave move, to his credit, he was also not afraid of exposing himself to his peers' honest feedback. He shared his work with fellow writers and friends Bret Harte and William Dean Howells, which was agonizing at times but necessary to improve the quality of his writing. And as long as their opinions weren't too demoralizing or otherwise slanderous, Clemens respected people who were honest, sincere, kind, and had pluck.

Clemens also listened to others when it came to settling on a title for his first book. "I want a name that is striking, comprehensive, & out of the common order," he wrote to friend Mary Fairbanks. "I had chosen 'The New Pilgrim's Progress,' but it is thought that many dull people will shudder at that, as at least taking the name of the consecrated book in vain. . . . I have thought of 'The Irruption of the Jonathans—Or, the Modern Pilgrim's Progress'—you see the second title can remain, if I only precede it with something that will let it down easy. Give me a name, please."[10] Not long after, he offered Bliss two options: *The Exodus of the Innocents* or *The Innocents Abroad*. Clemens preferred the latter, and so it was.

Don't Be Afraid to Make Trouble in Order to Protect Your Self-Interest

Increasingly hungry for income, Clemens was distraught when the publishing date of *The Innocents Abroad* was repeatedly pushed back due to delays in publishing other books ahead in the queue. He fired off a scathing letter to Bliss that dripped with sarcasm, omitting a salutation in order to set a hard tone immediately:

> I am not contending that I am hurt unto death simply because the delay for "Grant" damaged my interests; or because the delay for the "Metropolis" damaged my interests likewise; or because the

delay necessary to make me a spring vegetable damaged my interests . . . No. All I want to know is, —viz:—to wit—as follows:

After it is done being a fall book, upon what argument shall
you perceive that it will be best to make a winter book of it?
And—

After it is done being a winter book, upon what argument shall
you perceive that it will be best to make another spring book of it
again? . . .

All I desire is to be informed from time to time . . . so that I
can go on informing my friends intelligently—I mean that infatuated baker's dozen of them who faithful unto death, still believe
that I am going to publish a book.

Weeks and then months continued to go by with no explanation, so, concerned that his interests had been "entirely disre-
garded," Clemens took it upon himself to venture to Hartford
for a well-deserved explanation.[11] "Bliss said that the fault was
not his; that he wanted to publish the book but the directors of
his company were staid old fossils and were afraid of it," the author recalled. "They had examined the book and the majority of
them were of the opinion that there were places in it of a humorous character. Bliss said the house had never published a
book that had a suspicion like that attaching to it and that the directors were afraid that a departure of this kind could seriously
injure the house's reputation, that he was tied hand and foot and
was not permitted to carry out his contract." Well, for Clemens
the situation was unacceptable: A contract was a contract.

One of the American Publishing Company's directors, Mr.
Sidney Drake, invited Clemens on a buggy ride in hopes of ap-
peasing the aggravated author. Filled with contempt for Drake,
Clemens was hardly going to capitulate:

He was a pathetic old relic and his ways and his talk were also pathetic. He had a delicate purpose in view and it took him some
time to hearten himself sufficiently to carry it out, but at last he

accomplished it. He explained the house's difficulty and distress, as Bliss had already explained it. Then he frankly threw himself and the house upon my mercy and begged me to take away The Innocents Abroad and release the concern from the contract. I said I wouldn't—and so ended the interview and the buggy excursions.

Then I warned Bliss that he must get to work or I should make trouble. He acted upon the warning and set up the book and I read the proofs. Then there was another long wait and no explanation. At last toward the end of July (1869, I think) I lost patience and telegraphed Bliss that if the book was not on sale in twenty-four hours I should bring suit for damages.

That ended the trouble. Half a dozen copies were bound and placed on sale within the required time. Then the canvassing began and went briskly forward. In nine months the book took the publishing house out of debt, advanced its stock from twenty-five to two hundred and left seventy thousand dollars profit to the good. It was Bliss that told me this—but if it was true it was the first time that he had told the truth in sixty-five years. He was born in 1804.[12]

Of course, *The Innocents Abroad* was a hit. And Bliss took credit for discovering Clemens—as did dozens of other editors and publishers of various newspapers and magazines. "I came to believe that I had been more multitudinously discovered and created than any other animal that had ever issued from the Deity's hands," concluded Clemens. *Created* is the operative word. But it was Clemens who was consciously and conspicuously creating an image for himself with his rough and wild looks, incessant smoking of cigars, uncompromising attitude, and blistering commentary on the world.

Come January 1870, Clemens and Bliss had achieved a measure of detente, a condition facilitated by the success of the book. "Yes, I am satisfied with the way you are running the Book," Clemens extolled. "You are running it in staving, tip-top, first-class style." Digesting the various aspects of subscription sales,

Clemens appreciated the sales process for its military-like action and soaked it all in:

> What with advertising, establishing agencies, &c., you have got an enormous lot of machinery under way and hard at work in a wonderfully short space of time. It is easy to see, when one travels around, that one must be endowed with a deal of genuine gener-alship in order to maneuvre a publication whose line of battle stretches from end to end of a great continent, and whose foragers and skirmishers invest every hamlet and besiege every village hid-den away in all the vast space between.[13]

Clemens's calculated gamble of taking the 5 percent royalty paid off: The book netted him over $16,000, easily surpassing the $10,000 option he could have taken. In the United States alone, *The Innocents Abroad* sold over 82,000 copies in 18 months—a substantial success for that time—with an average retail price of four dollars.[14] His next book, *Roughing It*, pub-lished in 1872, sold over 75,000 copies its first year and netted him just over $20,000.[15] By 1874 about 240,000 of Clemens's books would be sold, which has been called "an astonishing achievement for that time." For Bliss and American Publishing, it meant a gross income of almost a million dollars—not bad for a modest Hartford outfit.[16]

Clemens Buys Stock in His Publishing Company to Insure They're Being Honest

Naturally, on the heels of *The Innocents Abroad*'s success, both Clemens and Bliss were anxious to crank out another book, the next being *Roughing It*. So Clemens wrote like a fiend and im-mediately passed along finished chapters to Bliss so he could incorporate them into the prospectus used by his sales agents. "If you want to issue a prospectus and go right to canvassing," a marketing savvy Clemens wrote to Bliss in May 1871, "say the word and I will forward some more MS—or send it by hand—special messenger. Whatever chapters you think are unquestionably good, we will retain of course, so they can go into a prospectus as well one time as another. The book will be done soon, now. I have 1200 pages of MS already written and am now writing 200 a week—more than that, in fact; during the past week wrote 23 one day, then 30, 33, 35, 52, and 65.—How's that?"[17] This letter was one of many in which Clemens boasted about his capacity to churn out manuscript.

Already with an eye on future contract negotiations with the tight-walleted New Englander, Clemens concluded his letter to Bliss with a blast of self-promotion: "The reaction is beginning and my stock is looking up. I am getting the bulliest offers for books and almanacs; am flooded with lecture invitations, and one periodical offers me $6,000 cash for 12 articles, of any length and on any subject, treated humorously or otherwise." This reminder of his growing reputation would put pressure on Bliss to ante up a heftier royalty rate. Clemens wanted 10 percent, but Bliss claimed his firm would not earn any profit if they acquiesced to his demands. To bolster his argument, the publisher laid out the facts and figures and asked Clemens to put himself in their place.[18]

Refusing to pander to Bliss, instead Clemens summoned him to the Langdon home in Elmira for contract talks, which put the publisher on his heels. The very fact that Bliss accepted placed him at a disadvantage: By making the arduous trip he was essentially conceding to Clemens, who was quickly learning how to control the businessmen around him. However, Clemens later admitted that he still had much to learn about publishing at the time of this negotiation:

I sent for Bliss and he came to Elmira. If I had known as much about book publishing then as I know now, I would have required of Bliss seventy-five or eighty per cent of the profits above cost of manufacture, and this would have been fair and just. But I knew nothing about the business and had been too indolent to try to learn anything about it. I told Bliss I did not wish to leave his corporation and that I did not want extravagant terms. I said I thought I ought to have half the profit above cost of manufacture and he said with enthusiasm that that was exactly right, exactly right.

He went to his hotel and drew the contract and brought it to the house in the afternoon. I found a difficulty in it. It did not name "half profits," but named a seven and a half per cent royalty instead. I asked him to explain that. I said that that was not the understanding. He said "No, it wasn't," but that he had put in a royalty to simplify the matter—that seven and a half per cent royalty represented fully half the profit and a little more, up to a sale of a hundred thousand copies, that after that the publishing company's half would be a shade superior to mine.

I was a little doubtful, a little suspicious, and asked him if he could swear to that. He promptly put up his hand and made oath to it, exactly repeating the words which he had just used.[19]

While the offer of 7.5 percent royalty on the retail price, which Bliss claimed amounted to half the book's profits, appeared generous, Clemens clearly did not trust the conniving publisher. Even after making Bliss take an oath of honesty, he still harbored doubts. From his mining days, he was wary of business partners offering a percentage of profits—that could mean almost anything depending on how the numbers were manipulated—so an emboldened Clemens demanded that Bliss open the company's books to him. In March 1872, the justifiably paranoid author traveled to Hartford and together they went over the accounting books. Clemens came away pleased that Bliss had convinced him "by good solid arguments and figures instead of mere plausible generalities" that he was not being swindled, "for that was just and business-like."[20]

To further protect his interests, in 1872 Clemens purchased $5,000 worth of the American Publishing Company's stock and insisted he be given a seat on the board of directors.[21] Although he refrained from becoming involved in daily management issues, in June 1876 he thought the company was operating a little too extravagantly, with unnecessary expenses cutting into both his royalties and his stock dividends. In a letter to Bliss, Clemens strongly suggested the company—which, he believed, was overextending itself—sell its newly acquired plush offices at 294 Asylum Street, publish only "one or two books at a time" and scale back operations: "If the directors will cut the business down two-thirds, & the expenses in one half, I think it will be an advantage to all concerned, & I feel persuaded that I shall sell more books."

Bliss responded by trying to make Clemens feel guilty: "I am sorry you found it necessary to talk against my management outside of our board as I have several times heard you have. Even the poor drunken Williams comes and boastingly taunts me. . . ." Apparently, Bliss didn't mind talking behind Williams' back. Wisely, Clemens didn't bother to deny the claim: "I listen to a director of the company and others, and under irritated impulse, talk and act unwisely, and get sorry at leisure." But fairly relentless, he hammered home his point: "The business seems to be a great unpaying thing, whereas the reverse would be the case if it were shrunk up, perhaps. I don't know it, I simply suggest it. And with the suggestion I stop. My duty as a director and stockholder ends there."[22]

Clemens Takes a Mercenary View and Attacks Enemies Who Are Infringing on His Copyrights

Exceptionally competitive, Clemens considered alleged friend Bret Harte one of his primary opponents he wanted to beat in terms of book sales and revenue. Toward that end, he kept tabs on his competitor's contracts. "Bret Harte has sold his novel (same size as mine, I should say) to Scribner's Monthly for $6,500 (publication to begin in September, I think,) and he gets a royalty of 7½ per cent from Bliss in book form afterwards," he wrote to their mutual friend William Dean Howells, editor of the *Atlantic* magazine, in a July 1875 letter. "He gets a royalty of ten percent on it in England (issued in serial numbers) and the same royalty on it in book form afterwards, and is to receive an advance payment of five hundred pounds the day the first No. of the serial appears. If I could do as well, here, and there, with mine, it might possibly pay me, but I seriously doubt it though it is likely I could do better in England than Bret, who is not widely known there."

Painfully self-conscious of his suspect motivations, Clemens concluded, "You see I take a vile, mercenary view of things—but then my household expenses are something almost ghastly." In addition to keeping Livy comfortable, Clemens was also supporting his mother and supplementing his brother Orion's meager income. Watching his older brother Orion fail in venture after venture—politics, printing, newspaper editor, and running a boarding house—drove Clemens all the harder because his brother's situation served as a constant reminder of their father's failings.

On another battlefront, Clemens was fiercely concerned about the enforcement of stricter copyright laws to protect his work, which had already been pirated in the United States, Canada, and Great Britain. Over the years he would make speeches, write essays, and appear before legislatures on both sides of the Atlantic to further the cause. He was also more than willing to employ a lawyer to go after those "idiots"—a term he used with impunity—whom he believed had infringed on his copyrighted material. "Osgood [a Boston publisher] and I are 'going for' the puppy G—on infringement of trademark," he explained to Howells in a somewhat cryptic July 1875 letter. "To win one or two suits of this kind will set literary folks on a firmer bottom. I wish

Osgood would sue for stealing Holmes's poem. Wouldn't it be gorgeous to sue R—— for petty larceny? I will promise to go into court and swear I think him capable of stealing peanuts from a blind peddler."[23] In this case, which involved a book of his sketches being published without permission, he forcefully instructed his friend James Osgood to go after publisher William Gill (a.k.a. "puppy G"): "What I desire, *now*, is to go for Mr. Gill once more, at law—and this time, let us mean '*business.*'" Clemens would tolerate no compromises: He demanded $11,000 in restitution and a written confession from the perpetrator Gill.[24] Despite being a humorist, Clemens was exceptionally earnest when it came to protecting his monetary interests.

In 1876, to secure copyright for the surefire hit *The Adventures of Tom Sawyer* in both the United States and Great Britain simultaneously, Clemens was even willing to delay the book's publication. "Well," he wrote Howells, "yesterday I put in the Courant an editorial paragraph stating that Tom Sawyer is 'ready to issue, but publication is put off in order to secure English copyright by simultaneous publication there and here. The English edition is unavoidably delayed.'"[25] The notice in the Hartford newspaper served to placate his ravenous fans and to generate a smackerel of publicity. Behind the scenes, Clemens also blamed the delay on Bliss's mismanagement—their contentious relationship, although very profitable, was nearing its end.

By Continuously Pushing for a Better Contract, Clemens Exposes a Double-Crosser

By 1878 Clemens's relationship with Bliss had deteriorated to a breaking point, as the author was certain he was being swindled by the sniveling, money-grubbing publisher. He began to quietly negotiate with Bliss's likable son Frank, who was forming his own publishing firm. The scheming author calculated such a move would be a real stab in Elisha's back. But his break from the elder Bliss never materialized as young Frank soon confessed he was in over his head. With the two antagonists reunited in 1879, the thorny question of royalties was again raised by Clemens, whose brother Orion had convinced him he was indeed being "handsomely swindled." In response, Clemens insisted that the language of their latest contract be changed:

> I said that I was not satisfied about those royalties and that I did not believe in their "half-profit" pretenses, that this time he must put the "half profit" in the contract and make no mention of royalties—otherwise I would take the book elsewhere. He said he was perfectly willing to put it in, for it was right and just, and that if his directors opposed it and found fault with it he would withdraw from the concern and publish the book himself—fine talk, but I knew that he was master in that concern and that it would have to accept any contract that had been signed by him. This contract lay there on the billiard table with his signature attached to it. He had ridden his directors roughshod ever since the days of The Innocents Abroad and more than once he had told me that he had made his directors do things which they hadn't wanted to do, with the threat that if they did not comply he would leave the company's service and take me along with him.

However, again Bliss hesitated to agree to this language being inserted; he insisted that the company's directors would never consent to such a concession. As Bliss continued with his explanation, it became apparent to Clemens that Bliss was playing both the author and the publishing company for his own profit:

> I reminded him that his company would not be likely to make any trouble about a contract which had been signed by him. Then,

with one of his toothless smiles, he pointed out a detail which I had overlooked, to wit: the contract was with Elisha Bliss, a private individual, and the American Publishing Company was not mentioned in it.

He told me afterward that he took the contract to the directors and said that he would turn it over to the company for one-fourth of the profits of the book together with an increase of salary for himself and for Frank, his son, and that if these terms were not satisfactory he would leave the company and publish the book himself, whereupon the directors granted his demands and took the contract. The fact that Bliss told me these things with his own mouth is unassailable evidence that they were not true. Six weeks before the book issued from the press Bliss told the truth once, to see how it would taste, but it overstrained him and he died.[26]

In fact, Bliss did die, in October 1880, which finally gave Clemens an unfettered opportunity to fully analyze the American Publishing Company's books without interference at the very next annual meeting of stockholders. A semi-formal affair, it was held at the home of his neighbor, fellow stockholder, and longtime director in the publishing company, Newton Case. When the books were analyzed without Bliss's censoring and spinning, it was discovered that Clemens was being paid about a sixth of the profits on certain books for which he had been promised one half in his contract. "Well, Bliss was dead and I couldn't settle with him for his ten years of swindlings," Twain noted angrily, but added sarcastically, "I feel only compassion for him and if I could send him a fan I would." (A fan for cooling himself, because Bliss was in hell, no doubt.)

In his autobiography, Clemens reflected on the situation and his next steps:

When the balance sheets exposed to me the rascalities which I had been suffering at the hands of the American Publishing Company I stood up and delivered a lecture to Newton Case and the rest of the conspirators—meaning the rest of the directors.

My opportunity was now come to right myself and level up matters with the publishing company but I didn't see it, of course. I was seldom able to see an opportunity until it had ceased to be one. I knew all about that house now and I ought to have remained with it. I ought to have put a tax upon its profits for my personal benefit, the tax to continue until the difference between royalties and half profits should in time return from the company's pocket to mine and the company's robbery of me be thus wiped off the slate. But of course I couldn't think of anything so sane as that and I didn't. I only thought of ways and means to remove my respectability from that tainted atmosphere. I wanted to get my books out of the company's hands and carry them elsewhere. After a time I went to Newton Case—in his house as before—and proposed that the company cancel the contracts and restore my books to me free and unencumbered, the company retaining as a consideration the money it had swindled me out of on *Roughing It, The Gilded Age, Sketches New and Old* and *Tom Sawyer.*

Mr. Case demurred at my language but I told him I was not able to modify it, that I was perfectly satisfied that he and the rest of the Bible Class were aware of the fraud practiced on me in 1872 by Bliss—aware of it when it happened and consenting to it by silence. He objected to my calling the Board of Directors a Bible Class. And I said then it ought to stop opening its meetings with prayer—particularly when it was getting ready to swindle an author.[27]

To correct an injustice, Clemens certainly was not afraid of going to the top and speaking his mind. The audacity of calling the Board of Directors a Bible Class put Case on his heels, giving the author the advantage, and he would be paid more for his 1880 book *A Tramp Abroad* than he would have otherwise. Although he had never trusted Bliss, he still kicked himself for being hoodwinked: "I don't know how a grown person could ever be so simple and innocent as I was in those days. It ought to have occurred to me that a man who could talk like that must either be a fool or convinced that I was one. However, I was the one. And so even very dimple and rudimentary wisdoms were not likely to find their way into my head."[28]

In a letter to Orion, Clemens displayed not one shred of sympathy for his longtime publisher:

> Bliss is dead. The aspect of the balance-sheet is enlightening. It reveals the fact, through my present contract, (which is for half the profits on the book above actual cost of paper, printing and binding) that I have lost considerably by all this nonsense—sixty thousand dollars, I should say—and if Bliss were alive I would stay with the concern and get it all back; for on each new book I would require a portion of that back pay; but as it is (this in the very strictest confidence) I shall probably go to a new publisher 6 or 8 months hence, for I am afraid Frank, with his poor health, will lack push and drive.

For *A Tramp Abroad*, Clemens received an extra $20,000, for which he credited the semidestitute Orion because his brother had warned him of possible improprieties at the American Publishing Company. Actually displaying a soft side, the normally rough-edged Clemens rewarded Orion with an increase in his monthly stipend: "Twenty thousand dollars, after taxes and other expenses are stripped away, is worth to the investor about $75 a month—so I shall tell Mr. Perkins to make your check that amount per month, hereafter, while our income is able to afford it. This ends the loan business; and hereafter you can reflect that you are living not on borrowed money but on money which you have squarely earned, and which has no taint or savor of charity about it— and you can also reflect that the money you have been receiving of me all these years is interest charged against the heavy bill which the next publisher will have to stand who gets a book of mine."[29]

Business and Billiards Don't Mix; Clemens Learns That Partnering with a Friend Is Not Ideal

While Clemens continued to shop around for a new publisher, he attempted to buy out his own contracts from American Publishing, but the board refused to entertain his proposition—his books accounted for nine-tenths of their income. Bliss had sold more than 330,000 volumes for Clemens over 10 years, making him the best-selling American author of his time. Regardless of such success, he knew it was best to sever ties; he understood that it was better to remove himself from a "tainted atmosphere" even if it resulted in no income for a period.

For his next publisher, Clemens settled on his friend and Boston publisher, James R. Osgood, who had sought out Clemens in the early 1870s in hopes of publishing his work. More significantly, Clemens restructured the traditional publisher-author relationship for his next books, *The Prince and the Pauper* and *Life on the Mississippi*, published in 1881 and 1883, respectively. He wanted more control over the profit equation, so this time the book would be manufactured at his expense, while Osgood would manage the subscription campaign and charge the author "a royalty for his services." In other words, Osgood would be paid a sales commission—nothing more—so he was highly motivated to make the book a commercial success. Meanwhile, Clemens would reap both his royalties and any other profits left over if he ran a tight ship.

Regardless of the new, dynamic arrangement, success for *The Prince and the Pauper* was mixed because not only did the salesmen working under Osgood lack oversight, but Clemens and Osgood enjoyed each other's company too much. They passed many hours together playing billiards, smoking cigars, and generally having a good time. While Osgood and he were fast friends, Clemens knew he had to go elsewhere—but where?[30]

QUIRKY HABITS & BRAZEN PHILOSOPHY

The Author's Stormy Work Habits

When it came to writing, Clemens's work rhythm had a pronounced ebb and flow to it. Too easily distracted by business or socializing, he might neglect a project for weeks, months, or even years, which he ultimately regretted. In an 1896 interview, he stated, "Well, the fact is that for many years while at home, in America, I have written little or nothing on account of social calls upon my time. There is too much social life in my city for a literary man, and so for twenty years I gave up the attempt to do anything during nine months of the twelve I am at home. It has only been during the three months that I have annually been on vacation, and have been supposed to be holiday-making, that I have written anything. . . . I wish now, that I had done differently and had persisted in writing when at home."

When it came to the process of writing a book, Clemens gave himself mixed reviews. In the 1896 interview, the self-effacing Clemens admitted:

> I have what would be called pretty lazy methods in the matter of preparation for my books. It is a troublesome thing for a lazy man to take notes, and so I used to try in my young days to pack my impressions in my head. But that can't be done satisfactorily, and so I went from that to another stage— that of making notes in a note-book. But I jotted them down in so skeleton a form that they did not bring back to me what it was I wanted them to furnish. Having discovered that defect, I have mended my ways a good deal in this respect, but still my notes are inadequate. However, there may be some advantage to the reader in this, since in the absence of notes imagination has often to supply the place of facts.

(Continued)

The Author's Stormy Work Habits *(Continued)*

I have said just now I was lazy in preparation, but I won't admit that I am lazy in writing. No, I don't write rapidly, for when I did that I found it did not pay. I used to spend so much time next day correcting the manuscript, that it went to the printer a veritable forest of erasures, interlineations, emendations, abolitions, annihilations, and revisions. I found I should save time by writing slowly and carefully, and now my manuscript gives the printer no cause to blaspheme.[31]

In fact, Clemens was not lazy when he finally set to writing. He attacked a project with ferocity, ripping off 30 pages a day for weeks—immersed in a chaotic tempest of creation. He would strip down to his pants and suspenders, smoke and curse viciously, and litter the floor with garbage. In one particular letter to his friend William Dean Howells, he boasted, "I've done two seasons' work in one, and haven't anything left to do, now, but revise. I've written eight or nine hundred MS pages in such a brief space of time that I mustn't name the number of days; I shouldn't believe it myself, and of course couldn't expect you to. I used to restrict myself to 4 or 5 hours a day and 5 days in the week, but this time I've wrought from breakfast till 5:15 p.m. six days in the week; and once or twice I smouched a Sunday when the boss wasn't looking. Nothing is half so good as literature hooked on Sunday, on the sly."[32]

While Clemens obsessively tracked his production, quality was extremely important too. In an 1871 letter to his publisher Elisha Bliss, Clemens provided some insight into his ultimate goal, which was for the reader to become so enraptured with his book that they wouldn't put it down until finished. "My present idea is to write as much more as I have already written," he explained, "and then cull from the mass the very best chapters and discard the rest. I am not half as well satisfied with the first part of the book as I am with what I am writing now. When I get it done I want to see the man who will begin to read it and not finish it."[33]

Just how far would Clemens go in culling? While in Europe working on various pieces, he trashed what was a fortune's worth: "In Rouen in '93 I destroyed $15,000 worth of manuscript, and in Paris in the beginning of '94 I destroyed $10,000 worth—I mean, estimated as magazine stuff. I was afraid to keep those piles of manuscript on hand lest I be tempted to sell them, for I was fairly well persuaded that they were not up to standard. . . . My wife not only made no objection but encouraged me to do it, for she cared more for my reputation than for any other concern of ours."[34] Throughout his career, Livy remained Clemens's conscience, editor, and toughest critic, a key element to his success.

chapter five

SUCKED INTO THE GILDED AGE: MONEY LUST AND THE MAKING OF AN INVENTOR

"Money-lust has always existed, but not in the history of the world was it ever a craze, a madness, until your time and mine."

*I*n 1873 Clemens published The Gilded Age, *co-authored with Charles Dudley Warner, in which he provides insights into get-rich-quick schemes, as well as living on credit and debt. He also became a venture capitalist and inventor. With help from his father-in-law, he bought into the Buffalo Express newspaper, but soon sold out. In 1871 he invented the Mark Twain's Elastic Strap, designed to hold up pants; in 1872, he invented a scrapbook that would prove very lucrative; and in 1874 he invested a hefty $23,000 in an insurance company start-up. In the early 1880s he developed a game, a perpetual calendar, and bed sheet clamps, all of which provided lessons on product development and marketing.*

At the same time that Clemens was seeking ever-greater profits by playing both sides of the publishing game, he also began to fancy himself a serious venture capitalist. As Clemens observed and digested the carnivorous monster of big business and corrupt government during President Ulysses S. Grant's administration (1869–1876), he was both mesmerized and repulsed by the money and power. Unable to resist the temptations, he would embark on a series of escapades that resulted in both failure and triumph.

It was a freewheeling period of the Industrial Revolution when tycoons like Andrew Carnegie, J. Pierpont Morgan, and John D. Rockefeller came to power and ruled the day—and made the rules as they went. Wall Street was burgeoning, which lent itself to a host of swindles as scoundrels like Jay Gould and Jim Fisk manipulated the market with great fervor. And the politicians in Grant's negligent administration held out their hands for payouts, while looking the other way. The get-rich-quick schemes and brazen bribery made for damn good material, all of which inspired Clemens and friend Charles Dudley Warner to co-write *The Gilded Age: A Tale of To-Day*, a satire that attacked the systematic corruption in business, politics, and the courtroom. Published in December 1873, the novel is considered one of best mirrors of the age and its namesake.

In developing the novel's characters, Clemens drew upon not only public figures but his own family members, which included his mother's cousin, who inspired the fictional Beriah Sellers, a backwoods dreamer who repeatedly claims, "There's millions in it!" Sellers intended to make a fortune in hog speculation, buying up wildcat banks, and patenting medicine. "It's everything in knowing where to invest," he proclaimed, a philosophy easily applied if you invest in anything and everything.[1]

Another character from the book exemplifying the times was Mr. Bolton, who juggles all sorts of schemes and is always just a breath away from making millions but doesn't have enough good money to throw after bad. "He had never been so sorely pressed," Twain and Warner wrote. "A dozen schemes which he had in hand, any one of which might turn up a fortune, all languished, and each needed just a little more money to save that which had been invested."[2] Clemens and Warner offered some wonderful outbursts on the financial madness that echo loudly today. Take their view on credit: "Beautiful credit! The foundation of modern society. That is a peculiar condition of society which enables a whole nation to recognize." And how about this zinger on debt: "I wasn't worth a cent two years ago, and now I owe two millions of dollars."[3] As for indebtedness, one *Gilded Age* character explained, "If you get into anybody far enough you've got yourself a partner."

The evils of beautiful credit were revealed the very year *The Gilded Age* was published: Thanks to risky bank loans made to overextended railroads that subsequently defaulted, a financial panic swept the country in late 1873. It was precipitated by the announcement on September 8 of the collapse of Jay Cooke and Company, a Philadelphia bank that had been financing the hopelessly indebted Northern Pacific Railroad. A three-year depression ensued and some 10,000 businesses failed—indeed ripe material for Clemens, who could only scoff at the fools.

A Self-Fulfilling Prophecy: The Allure of Wealth Is Difficult to Resist

Amazingly, *The Gilded Age* would prove to be a self-fulfilling prophecy for the author, who would find himself becoming a creature of the age. Yes, while Clemens was lampooning the period, he was also being drawn into the lavish lifestyle—more so because he had been denied any luxury in his early life. In the 1870s, as income now rolled in from his books, articles, and lectures, the allure of wealth would soon control him as he sought to make millions in various schemes and inventions to support his increasingly expensive tastes, which would soon include a Hartford mansion with 12 servants. And his writing would suffer.

Now complicating financial matters for the author was Livy, whom he had married on February 2, 1870. It didn't hurt that she came with a handsome dowry and would soon inherit an astounding $300,000 on her father's death; however, she was an heiress accustomed to a luxurious lifestyle and Clemens felt pressure to maintain the lavish standard.[4] As early as 1868, not long after his courtship began, Clemens had written to his mother, "Livy thinks we can live on a very moderate sum and that we'll not need to lecture. I know very well that she can live on a small allowance, but I am not so sure about myself."[5] At least he was honest with himself.

Sure enough, on subsequent trips to Europe, Clemens took suites in the ritziest hotels, placed no restraints on spending, and rubbed elbows with Europe's aristocracy. On an 1878–1879 European junket, which took them through Germany, Switzerland, Italy, Belgium, Holland, and England, Clemens wrote to Howells about their 31-foot-long bedroom and parlor with 2 sofas and 12 chairs in a Hamburg, Germany hotel—never mind the culture. (He despised the German language anyway.)[6]

Another force that still drove Clemens to "get rich" was his family's damnable Tennessee land, which, in the 1870s, continued to haunt him as a visceral reminder of his father's failure. His brother Orion had had several opportunities to sell the land, but continued to bungle it. At wit's end, Clemens wrote to him, "If any stupid fool will give 2,000 for it, do let him have it—shift the curse to his shoulders . . . this is the last time I will ever have anything to do with . . . that doubly and trebly hated and accursed land."[7] A month later, he wrote, "I don't want to be consulted at all about Tenn. I don't want it even mentioned to me. When I make a suggestion it is for you to act upon it or throw it aside, but I beseech you never to ask my advice, opinion or consent about that hated property."[8] And still later, Clemens hired an agent to sell the land and forwarded the agent's bill to Orion: "Hoping that the Tennessee Land is now in hell, please pay the enclosed bill."[9] Clearly, he was determined to shirk the curse one way or another—one way being to become a successful capitalist.

An Old Friend's Success and a Concerned Father-in-Law Inspire Clemens to Enter Business

Two years prior to marrying Livy, in 1868 Clemens's interest in venture capitalism was kindled when Frank Fuller, the author's friend and booking agent for lectures, started "making money hand over fist in the manufacture and sale of a patent odorless India rubber cloth, which is coming greatly into fashion for buggy-tops and such things."[10] The other things included condoms, samples of which Clemens requested . . . in jest. Their friendship dated back to 1862, when the two met in hardscrabble Nevada Territory and Clemens, in the capacity as his brother's secretary, gave Fuller, who was three years his senior and then acting governor of the Utah Territory, a tour of the Esmeralda silver mining camps. The next year Fuller found himself staking a claim. After a brief stint in mining, at the close of the Civil War Fuller returned to New York City and became a successful entrepreneur. As Clemens observed his friend's success and that of the age's prominent tycoons, he could no longer resist the temptation to get in on the action. Fortunately, he was savvy enough to forego the condom business and stick to something he knew more intimately (at least in a business sense): newspapers.

"I am offered an interest in a Cleveland paper which would pay me $2,300 to $2,500 a year, and a salary added of $3,000," he wrote to his mother in 1868. "The salary is fair enough, but the interest is not large enough, and so I must look a little further. The Cleveland folks say they can be induced to do a little better by me, and urge me to come out and talk business. But it don't strike me—I feel little or no inclination to go."[11] Not one to play second fiddle, Clemens wanted a large enough interest to control the content and design of the paper.

The following year Clemens purchased a one-third interest in the Buffalo *Express*, Buffalo being not far from Livy's hometown of Elmira. The price tag was $25,000 with $15,000 down, a little out of his reach, but Livy's father, Jervis, who had connected him with the paper to begin with, loaned him $12,500 to consummate the deal. Clearly, it was an incentive to induce the vagabond writer to settle down. There was another motivational fact on Jervis's part: He was weary of the *Express* attacking his coal cartel and hoped Clemens would blunt further criticism of the Langdon family. Demonstrating he was morally disposed to big business—or at least indifferent—the author insured Jervis's business dealings were no longer front-page material.

Clemens became the managing editor on August 15, 1869, and immediately recognized the need to buckle down and focus on the task at hand. He wrote to his publisher Elisha Bliss (still alive and kicking in 1869) that it was "an exceedingly thriving newspaper. We propose to make it more so. I expect I shall have to buckle right down to it and give up lecturing until next year."[12] He cleaned up the typesetting, redesigned the paper to improve its appearance, and fired off some juicy editorials to attract attention and grow readership. But by 1871, the restless Clemens knew the paper would not hold his interest and was unable to adapt to the Siberia-like town, so he and Livy put their Buffalo house on the market and sold his share in the *Express* for $15,000. The investment was essentially a wash because he still owed $7,500 to the previous shareholder and there was the loan from Jervis Langdon (who would not collect on it, as Clemens's kind editorials were payment enough).[13]

A Strategic Move, Literally Speaking, to Become Better Attuned to the Publishing Industry

Clemens was intent on moving to Hartford, Connecticut, a thriving city where he could better keep an eye on his slippery publisher Elisha Bliss. It also put him square between his publishing contacts in New York and Boston, each city accessible with relative ease. In Hartford, he further indulged in the Gilded Age: He and Livy built a mansion that would cost more than $40,000, be filled with furniture and decorations shipped back from Europe, and require a staff of 12 to manage. This luxurious lifestyle—hardly typical of an author—only added to the pressure on Clemens to secure riches.[14] Fortunately, over the coming year, Clemens would make over $10,000 on lecture fees—an astounding sum for the day—to help pay for the house.

Clemens Allows His Creativity to Wander, Resulting in a Melding of Edison and Shakespeare

As a writer, Clemens was creative, no doubt, but now, as he settled into a comfortable existence, he let the creativity wander into the arena of mammon. "As we shall presently see," his great nephew Samuel Charles Webster once wrote, "he tried to be an Edison as well as a Shakespeare, and a few other great men besides."[15] He did indeed at times fancy himself a Thomas Edison, albeit on a slightly more modest scale. Over two decades, the 1870s and 1880s, he would come up with a series of what can be loosely called inventions and actually secure patents for three, with one earning him some decent income. At the same time, his writing would suffer to such a degree that his family would become concerned.

Clemens held inventors in high regard and was quoted as saying that they "are the creators of the world—after God." On the other hand, he also acknowledged that many inventions are not necessarily the result of brilliance: "Name the greatest of all inventors. Accidents."[16] His own first two inventions were the result of seeing a need in his everyday life and acting on it. He first dabbled in this realm in 1871 when he conceived of Mark Twain's Elastic Strap, which was a vest strap that attached a man's pants to his vest to hold them up. This was in the day before belts and modern suspenders.

The problem of holding one's pants up had troubled him for years (although it does not seem to trouble twenty-first century youth, who pride themselves on their colorful boxers). Then his elastic strap epiphany came to him one morning while lying in bed. In a letter to the U.S. Patent Office, he wrote that "on the 13th of August last, as I lay in bed, I thought of it again, & then I said I would ease my mind and invent that strap before I got up—probably the only prophecy I ever made that was worth its face." Determined to see his idea through, he easily envisioned the elastic strap, but needed to work out the precise design.

"While I dressed," he explained, "it occurred to me that in order to be efficient, the strap must be adjustable & detachable, when the wearer did not wish it to be permanent. So I devised the plan of having two or three buttonholes in each end of the strap, & buttoning it to the garment—whereby it could be shortened or removed at pleasure. So I sat down & drew the first of the accompanying. . . . While washing (these details seem a little trivial, I grant, but they are history & therefore in some degree respect-worthy), it occurred to me that the strap would do for pantaloons also, & I drew diagram No. 2."

While lying in bed, while dressing, while washing—this was when the ideas popped into his head. It was when he was relaxed but mulling over a concept, before the day's responsibilities imposed upon him, before his mind became cluttered with daily minutia, that his creative conscious was best able to explore solutions. It was also a result of keeping the concept on the back burner all those years, patiently letting it stew, until a solution presented itself. Clemens never liked to give up on an idea, no matter how trivial it may appear.

On September 9, 1871, our literary Edison traveled to Washington to apply for his patent in person, but upon arrival he discovered that a would-be competitor, Henry C. Lockwood of Baltimore, had applied for a similar patent. To settle the matter, the Patent Office asked each man to write a history of their process with accompanying documentation to discern who thought of it first. On October 6, Clemens wrote a short essay entitled "Concerning Mark Twain's Elastic Strap" and mailed it to Washington. Either his meticulous punctuation or his actual documentation won the day and he was granted patent No. 122,992, on December 19, 1871. He never made a dime on this playful diversion, but the episode does provide a glimpse of how his fertile mind worked.[17]

Fulfilling a Practical Need, Clemens Invents the World's Only Rational Scrapbook

Clemens's next invention yielded a healthy return in cold cash, the idea germinating in his compulsive need to document his accomplishments. The author was the consummate scrapbook keeper, cutting out articles about himself and other people, places, and events of interest from newspapers and magazines. However, he found the whole process of gluing items into a book tedious and destructive to the "scraps" you were trying to preserve. In the summer of 1872, he struck upon an idea: The scrapbook pages could have strips coated with a glue-like compound that simply required a little moisture.

On August 11 he wrote excitedly to his brother Orion, explaining how "in wetting the paper you need not wet any more of the gum than your scrap or scraps will cover—then you may shut up the book and the leaves won't stick together." Learning from the elastic strap episode, he ordered Orion to keep his letter for documentation purposes: "Preserve, also, the envelope of this letter—postmark ought to be good evidence of the date of this great humanizing and civilizing invention." The Patent Office, apparently also recognizing the unique civilizing nature of this invention, awarded him a patent.

Even before he was granted the patent, Clemens had thought through the entire business, too, from the manufacturing to the finished product's name. "I'll put it into Dan Slote's hands and tell him he must send you all over America," he explained to Orion, who was once again fishing for a business, "to urge its use upon stationers and booksellers—so don't buy into a newspaper.

The name of this thing is 'Mark Twain's Self-Pasting Scrapbook.'"[18] Slote was his old traveling buddy from the pilgrim boat, and Slote's family was a partner in a New York City stationery business—Slote, Woodman & Company—so it appeared to be a savvy move to have him publish and distribute the scrapbook. Unfortunately, Clemens would discover that doing business with friends was not a good way to remain friends.

According to his contract with Slote, the inventor was to receive one-third of the profits; but again, as in book publishing, determining the bottom-line profit was not always straightforward and would lead to disagreements between the two friends. Nevertheless, the self-pasting scrapbook was a hit: At its peak it would sell more than 50,000 copies a year; over six months in 1878 it made a profit of $12,000; by 1901, at least 57 different types of his albums were available; and in total Clemens would pocket a tidy $50,000. However, trouble between Clemens and Slote started in that bountiful year of 1878, when Slote asked Clemens to loan the firm $5,000. Shortly after Clemens fronted him the money in July, the company failed—a surefire way to strain a relationship.[19] In his autobiography, a smug and chagrined Clemens recalled the entire episode:

> I invented a scrapbook—and if I do say it myself, it was the only rational scrapbook the world has ever seen. I patented it and put it in the hands of that old particular friend of mine who had originally interested me in patents and he made a good deal of money out of it. But by and by, just when I was about to begin to receive a share of the money myself, his firm failed. I didn't know his firm was going to fail—he didn't say anything about it. One day he asked me to lend the firm five thousand dollars and said he was willing to pay seven per cent. As security he offered the firm's note. I asked for an endorser. He was much surprised and said that if endorsers were handy and easy to get at he wouldn't have to come to me for the money, he could get it anywhere. That seemed reasonable and so I gave him the five thousand dollars. They failed inside of three days. . . .[20]

In 1880, Clemens's relationship with Slote would become more complicated as the two traded accusations. It came as no comfort that Slote was not the only friend who would entangle Clemens in financial disasters, the next escapade involving far more than $5,000.

Funding a Start-Up That Makes Money on Fear: Clemens Invests in a Friend's Insurance Company

An old friend of Clemens from the Nevada Territory mining days, John P. Jones, had struck it rich when he laid claim to what turned out to be a bonanza mine that was part of the Comstock vein, one of the largest silver lodes in the world. Determined to win more riches, in 1872 Jones—who had a rapidly receding hairline but sported a long, conical beard that ended in a sharp point—was elected Nevada senator in a hard-fought battle, on which he spent a substantial amount of money. In the spirit of the Gilded Age and playing the game of cronyism to the hilt, he subsequently founded the Hartford Accident Insurance Company in Hartford, Connecticut, the insurance capital of the country.

Expecting to make money hand-over-fist, once he incorporated his firm in June 1874, he sold a total of $23,000 in stock to Clemens. Jones promised to protect him from loss, and asked him to serve as a director. Throwing his usual enthusiasm behind the venture and always quick to take advantage of a marketing opportunity that benefited himself, at an 1875 business dinner, Clemens made a brief speech on the merits of the insurance industry that he intended to be more humorous than earnest:

> Certainly there is no nobler field for human effort than the insurance line of business—especially accident insurance. Ever since I have been a director in an accident-insurance company I have felt that I am a better man. Life has seemed more precious. Accidents have assumed a kindlier aspect. Distressing special providences have lost half their horror. I look upon a cripple now with affectionate

interest—as an advertisement. I do not seem to care for poetry any more. I do not care for politics; even agriculture does not excite me. But to me now there is a charm about a railway collision that is unspeakable. . . . I will remark here, by way of advertisement, that that noble charity which we have named the Hartford Accident Insurance Company is an institution which is peculiarly to be depended upon. A man is bound to prosper who gives it his custom. No man can take out a policy in it and not get crippled before the year is out.[21]

Unfortunately, after 18 months the "noble charity" collapsed and Clemens found himself out $23,000. It took several years for him to negotiate the return of his money, which had been guaranteed, but finally, on March 13, 1878, he traveled to the Rossmore Hotel in New York to meet with one of Jones's associates to successfully wrap up the sullied business. A week later Clemens jotted down in his notebook: "How Jones was grandly going to make all his kin rich—broke up all their business to flock at his heels, & killed them broken hearts. He meant well, but he was a fool."[22] The insurance business was too complicated to be a mere passing hobby of a Nevada senator expecting to make a quick killing.

By March 26 Jones refunded all of the money to Clemens, who recalled, "With that check in my pocket I was prepared to seek sudden fortune again. The reader, deceived by what I have been saying about my adventures, will jump to the conclusion that I sought an opportunity at once. I did nothing of the kind. I was the burnt child. I wanted nothing further to do with speculations."[23]

While Clemens Considers Himself an Informed Investor, He Learns That Sometimes the Ignorant Succeed

Of course, as fate would have it, Clemens's now gun-shy attitude would cost him. While at the Hartford *Courant*'s newspaper offices, he met a young man who tried to sell him some stock in a company making a newfangled contraption called a telephone:

> I declined. I said I didn't want anything more to do with wildcat speculation. . . .
>
> That young man couldn't sell me any stock but he sold a few hatfuls of it to an old dry-goods clerk in Hartford for five thousand dollars. That was that clerk's whole fortune. He had been half a lifetime saving it. It is strange how foolish people can be and what ruinous risks they can take when they want to get rich in a hurry. I was sorry for that man when I heard about it. I thought I might have saved him if I had had an opportunity to tell him about my experiences.
>
> We sailed for Europe on the 10th of April, 1878. We were gone fourteen months and when we got back one of the first things we saw was that clerk driving around in a sumptuous barouche with liveried servants all over it—and his telephone stock was emptying greenbacks into his premises at such a rate that he had to handle them with a shovel. It is strange the way the ignorant and inexperienced so often and so undeservedly succeed when the informed and the experienced fail.[24]

Dealing with the various business distractions, along with being inundated by fan mail, took its toll on Clemens. In March 1878, before sailing for Europe, the 42-year-old celebrity wrote to his mother: "Life has come to be a very serious matter with me. I have a badgered, harassed feeling, a good part of my time. It comes mainly of business responsibilities and annoyances, and the persecution of kindly letters from well meaning strangers— to whom I must be rudely silent or else put in the biggest half of my time bothering over answers." He hoped to find some tranquility in Europe for writing.[25] In fact, after publishing *The Gilded Age* in 1873, it was three years until his next book, *The Adventures of Tom Sawyer* (1876), and another long four years until the one after that, *A Tramp Abroad* (1880), was published.

His Inventions Make It Necessary to Set Aside Huckleberry Finn

The very year he confessed to his mother that he was feeling harassed by business responsibilities, Clemens's hyperactive mind cooked up a couple more ideas that would hound him for years. "Hound," because once he generated an idea for an invention or an investment, he couldn't let it go, regardless of its merits, and his inability to walk away, thus cutting losses, would prove to be his Achilles' heel.

In May 1878, Clemens noted in his personal journal that he had invented a notebook designed with a tab protruding from the top corners of each leaf so the writer could find his place. As trivial as the idea sounds, he insisted on manufacturing his design and used the notebooks himself.[26] While the benign notebook cost him little in time and money, that same year a far more time-consuming project barged into his head: a historical-biographical game that would evolve *over a dozen years plus* as he refined, manufactured, and marketed what would eventually be called "Mark Twain's Fact and Date Game."

Five years after first thinking of creating such a game, Clemens wrote to his brother Orion in July 1883 that he was out walking when "I struck an idea for the instruction of the children, and went to work and carried it out."[27] Now his idea was to help children improve their memory by concentrating on historical characters and facts, with players' pieces moving forward on the game board when they answered trivia questions correctly. Over the summer and into the fall, Clemens filled his notebook with thoughts on the game or "Memory Improver" and hired Orion to help assemble the needed information.[28]

Refining the game wasn't as easy as he thought and took more effort than he realized; later in the summer he wrote to Howells, "If you haven't ever tried to invent an indoor historical game, don't. I've got the thing at last so it will work, I guess, but I don't want any more tasks of that kind. When I wrote you, I thought I had it; whereas I was only merely entering upon the initiatory difficulties of it. I might have known it wouldn't be an easy job, or somebody would have invented a decent historical game long ago—a thing which nobody had done."[29]

By August 1883 Clemens had enough of the game designed to apply for patents in the United States, Canada, and England—although he continued to perfect it through the fall of 1883.[30] Yet again, the author anticipated a windfall: The next year he wrote to Charles Webster, whom he had hired as his business manager to handle the details of such projects, "There's bushels of dividends in those games."[31] Meanwhile, his future masterpiece, *The Adventures of Huckleberry Finn*, which he had hoped to complete in two months, would continue to languish as he focused his energies on the game. It was a confounding state of affairs (i.e., *Huck Finn* being set aside), especially when you consider what Ernest Hemmingway said of the book: "All modern American literature comes from one book by Mark Twain called Huckleberry Finn." Begun in 1876, the novel would not be published until 1885.

The game would not make it to market until 1891 as the inventor continued to tinker with it, but even after all those years, Clemens never lost his enthusiasm for it. "Come quickly," he wrote to his latest business manager, Fred Hall, that year, "and discuss my historical game. It is the important feature right now."[32] Reception of the game was cool, however; just a few retailers were willing to take it—on consignment only. The directions were too complicated, and, according to one critic, "The game looked like a cross between an income tax form and a table of logarithms."[33] Recognizing that without the shopkeepers' endorsement, the game was finished, Clemens lamented to Hall: "The fatalest objection of all is that the trade see no promise in the Game. Therefore, my advice is that you put it aside until some indefinite time in the far future—it isn't worth trouble, now, when you can employ your time more profitably on other things. Besides, I am sorry I put my *name* to the Game; I wish I hadn't."[34]

In addition to having overengineered the game, rather than keeping it dumbed down for an American audience that didn't like to think too much, what else had gone wrong? For starters, Clemens should have test-marketed it with shopkeepers years earlier. By involving his potential customers early on in the process, he could have tweaked the game to make it more attractive, or determined it was not worth pursuing. Finally, why was he sorry he had put his *name* to the game? Well, the public perception that he was prostituting himself might have been a factor for a man who had come to relish universal adoration. Also, the game was a serious venture, but Clemens was a humorist, so the public didn't know what to expect and was therefore hesitant to buy it. Imagine Mark Twain—whiskey drinker and cigar smoker— posing for "Got Milk?" ads. Compatible consistency of deliverer and message it would not be. On the other hand, his core idea of a historical trivia game was on the mark—the explosive sales of Trivial Pursuit a century later would prove that true.

As Clemens Strays Away from His Expertise, Success Becomes Far Less Likely

In the fertile mid-1880s, several more brainstorms took hold of the author's fractured, kaleidoscope-like imagination. The summer of 1884 found Clemens working on a portable calendar— later called a perpetual calendar—which displays the numerical days of the month only, rather than the days of the week, so that it can be used over and over, recycled from one year to the next. Sufficiently keen on the idea, he assigned Webster the task of securing a patent for it. Apparently no patent was awarded and the calendar never materialized. On a practical level, organizing one's life around the days of the week far outweighed the money-saving recyclable aspect. Again, on the other hand, over a century later there are a plethora of fancy perpetual calendars for sale, so Clemens's idea had real merit.

In July 1884, Clemens realized another invention opportunity after his niece Annie, who was married to his business manager at that time, Charles Webster, gave birth to a baby boy who was subsequently prone to kicking off his bed covers. As Clemens mulled over the young lad's subversive behavior, he envisioned a solution for this seemingly mundane everyday annoyance: a bed-clamp to keep babies from kicking off their covers, a vice-like device that would clamp the bed sheets to the crib or bed. Not one to dally, by October Clemens had discovered that a patent already existed for such an item and a company was manufacturing it; however, he was able to secure an option on buying out the company's interest in bed clamps. He was convinced that the unnamed manufacturer was selling their bed clamps too cheaply: "The only fault it has is that it is too cheap—90 cents to $1.15. . . ." he wrote to Charles Webster. "But have invented a more expensive & more convenient one, & presently when I see you we will talk about it."[35]

Immersed in managing Clemens's money, checking his royalties, paying the bills, Webster was not enthusiastic about this new venture and warned Clemens: "You haven't asked my opinion, but I will say; I have no doubt that it will prove a failure. It is so entirely foreign to our business that I think it is unwise to go into it."[36] Aye, the old "put your eggs in one basket and watch that basket" maxim. Nevertheless, it became Webster's job to analyze how high they could price bed clamps and to estimate the potential profit.

He returned with some vague figures, which prompted Clemens to sound off: "Try again. *Tabulate* the expenses of all kinds, in an intelligible way. And state some kind of idea of what that *entire* expense will *be*, in dollars & cents; for '& expenses' means nothing." When his business manager asked for more input, more clarification from Clemens, he received a blunt response. "No," Clemens wrote back, "it is business—and so I don't want anything to do with it. You are there to take care of my business, not make business for me to take care of."[37] Even though Clemens himself was creating more business for himself by initiating these projects, clearly, in January 1885, the humorist had again lost his patience in dealing with the business of business.

Not long after, the bed clamp business died a quiet death with little fight from Clemens, who confided in Webster that he was once again tired of being hounded by business problems: "I won't talk business—I will perish first," he wrote while in a particularly aggravated state of mind. "I hate the very idea of business, in all its forms."[38] Of course, his proclaimed annoyance with business was just idle talk because, at the same time that he was diverted by these inventions, he started building a prodigious securities portfolio, investing in companies, and, in 1884, would establish his own publishing house.

QUIRKY HABITS AND BRAZEN PHILOSOPHY

Managing a Glut of Loathsome Correspondence

"Do something every day that you don't want to do; this is the golden rule for acquiring the habit of doing your duty without pain."

As his fame and notoriety spread, Clemens received an increasing glut of letters from earnest but annoying colleagues, rabid fans who suggested new book ideas, aspiring writers who sought advice, and nut-jobs who wanted a handout. He hardly had time to write his family (and was forced to apologize to his mother for his wayward ways) let alone all these other damned human beings. Clemens could not even tolerate brief telegrams, and more than once he instructed his business manager to use the telegraph less in communicating with him.

"My correspondence is the despair of my life," Clemens wrote to his sister. "I count only those people my friends who release me from the sense that I must some time or other write them."[39] To his business manager Webster he wrote: "Whenever you receive letters addressed to me, always read them, whether marked private or not—& don't send them to me unless they are unanswerable by you."[40] Thankfully he was spared e-mail signed with a ":)," which is surely the scourge of the corporate world, sucking away valuable time (and leaving a tidy trail for snooping district attorneys).

In the following all-too-brief excerpt of his essay "One of Mankind's Bores," Clemens offers his whimsical attitude toward odious correspondence. Ultimately, he learned to set aside dedicated time, attack his pile of letters, and get it out of the way, so it didn't weigh on his mind.

One of Mankind's Bores

I suppose that if there is one thing in the world more hateful than another to all of us it is to have to write a letter. A private letter especially. And business letters, to my thinking, are very little pleasanter. Nearly all the enjoyment is taken out of every letter I get by the reflection that it must be answered. And I do so dread the affliction of writing those answers, that often my first and gladdest impulse is to burn my mail before it is opened. For ten years I never felt that sort of dread at all, because I was moving about constantly,

(Continued)

Managing a Glut
of Loathsome Correspondence *(Continued)*

from city to city, from State to State, and from country to country, and so I could leave all letters unanswered if I chose, and the writers of them would naturally suppose that I had changed my post-office and missed receiving my correspondence. But I am "cornered" now, I cannot use that form of deception any more. I am anchored, and letters of all kinds come straight to me with deadly precision.

They are letters of all sorts and descriptions, and they treat of everything. I generally read them at breakfast, and right often they kill a day's work by diverting my thoughts and fancies into some new channel, thus breaking up and making confusion of the programme of scribbling I had arranged for my working hours. After breakfast I clear for action, and for an hour try hard to write; but there is no getting back into the old train of thought after such an interruption, and so at last I give it up and put off further effort till next day. One would suppose that I would now answer those letters and get them out of the way; and I suppose one of those model young men we read about, who enter New York barefoot and live to become insolent millionaires, would be sure to do that; but I don't. I never shall be a millionaire, and so I disdain to copy the ways of those men.[41]

When Clemens finally got around to replying to those deserving letters, it would take him five or six hours to answer no more than nine letters as he toiled away under duress. As for those who never received a response, the above essay served as a broad apology.

chapter six

SEEING AND SEIZING OPPORTUNITIES: VENTURE CAPITALIST AND WALL STREET SPECULATOR

"There are two times in a man's life when he should not speculate: when he can't afford it and when he can."

S*mitten with technology, Clemens embraced the newfangled telephone, the typewriter, and the phonograph. He also invested in emerging technologies, which included funding the development of the Kaolatype, a new engraving process, from 1879 to 1883. In dealing with his deceitful Kaolatype partners, he adroitly used Machiavellian tactics. In 1881 Clemens hired his first full-time business manager to help manage his burgeoning investments. Around that time, he invested in a watch company, a steam engine, and a redesigned typesetting machine invented by James Paige, which he assumed control of. In the early 1880s his portfolio of stocks and bonds grew substantially as he learned to play the insider's game and to invest in companies of the "staying kind."*

Clemens's life had various compartments—the writing, the inventions, the investments, the socializing—all overlapping and intruding on each other, which disrupted the continuity of his life. This disruption is all the more apparent as we again step back to the late 1870s, when Clemens had plenty of discretionary funds to invest not only in his own inventions, but in other people's inventions and in stocks and bonds. He envisioned himself as a venture capitalist and a Wall Street investor. He continued to seek the big score that would put any money worries forever behind him and elevate him to the same social standing as his father-in-law, Jervis Langdon. He would then be accepted as part of the social elite, as opposed to a humorist who entertained high society. Later adding to this self-imposed pressure, in 1880 Clemens had four mouths to feed besides his own: wife Livy and three daughters, Susy, Clara, and Jean, ages eight, six, and one, respectively.

In addition to the familial pressure, Clemens, having an always active mind, simply couldn't stand being on the sidelines while the tycoons of the age amassed huge fortunes; he had to be involved in their game. The risks gave him pleasure, but success would depend on him not acting compulsively on his imagination, which would be sorely enticed by the promise of a glorious future filled with the magnificent machines of the Industrial Revolution. Indeed, Clemens, who was one of the first Hartford residents to have a telephone installed in 1877, was fascinated by technology, leading to results both good and bad: The wonders of new technology would enrich his life but also prompt him to make some risky, impulsive investments.

Embracing Technology (for the Love of It—and Money): The Typewriter and Phonograph Entice Clemens

To garner a hint of the manic behavior that was to come, we only need to consider Clemens's instantaneous fixation on the typewriter, a real humdinger of a futuristic machine that was mass-produced for the first time in 1873. He first encountered it during an 1874 trip to Boston where, on seeing it displayed in a window, he went into the shop and watched as the "type-girl" banged out 57 words in a minute. Obsessed with his personal production, he immediately envisioned the machine taking him to new records in churning out manuscript and compulsively bought one for $125.[1]

Unfortunately, while he enjoyed using the machine, it proved to be more trouble than it was worth: Every letter he generated using the typewriter prompted the recipient to write back, inquiring about the typewriter, which meant Clemens had to write more odious letters. Adding to his frustration, one of the machine's manufacturers had promoted the fact that Clemens had bought one, which created more inquiries—so many, in fact, that he asked the manufacturer to "not use my name in any way. Please do not even divulge the fact that I own a machine. I have entirely stopped using the typewriter, for the reason that I never could write a letter with it to anybody without receiving a request by return mail that I would not only describe the machine, but state what progress I had made in the use of it, etc., etc. I don't like to write letters, and so I don't want people to know I own this curiosity-breeding little joker."[2]

Clemens proceeded to trade the torturous typewriter for a saddle. However, he would again use it: In the summer of 1882, Clemens employed typists to type his manuscript for *Life on the Mississippi* and for *Huckleberry Finn*. The clean copy, much tidier than his hand-written manuscript, allowed him to make better edits: "The pages of the sheets begin to look as natural, and rational, and void of offense to his eye as do his own written pages, and therefore he can alter and amend them with comfort. . . . I shall not be likely to ever use any other system."[3]

To increase productivity, Clemens also experimented with the newfangled phonograph, a model of which Thomas Edison had started producing in 1878, although it would require another decade of improvements before the general public was ready to embrace it. On October 8, 1887, the renowned inventor formed The Edison Phonograph Company to market his machine and the next spring he introduced a new model simply called the Improved Phonograph. The very month it hit the market, Clemens wrote to Thomas Edison in hopes of getting "my hands on a couple of phonographs *immediately*, instead of having to wait my turn."[4] Three years later, when suffering from rheumatism in his right arm, which made writing painful, he looked to the machine to solve his dilemma. "I feel sure I can dictate the book into a phonograph if I don't have to yell," he wrote Howells on February 28, 1891. "I write 2,000 words a day; I think I can dictate twice as many." After filling about four dozen wax cylinders, however, Clemens determined that you can't dictate a book because the process suppressed ideas that required mulling over and it was too difficult to elaborate on thoughts.[5]

Nevertheless, Clemens was forever enticed, even hypnotized, by new technologies and considered himself a forward-thinking man. So, while he fiddled with his own inventions and games, he would also invest heavily in machines, patents, and processes that he devoutly believed would change the future and make him rich beyond his dreams.

Clemens Hopes to Make a Mighty Fortune by Investing in a New Engraving Technology

Clemens's first investment as a venture capitalist was in the futuristic-sounding Kaolatype, a process for engraving that used clay-based molds that artists could draw directly upon to speed up and improve the quality of the production of engraved illustrations. However, there was an immediate barrier to overcome: His buddy Dan Slote controlled the patent. Even though Clemens was not entirely trusting of how Slote had been managing the scrapbook—with the failure of his company but subsequent reorganization—the two now became more deeply involved as business partners.

"Dan Slote has the best process in the world," Clemens crowed to his publisher in June 1879, "but I suppose we can't use that, because in his process the pictures are not transferred, but drawn on a hard mud surface. It looks like excellent wood engraving whereas all these other processes are miserably weak and shammy."[6] And to his sister Pamela he wrote, "I got up a kind of marvelous invention the other day, & I could make a mighty fortune out of it. . . ."[7]

To manufacture and market the process, Slote formed the Kaolatype Engraving Company, located at 104 Fulton Street, New York, and issued 1,000 shares of stock to raise $25,000 in capital. For $20,000 in cash, Clemens took 800 of Slote's 1,000 shares and was made president—he intended to control the operation, unlike when he had simply handed his scrapbook over to Slote. Clemens considered it a safe investment in a business he understood and invited his publisher Elisha Bliss to join the firm: "I have put off one man who had a disposition to buy some stock at par, because he is a stranger to this sort of business and could be of no use to us."[8] Demonstrating a savvy business sense, Clemens was not only in a realm he understood—publishing—but was looking for investors who had some particular knowledge to bring to the table.

To cast a wider money net, the ambitious Clemens immediately sought to extend the usefulness of the process; he envisioned applying it to brass molds to be used for stamping book covers, for wallpaper stamps, for calico printing, and for making embossed work on leather. On February 26, 1880, he wrote to Orion excitedly, "Yesterday I thought out a new application of this invention which I think will utterly annihilate & sweep out of existence one of the minor industries of civilization, & take its place. . . ."[9] According to his calculations, this would increase the value of the Kaolatype a hundredfold. "But every brass-expert laughed at the idea & said the thing was absolutely impossible," he later wrote to Orion. "But at last I struck a young German who believed he could do it. I have had him under wages for 3 months, now, night & day, & at last he has worked the miracle. In the rough, it is true; but all new things are in the rough."

Persistence appeared to pay off. Clemens signed a contract with a German metallurgist, Charles Sneider, who would pay him $5,000 for the patents once he had perfected the process of using brass-plates. As for profits, Twain, Slote, and the German were to split them evenly, a wise move to keep the latter two vested in the success of the invention.[10]

Clemens had the right attitude, but had he picked the right invention for making millions? He would find out the following year.

In the winter of 1880–1881, 12 months into the project, Clemens justifiably wanted some evidence as to Sneider's progress, so twice in February 1881 he made arrangements to visit and see a demonstration. However, each time he ran into roadblocks that should have been huge red flags waving in his face. As he explained to Howells, "the first appointment was spoiled by his burning down the man's shop in which it was to be done, the night before; the second was spoiled by his burning down his own shop the night before. He unquestionably did both of these things."[11] The two fires were indeed a little too convenient, and Clemens began to suspect that he was being swindled; but in March 1881 Slote sent him a set of sample impressions that impressed Clemens enough to renew his enthusiasm.

That month Clemens also funded the construction of a building in New York to house his brass-casting works, even though, at the same time, he was concerned about the project's rising costs.[12] In 1881 he put at least another $3,000 into Kaolatype in what would be estimated to be a total $40,000 investment.[13] By the end of March, Clemens's patience was wearing thin and business was again hindering his writing. "I hope that before April is over we shall see palpable & demonstrable (not theoretic & imaginative) reasons for going on;" he warned Slote, "but my hopes are not high—they have had a heavy jolt. I feel pretty sore & humiliated when I think over the history of the past few months. The book I was at work on & intended to rush through in two months' time, is standing still. One can't write a book unless he can banish perplexities & put his whole mind on it."[14] Clemens had become consumed by the business, while his writing career played second fiddle.

To Limit the Increasing Distractions, Clemens Hires His First Full-Time Business Manager

Frustrated by ongoing distractions, which were becoming more than he could handle alone, Clemens comprehended that he needed to hire a manager to handle far more than just his lecture tours; he needed an able lieutenant to manage his burgeoning business affairs so he could focus on his writing. His answer came in the form of an engineer peddling stock in a watch-making firm who also happened to be his nephew-in-law. In March 1881, the previously mentioned Charles Webster visited with Clemens to promote the Independent Watch Company of Fredonia, in hopes his famous uncle would invest. A 29-year-old trained engineer from good Connecticut stock, Webster was married to Clemens's niece Annie Moffett. He had a straight nose, earnest gaze, full beard, hair thinning at the temples, and an unhealthy complexion; his features were a mix of mouse-like and bookish. But he was honest looking, and willing to take orders and accommodate Uncle Sam's various whims, so it was at this time that Clemens hired Webster.

Incidentally, while Clemens was intrigued by the watch-making investment, he explained to his sister Pamela that "I've got to stay out of it, for the reason that the enterprises above mentioned are going to call for the most of our ready money."[15] For the moment, he stayed focused on the Kaolatype—for now.

Not afraid to delegate power, on April 29, 1881, Clemens appointed Webster vice president of the Kaolatype company and gave him full authority to deal with all matters, including hiring and firing and the flow of money: "No money of the Company is to be paid out in any circumstances without your distinct authority."[16] His first week on the job, the annoyingly inquisitive Webster discovered evidence suggesting that both Slote and Sneider were most likely swindling Clemens. Apparently, Sneider had long ago invented the process for creating the brass plates and was simply living off Clemens's money while tinkering around.[17] The two crooks would quickly discover that the humorist was not to be meddled with.

Machiavellian Tactics Are Used to Attack a Pair of Scoundrels

Always very reactionary when feeling threatened, Clemens's modus operandi was to use threatening lawyers with abandon, as he did now. Employing a classic Machiavellian tactic, Clemens decided to divide and conquer his supposed partners and apparent enemies. He would file a lawsuit against Sneider first, pretending that Slote was still his buddy, and then go after Slote. In a May 6 letter to Webster, Clemens informed him of his plans to have Sneider arrested "on a charge of obtaining money under false pretenses." A week later he elaborated: "Yes, it will doubtless be well to finish with Sneider & then tackle Dan," Clemens explained to Webster. "In order to force Sneider, though, you may find it necessary to hint to Dan that if S.'s case comes into court Dan will probably be proceeded against as a *party* to the swindle. Dan hopes to get out by simply *dropping* S. & leaving us to force him to terms."

On May 18, Webster reported: "The bubble has burst. Sneider has confessed . . . that the whole thing was a swindle from the beginning. . . . Sneider says he's going to commit suicide."[18] Clemens now demanded that Slote cover half of the expenses of any legal action against Sneider. Then, in his subsequent campaign against Slote, he desired nothing less than all of Slote's stock in the firm, repayment of all Clemens's Kalaotype funding, reimbursement for legal expenses, and reimbursement of the $5,000 Clemens had given his firm in 1878.[19]

Ah yes, the humorist was ruthless—all the more so because as a young man he had sworn he would never trust anyone, but he had trusted Slote, only to be compromised by his partner's deceit. Further compounding the author's unforgiving ire, the scrapbook was now paying him just $1,800–2,000 a year, while he expected three times as much from Slote. On reflection, he wrote, "Slote took advantage of my utter confidence in his honesty to cheat me."[20] Partly a result of Clemens's unrelenting, remorseless campaign against him, Slote died a broken man in February 1882. Clemens did not go to the funeral.

Although he had been swindled, Clemens still devoutly believed in the Kaolatype project's worth. To find new partners and money, in the summer of 1881 he asked Webster to value the company. He himself had put upwards of $10,000 into it, with expenses mounting at his brass works, but adroitly understood that it was difficult to value the company until the "brass experiments *give* it value." Once the company was valued he wanted to give Webster $1,000 total in stock, to make him vested in its success.[21] Clemens was convinced Webster was doing a fine job making connections with possible customers and investors, but he openly claimed the right to complain: "Yes, it will cost some money to make it pay—but it shall pay. I shall retain the privilege of complaining over the money-drain; a privilege which I seldom exercise, whereas any other man would abuse it."[22] At least Webster knew where he stood.

Clemens's Letter Writing Helps to Measure the Distractions

As a gauge for how much time Clemens was dedicating to his business ventures, consider that in 1881 he wrote 54 letters to Webster, versus a mere 17 to his good friend Howells, and 43 to James R. Osgood, who was his publisher at the time. (These numbers come from the letters cataloged by the Mark Twain Papers and Project.)[23] Some letters to Webster about the Kaolatype ran 2,000 words—a modest essay's worth. In light of Clemens's profession of author, this disparity in letter writing is surprising. The imbalance continued into 1882 and 1883, the latter being the year Clemens finally finished *Huck Finn*—and the delays in bringing this book to market had nothing to do with obsessive wordsmithing.

By Treating the Kaolatype Like a Sick Patient, Clemens Hopes to Better Monitor the Situation

By November 1881, Clemens was finally losing his patience with the dawdling development of the Kaolatype, which was not yet refined enough for commercial sales, and demanded both action and more definitive status reports. From Hartford he cabled Webster in New York: "Put a hundred men on it and telegraph me result of some sort or another in twenty-four hours."

Webster, who was also monitoring the author's royalties and managing his personal finances, responded that he, too, was losing patience: "It's just as hard to report results you can't get as to get 100 skilled men in twenty-four hours."[24]

Clemens now considered the Kaolatype a sick patient and demanded more from Webster: "Now what I have felt the want of, in *you*, the doctor, is *reports*, REPORTS, man! . . . I don't require *long* reports—a remark like the one just *quoted* is plenty for a day: it keeps the parent posted as to the condition of the sick child."[25] He wanted statistics made "simple and easy" so he could understand the costs involved with the various aspects of the project. He also accused Webster of dragging his feet over adapting the process to brass stamps.[26]

While he was correct about the importance of clean, concise reports, Clemens could have been a little more diplomatic rather than hammering Webster with blunt language. His harried manager responded, "You may think I am slow about the brass business but I have worked until nearly 1 a.m. for four nights and then gone home over four miles to my apartment and arrived at the office next morning at 8 a.m. . . . and if I keep this up much longer I will be on my back that's all there is about it."[27]

For two years Clemens continued to fund the Kaolatype business, ample time for a chance at success. Then, in 1883, Clemens wanted to use the Kaolatype process for *Life on the Mississippi*, which was to have more than 300 illustrations; however, the artists involved refused to use it because they felt that their artistry would be compromised by making the direct impression in the molds, which allowed little room for error. Requesting the artists to use the Kaolatype was the true test, and it proved the process a failure. Clemens knew to pull the plug on it; however, this disappointing conclusion begs the question of whether he should have had the artists—the end users who know best—more involved from the start.

With $50,000 out the door, Clemens took his usual flip attitude—spinning a little fiction into the event—when reflecting on the doomed Kaolatype:

An old and particular friend of mine [Slote] unloaded a patent on me, price fifteen thousand dollars. It was worthless and he had been losing money on it a year or two, but I did not know those particulars because he neglected to mention them. He said that if I would buy the patent he would do the manufacturing and selling for me. So I took him up. Then began a cash outgo of five hundred dollars a month. That raven flew out of the Ark regularly every thirty days but it never got back with anything and the dove didn't report for duty. . . . I gave it (the patent) away to a man whom I had long detested and whose family I desired to ruin. Then I looked around for other adventures.[28]

Those other adventures included additional investments in patents, companies, and his own inventions—experiences that sometimes proved to be more instructive than lucrative.

Sometimes a Good Argument Clears the Air and Makes for a Better Business Relationship

While the great American novel *Huckleberry Finn* languished in a desk drawer, and while Clemens was trying to make a go of the Kaolatype, the watch company temptation that Webster had peddled proved too much to resist. In 1881 and 1882, Clemens invested $5,000 in the Independent Watch Company of Fredonia, New York, including buying his sister's stock at par, and he loaned the venture another $3,600.

What Webster and he didn't realize was that the firm's cofounders were mere confidence men—patent medicine salesman as of 1880. To lend legitimacy to their latest scheme, Edward D. and Clarence M. Howard had paid for Webster's travel expenses to initially visit with his uncle-in-law to secure Clemens's endorsement; they were anxious for the renowned author to invest and even promised to name a watch after him. Who could resist such flattery? But then, in the summer of 1882, before the firm had even made a watch, the conniving brothers declared a bogus stock dividend to line their pockets and proceeded to unload their worthless stock on unsuspecting victims.

In Fredonia, word spread of the swindle and the Clemens family was soon in an uproar because Webster had drawn them into the sordid affair. Accusations were fired from all sides about his integrity and who was to blame for giving Annie permission to marry him. Clemens defended his business manager's reputation and record. In August 1882, he put a positive spin on the episode in a letter to his niece: "Well, Annie, you see there's nothing so wholesome as an occasional storm. It clears the atmosphere."[29] The next month Webster made good and recouped the family's money. "You did miraculously well with the Watch thieves," Clemens wrote. "It was an ugly job well carried through." No lawyers were needed this time.[30]

Statistics Make Clemens Drunk and Dizzy When Evaluating a New Investment

Meanwhile, back in Hartford, über-entrepreneur and condom distributor Frank Fuller was shopping around for another sexy investment. Clemens's "old friend"—although definition of *friend* was a stretch at times depending on the scheme—approached him about investing in the development of a machine that "would get out 99 per cent of all the steam that was in a pound of coal."[31] A firm called the New York Vaporizer Company had been created to manufacture this bedazzling machine, but it sounded too good to be true, so Clemens wisely reviewed the invention with an engineer, a certain Mr. Richards of the Colt Arms Factory.

Richards doubted that such a machine could be built and laid out the facts, which only confounded Clemens:

He showed me a printed book of solid pages of figures, figures that made me drunk and dizzy. He showed me that my man's machine couldn't come within 90 per cent of doing what it proposed to do. I went away a little discouraged. But I thought that maybe the book was mistaken and so I hired the inventor to build the machine on a salary of thirty-five dollars a week, I to pay all expenses. It took him a good many weeks to build the thing. He visited me every few days to report progress and I early noticed by his breath and gait that he was spending thirty-six dollars a week on whisky, and I couldn't ever find out where he got the other dollar.[32]

Clemens would eventually find himself out $5,000 thanks to friend Fuller.[33]

Nevertheless, a dreamer hopelessly addicted to speculation and now mesmerized by the power of steam, in March 1881 he explained to his sister Pamela that he had invested in a steam engine "on the mere *prospect* of a profitable business. . . . No guaranty, I took all the stock I could get yet." Specifically, he invested in the Hartford Engineering Company, which was developing a steam-powered pulley. He owned 145 shares, which made him the second-largest shareholder, and he would ultimately lose $12,500 on this venture.[34] Thanks to the trickle-down theory in economics, at least someone somewhere was benefiting.

Rest assured, at the same time that Clemens was playing venture capitalist with little to show for it, he was investing tens of thousands of dollars in stocks and bonds in various companies that were largely blue chip deals, which would yield a healthy return—but we'll get to that shortly.

Clemens Becomes Obsessed with a Typesetter and Mesmerized by Its Inventor

One more major adventure initiated at this time best exemplifies Clemens's infatuation with technology and involves a sordid love affair he had with a typesetting machine. It is an epic story that spanned 15 years and promised great riches. Of course, the riches would depend on whether Clemens had picked the right horse. The story begins with James William Paige, an inventive genius and hired gunslinger who had come to Hartford in 1876 to perfect a typesetting machine being developed by the Farnham Type-Setter Manufacturing Company.

Clemens first heard of Paige in 1880 while playing billiards and smoking cigars at home with Hartford jeweler Dwight Buell. Buell told him how Paige was working on a typesetting machine that could do the work of four men. It could set entire words instead of letters. Without further ado, visions of revolutionizing the printing industry a la Gutenberg and securing financial independence danced through Clemens's mind. He promised $2,000 on the spot. Later he visited the Samuel Colt Arms Factory, where Paige was set up. While small in stature, the confident inventor was bright-eyed, smartly dressed and— most importantly—guaranteed great riches. There was millions in it, no doubt. Fairly hypnotized by the man and his brilliance, Clemens anted up another $3,000 to bring his initial investment to $5,000.[35]

In April 1881 Paige claimed his machine was perfected. More complicated than a human being, it had 18,000 separate parts, and when the patent application was eventually submitted to the government it would include 204 sheets of drawings. Regardless of how sophisticated the machine was, Webster warned Clemens that typesetters were "scattered all over the country as thick as weeds."[36] There were numerous competitors out there, all seeking to design faster machines as the newspaper and magazine industry exploded. It would prove to be a dog-eat-dog battle. But Clemens thought Paige's machine had the advantage: He jotted in his notebook, "This type-setter does not get drunk. . . . He does not join the Printer's Union."[37] However, contrary to Paige's claims, it was also not yet perfected and more tinkering was required.

In spite of the machine's sobriety, Clemens, who envisioned himself seizing control of the project and bringing it to market with a triumphant flourish befitting kings, figured he needed to organize a new and more sophisticated company to impress potential investors and customers. But a partner with leverage was needed. Who better than William Hamersley, a slick Hartford lawyer and current president of Farnham Type-Setter? The lawyer could certainly extract Paige from any obligations owed Farnham when the time came, and he was also well connected with big New York City money. All-in-all, it appeared to be a savvy move on Clemens's part. In late 1881 Clemens and Hamersley schemed away; their initial plan was to capitalize the new company with $300,000, but then they increased it to $500,000. Clemens believed it would be far easier to find capitalists to fund this venture than the Kaolatype, and he expected to clear a whopping $2 million over the next four or five years.[38]

Not particularly anxious to add to his own burdens, Clemens again brought in the vigilant Webster to handle everyday headaches. "I didn't want to get Hamersley's business *added* to mine—I didn't want any more burdens—didn't even want to *talk* with anybody anymore," he informed Webster in October.[39] He was convinced that the machine could be perfected and told Webster that they should "hang along, and not drop it" as Paige persisted with his tinkering.[40] Patience is a virtue, they say.

Brimming with confidence in his ability to rustle up New York City capital too, Webster informed Clemens, "If any man can get money, I can." However, this could only be done, Webster warned, if the machine could stand a test evaluated by an independent expert.[41] Clemens and Hamersley both agreed it was a prudent move to bring in an expert, and, always waxing euphoric, Clemens was convinced the report would be favorable "if he is an old practical typesetter (like myself,) for he will perceive the value of the thing." Clemens also stated that a foreman with the New York *Herald* had already examined the machine and said he would advise the *Herald* to purchase 30 machines for a total of $150,000.[42]

On December 2, 1881, a group of experts came to evaluate the typesetter, including representatives from the *Boston Journal*, the *New York Times*, and Harper Brothers. According to Webster, the Boston man was duly impressed, declaring the machine "might as well talk as it had done everything else." The New York man also gave the machine high marks.[43] Still, a more arduous test would be required. The men wanted to run it for a week straight.

On the eve of what appeared to be commercial success, Clemens was prepared to sink even more money into the project, but first he had his law firm, Alexander & Green, investigate Paige to make sure he wasn't a swindler in the mold of metallurgist (or alchemist) Sneider. The report came back positive, except, in their opinion, the machine was not ready for the market; it was not ready for investors.[44] Certainly, Clemens had done due diligence, the machine had real promise, and he was quite justified in his investment.

By early 1883, the firm would have a board of directors in place, some 60 stockholders, and a plan to raise capital of $1 million. The foundation had been set. Now it was time to go public. But there was one obstacle: James Paige was proving to be the consummate tinkerer and perfectionist. The inventor's obsessiveness would result in delay after delay.

Addicted to Speculation, Clemens Builds His Portfolio

As the Paige adventure unfolded, along with his more impulsive investments, Clemens was acutely aware that speculation could ruin a man. While on his 1878–1879 European junket, he had noted in his journal, "A Munich friend tells me a pathetic story of the destruction of a lunatic who was ruined by vast speculations. He was always getting new maggots into his head—at last imagined he had bought a comet and it cost so much to keep it—could get no insurance on it &c."[45]

He also offered a glimpse of his awareness of the difficulty of keeping a nest egg intact when he jotted down some thoughts on Communism at that time: "Communism is idiotcy. They want to divide up the property. Suppose they did it—it requires brains to keep money as well as make it. In a precious little while the money would be back in the former owner's hands & the Communist would be poor again. The division would have to be re-made every three years or it would do the communist no good."[46]

By the time Clemens was in his 40s, the white suit was his signature outfit. (COURTESY OF THE MARK TWAIN HOUSE & MUSEUM, HARTFORD, CT)

All that said, Clemens did not shy from speculation: "I must speculate in something, such being my nature," he wrote to Howells in August 1883.[47] Whether he was conscious of it or not, that nature was inherited from his father. That speculation now included a portfolio of more than $100,000 in 1882, a portfolio he had been building since his move to Hartford. Using both local bankers and brokers, he had made various investments that ran the spectrum in terms of risk, from blue chip to chancy dogs that might come back to bite him. In his journal, he left a relatively complete snapshot of his portfolio as of May 1882:

Co-Op. Dress Assn Certif of stk #No. 2. (ticket No. 2002)	$ 25
Am. Bk. Note Co. certif. #1701 20 shs ($1000)	1,000
Ditto #1740–(80 shs)	4,000
N.Y. Central & Hud River 50 shs (A31929)	5,000
Adams Express #9261 (50 shs)	5,000
Norfolk & Western Bonds, Nos. 325, 326, 327, 1618, 1619	5,000
Little Rock M.R. & T. Bonds, 883, 884, 881, 880, 879	5,000
Little Rock M.R. & T. Bonds, 1531, 1530, 1532, 1533, 1534	5,000
Independent Watch Co.	5,000
N.Y. Vaporizing Co.	5,000
Hartford Engineering Co. 145 shs (No. 26)	14,500
Am. Exchange in Europe 500 shs 24001 to 24500	5,000
Conn. Fire Ins. 12 shs (No. 1515)	1,200
Jewell Pin Co 15 shs No. 19	1,500
Farnham Type-Setter Mf Co, 200 shs (No. 6)	5,000
Kaolatype Eng Co, 120 shs (No. 6)	3,000
Crown Pt. Iron Co. (No 339) 100 shares	10,000
Hartford Sanitary Plumbing Co. 40 shs	1,000

Watch Co (Howard Bros) Note in JL & Co's hands due Sept. 1883	3,600
St Paul Roller Mill stk	5,000
New stk Am Ex in Europe	5,000
Metford, 100 shs	3,125
Burr Index Co	2,500.[48]
Total	$100,450

That $100,000 would be worth almost *$2 million* today. Not bad for an author hailing from modest Hannibal, Missouri.

The exploding network of railroads—the Gilded Age's equivalent of Internet play and eventual dot-bombs—provided huge returns for those investors who timed the market with clairvoyance. With more than $20,000 in the railroads, Clemens did indeed follow them closely. In 1881 he tracked the prices of Missouri & Pacific Railroad, and Lake Shore & Michigan Southern Railroad stocks in his notebook.[49] Apparently he exercised some self-restraint because he did not purchase either stock. It was a wise choice, because the rapacious Cornelius Vanderbilt had gained control of the Lake Shore & Michigan, while the equally greedy Jay Gould had seized control of the Missouri Pacific. No doubt the same manipulative havoc the two tycoons had wreaked on the Erie Railroad would infect their new investments. At the same time, Clemens was following the more financially sound Western Union, which he would buy later.

Initial Insider Information Does Not Always Guarantee Success Because Someone Still Has to Watch the Market Carefully

Fully comprehending the importance of insider information, Clemens listened to friends in the know, like Frank Fuller, who in March 1882 encouraged him to invest in the Indiana,

Bloomington & Western Railroad. Fuller reported that it was "a stock not now generally believed in" although he was certain it "will take a considerable rise very soon." Quick to seize on the opportunity to buy into the undervalued company, Clemens purchased 100 shares, which Fuller watched for him, ready to pull the sell trigger.[50] While this stock provided a windfall in 1882, two years later Clemens wrote ruefully, "I'm out of luck this year." His Union Pacific railroad stock, which he could have sold at $56 for a profit of $3,400, was now down to $47.[51]

Railroad stocks were suffering, period, thanks to a May 1884 financial panic, which was precipitated by the failure of the brokerage house Grant and Ward, funded by Ulysses S. Grant and his son Buck, in partnership with Ferdinand Ward. Ward had bilked the firm and its customers, thus bankrupting the company and setting off a domino effect. A half dozen other stock exchange houses and more than 40 banks subsequently failed. Last but not least, former President Grant faced personal bankruptcy, but would save his family from poverty by writing his memoirs (to be published by none other than Samuel L. Clemens).

From such experiences—the 1884 panic and those like it—came one of Clemens's better known money maxims: "Prosperity is the best protector of principle." That is, when the country is financially healthy, individuals stay honest.

While the gyrating railroad stocks gave him fits, Clemens also had his blue chips, such as the $5,000 in American Bank-Note Company stock, a stock he held for years as he judged it the "staying kind."[52] Well managed, American Bank-Note was attempting to consolidate all leading engraving companies into one organization, and it already controlled the production of all postage stamps, as well as printing bank notes and securities. Investing in a monopoly was a wise move on Clemens's part, and American Bank-Note is still around today.

Another blue chip investment was his $10,000 in the American Exchange, a New York bank, which was paying healthy dividends.[53] Adams Express, a freight-shipping firm, was a solid company, too. Incidentally, a teenage Andrew Carnegie made his very first investment in Adams Express, in the mid-1860s, and this little nest egg would eventually grow to fund his steel empire.[54] Other safe bets included the $10,600 in Crown Point Iron Company, which was owned by his buddy Senator Jones.[55] Again, Clemens was more than willing to ride the coattails of his filthy rich friends.

Clemens continued to be on the lookout for investment opportunities in new technology with practical, everyday value—something the general public would consume. In 1884 he struck upon one such possibility when he heard about hand grenades that were filled with a fire retardant. In June he ordered six dozen, and apparently was forced to use them at least once to extinguish a fire in his house—no small surprise considering his propensity to fall asleep while smoking a cigar. Intrigued by the hand grenades, in October of 1884 he had Webster investigate the manufacturer to determine if it was worth investing in the company. Several months later, still curious as to the condition of the company and the stock price, he followed up with Webster but now wanted to know "how there come to be two hand-grenades in the field, looking just alike but differently named?"[56] There is no evidence that he invested in the company, apparently having learned that two identical competing products don't make the best investment as they slug it out for market share.

While Clemens was quick to heed the advice of his rich friends, he also relied on savvy Wall Street brokers, which helped temper his more compulsive side. In Hartford he used George P. Bissell & Company, a banking firm, with diligent Mr. Bissell himself putting the author into the profitable American Bank-Note Company and the Hartford Fire Insurance Company, the latter run by Yale graduate and family member Richard M. Bissell. Not afraid to spread his business around and risk offending one stockbroker or another, Clemens also used the Hartford brokerage firm of Hubbard & Farmer.

It was when he strayed outside a traditional brokerage firm that he tended to get into trouble. On one occasion in financially rocky 1884—even though Clemens claimed he had "sworn off permanently from stocks (speculative ones)"—he relied on his friend, Dean Sage, an executive at a lumber manufacturing firm, to buy him 300 shares of Oregon Trans-Continental at $73 each. It appeared to be a good deal, considering Dean Sage was related to multimillionaire Wall Street investor Russell Sage, the latter a big Twain fan who was no doubt providing Dean with reliable insider information. In fact, the stock went up to 98 but then collapsed to 15. Meanwhile, Dean Sage had fallen ill, was out of the office, and unable to sell the stock as it dropped like a rock, leaving Clemens caught short.[57] If only Dean had been a member of a brokerage firm, someone would have been covering his ass.

Clemens Advises to Not Rely on a Religious Newspaper for Investment Advice

Feeling a financial pinch in 1885, Clemens was now a little gun-shy when it came to Wall Street. A self-deprecating, satirical, and cynical attitude on investing emerged, evident in how Clemens responded to a poor reverend looking for advice. The minister had purchased some stocks recommended by Hartford banker Bissell and advertised in a religious paper. "After I made that purchase they wrote me that you had just bought a hundred shares and that you were a 'shrewd' man," the minister wrote to Clemens. The stocks did not fare well, however. There would be no sympathy from Clemens on that score:

> Bissell was premature in calling me a "shrewd man." I wasn't one at that time, but am one now—that is, I am at least too shrewd to ever again invest in anything put on the market by Bissell. I know nothing whatever about the Bank Note Co., and never did know anything about it. Bissell sold me about $4,000 or $5,000 worth of the stock at $110, and I own it yet. He sold me $10,000 worth of another rose-tinted stock about the same time. I have got that yet, also. I judge that a peculiarity of Bissell's stocks is that they are of the staying kind. I think you should have asked somebody else whether I was a shrewd man or not for two reasons: the stock was advertised in a religious paper, a circumstance which was very suspicious; and the compliment came to you from a man who was interested to make a purchaser of you. I am afraid you deserve your loss. A financial scheme advertised in any religious paper is a thing which any living person ought to know enough to avoid; and when the factor is added that M. runs that religious paper, a dead person ought to know enough to avoid it.[58]

When Clemens responded so blithely to the poor reverend, he was not only up to his eyeballs in the Paige typesetter business, but he had also embarked on a new and very public venture from which he would reap tens of thousands of dollars. In a very manic 1884, Clemens established his own publishing firm to produce and sell his books. While publishing his own books promised greater wealth, it would not be easy playing both author and publisher—the conflicts of interest would require a high-wire juggling act that would threaten his way of life.

QUIRKY HABITS AND BRAZEN PHILOSOPHY

The Half-Soled Stockbroker

"Honesty is the best policy—when there is money in it."

In Clemens's day the stock market was extremely volatile, and manipulation by scoundrels like Jim Fisk and Jay Gould was rampant. Today it is nearly impossible for one person to manipulate the entire market, although we do have our Enrons, terrorist attacks, earnings warnings, and sun spots that can send the market into an unreasonable tailspin. And then there are the allegedly objective analysts promoting specific companies so their mutant brokerage/ investment banking firms get juicy deals from said companies. So much for modern protections designed to safeguard the little guy.

From his Wild West days, Clemens was wary of scheming mining stock promoters, and this caution carried over to his attitude toward stockbrokers and, years later, Wall Street. Long before he had ample cash to invest, in 1864 he visited with the San Francisco Board of Brokers—The Lion's Den, or the Den of Forty Thieves, as he also called it—and then wrote an article about the experience, "Daniel in The Lion's Den—And Out Again All Right." While observing the hustle and bustle and chattering, Clemens determined that the brokers were speaking the Kanaka language, which he had heard in Hawaii, but an acquaintance assured him that it was English. More poignant today than ever are Clemens's critical opinions on those stockbrokers, whom he was certain were born with souls—but then something simply went wrong.

(Continued)

The Half-Soled Stockbroker *(Continued)*

Daniel in The Lion's Den—And Out Again
All Right

Some people are not particular about what sort of company they keep. I am one of that kind. Now for several days I have been visiting the Board of Brokers, and associating with brokers, and drinking with them, and swapping lies with them, and being as familiar and sociable with them as I would with the most respectable people in the world. I do this because I consider that a broker goes according to the instincts that are in him, and means no harm, and fulfils his mission according to his lights, and has a right to live, and be happy in a general way, and be protected by the law to some extent, just the same as a better man. I consider that brokers come into the world with souls—I am satisfied they do; and if they wear them out in the course of a long career of stock-jobbing, have they not a right to come in at the eleventh hour and get themselves half-soled, like old boots, and be saved at last? Certainly—the father of the tribe did that, and do we say anything against Barabbas for it to-day? No! we concede his right to do it; we admire his mature judgment in selling out of a worked-out mine of iniquity and investing in righteousness, and no man denies, or even doubts, the validity of the transaction. Other people may think as they please, and I suppose I am entitled to the same privilege; therefore, notwithstanding what others may believe, I am of the opinion that a broker can be saved. Mind, I do not say that a broker will be saved, or even that it is uncommon likely that such a thing will happen—I only say that Lazarus was raised from the dead, the five thousand were fed with twelve loaves of bread, the water was turned into wine, the Israelites crossed the Red Sea dry-shod, and a broker can be saved. True, the angel that accomplishes the task may require all eternity to rest

himself in, but has that got anything to do with the establishment of the proposition? Does it invalidate it? does it detract
from it? I think not. I am aware that this enthusiastic and
may-be highly-colored vindication of the brokers may lay
me open to suspicion of bribery, but I care not; I am a native
of Washoe, and I will stand by anybody that stands by
Washoe. . . .

However, I cannot leave the subject without saying I was
agreeably disappointed in those brokers; I expected to see a
set of villains with the signs of total depravity hung out all
over them, but now I am satisfied there is some good in
them; that they are not entirely and irredeemably bad; and I
have been told by a friend, whose judgment I respect, that
they are not any more unprincipled than they look. This was
said by a man who would scorn to stoop to flattery. At the
same time, though, as I scanned the faces assembled in that
hall, I could not help imagining I could see old St. Peter ad-
mitting that band of Bulls and Bears into Paradise—see him
standing by the half-open gate with his ponderous key
pressed thoughtfully against his nose, and his head canted
critically to one side, as he looks after them tramping down
the gold-paved avenue, and mutters to himself: "Well, you're
a nice lot, any way! Humph! I think you'll find it sort of
lonesome in heaven, for if my judgment is sound, you'll not
find a good many of your stripe in there!"[59]

chapter seven

BOLD VISION AND IMAGINATION: HOW TWAIN MADE GENERAL U. S. GRANT—AND HIMSELF—RICH

*"The happy phrasing of a compliment is one of the rarest
of human gifts and the happy delivery of it another."*

*T*o reap the benefits as author and as publisher, in 1884 Clemens
founded his own publishing house, Charles L. Webster & Company, to be managed by his nephew-in-law, Charles Webster. As the
firm's recognized leader, Clemens had to learn diplomacy and to embrace other intangible leadership skills, while implementing concrete
strategies such as a rewards program to motivate his salesmen. Originally intending to publish his own books, he soon took on Ulysses S.
Grant's memoirs, which would yield record book profits. Clemens's brilliant management of Grant's book would be studied more than a century later by academicians. By 1887 he knew he had to impose tighter
financial controls on his rapidly growing firm, and success bred conflict.

Clemens's good friend and billiards partner, James Osgood, had
failed miserably in the book subscription sales business; under
Osgood's direction, his books sold poorly. There would not be
another chance. In breaking up their partnership, however,
Clemens was careful not to hurt Osgood's feelings—he curbed
his typically flamboyant remarks. "Now I did not want to say
anything which could not be said through Webster," he wrote to

Osgood, "because I did not want to run the risk of saying or writing one word which might mar the pleasant relations existing between you and me. . . If it is necessary that we talk together, and if it seems to you best, we will do it; but let us not write about it—for writings do not successfully interpret the feeling of the writer."[1] Wisely, Clemens had filtered himself by using Webster as a go-between. At the same time, he understood a face-to-face was the best means of communication. As for poor Osgood, his publishing business would go bankrupt in May 1885.

Now, with *Huck Finn* finally coming down the pipe, Clemens had to have a publisher. Well, who better than himself? After all, in the publishing arena he was considered a brilliant marketing strategist, and he knew production inside and out thanks to his investigative efforts in trying to prove that Bliss and the American Publishing Company had been stealing from him by inflating production costs so the firm could pay less royalty. In 1881 he had seriously considered bringing a lawsuit against them over this issue, although he confided to Webster his real goal was to scare them into giving him control of his books.[2]

So, displeased with his publishers of the last two decades, in 1884, at the age of 49, Clemens founded his own publishing firm. It was part of a natural progression or evolution of his career as he sought self-reliance. Once and for all he could reap benefits from both ends, as author and publisher. He would display exceptional skills as a selfless leader who delegated responsibility and as a visionary marketer who pursued every opportunity with a militant determination. On the flip side, he would learn that success can breed failure.

Clemens Gives Webster a Share in the Firm's Success, But Fails to Make Him Also Assume Risk

To manage the firm, Clemens hired his ever-reliable nephew-in-law Webster. In a move to shield himself from undesirable public attention, he decided to name the business Charles L. Webster &

Company. This move served another purpose too: While checking his own ego, he played on Webster's by naming the company
after him—a good old trick for firing up the man's enthusiasm.
Fortunately, at age 32, Webster was somewhat prepared for the
grueling road ahead: On July 18, 1881, Clemens had put him "in
full control of my interests connected with the American Publishing Company," and in the fall of 1882 he had encouraged
Webster to bone up on the publishing business.[3]

There was one obstacle: What to pay Webster, who still knew
relatively little about actually managing a publishing house but
was eagerly willing to learn the trade on Clemens's dime. "He
thought he ought to have twenty-five hundred dollars a year
while he was learning the trade," Clemens reflected in his autobiography. "I took a day or two to consider the matter and
study it out searchingly. So far as I could see, this was a new
idea. I remembered that printers' apprentices got *no* salary."
Clemens figured, somewhat cynically, that anyone who made
such a demand "must surely be worth securing—and instantly—lest he get away."[4] Clemens agreed to pay Webster the
$2,500 and an annual bonus of one-third of the net profits up
to the first $20,000, then only a tenth thereafter.

Clemens was allowed to pocket the other two-thirds of the
profits. However, to keep the firm capitalized, he had to impose
restrictions on himself as to how much money he could take out
in a given year. He and Webster subsequently agreed that for any
capital he advanced the firm, Clemens would receive 8 percent
interest. A year later the contract was amended, increasing Webster's salary to $3,000 and reducing the interest Clemens earned
on his money to a more reasonable 6 percent.[5] To further secure
Webster's commitment to the firm's success, Clemens adroitly
offered him a tenth interest in the partnership. With his usual sea-
soning of sarcasms and jaded perspective, the humorist recalled:

I was coming to admire Webster very much and at this point in
the proceedings I had one of those gushing generosities surge up

in my system, and before I had thought I had tried to confer upon Webster a tenth interest in the business in addition to his salary, free of charge. Webster declined promptly—with thanks, of course, the usual kind. That raised him another step in my admiration. I knew perfectly well that I was offering him a partnership interest which would pay him two or three times his salary within the next nine months, but he didn't know that. He was coldly and wisely discounting all my prophecies about Huckleberry Finn's high commercial value. And here was this new evidence that in Webster I had found a jewel, a man who would not get excited; a man who would not lose his head; a cautious man; a man who would not take a risk of any kind in fields unknown to him. Except at somebody else's expense, I mean.[6]

While Clemens had certainly dangled a carrot by offering a generous bonus, his mistake in terms of motivating Webster was his failure to also wield a stick. Webster should have had to put capital into the firm, too, so that he would suffer if the business went south. Instead, he was in a cozy position where he couldn't possibly fail, monetarily speaking.

The first project on the docket was *Huck Finn*, which Clemens had prophesied would be a great success. With manuscript and capital in hand, Webster, who was still managing Clemens's other ventures like the memory game and typesetter, went to work with his usual diligence. He showered Clemens with so many income, expense, manufacturing, sales, and sundry other reports that the author nearly went mad from information overload. After reviewing reams of accounting, he exclaimed, "Great guns, it makes my head ache!" Before long he demanded very clean and simple weekly reports that provided an update on each item, from *Huck Finn*'s publishing costs to the status of his memory-builder game. He advised Webster to create a checklist for the many projects and stick it to his wall where he could see it every day as a reminder. While Clemens wanted to be updated, he believed in delegating and didn't want to be bothered with trivial decision-making. "You are there to take care of my business," he told Webster, "not make business for *me* to take care of."[7]

Clemens Wisely Takes a Hands-Off Approach to His Artists and Allows Them to Obey Their Own Inspiration

Clemens not only was more than willing to delegate authority and to empower Webster, but he also perceived the importance of sensitively handling others involved in the *Huck Finn* project. When the drawings for the book, made by a hired artist, were submitted, Clemens was not pleased. He considered them "forbidding and repulsive" and suggested to Webster that an "artist shouldn't follow a book too literally." While he thought the pieces had to be redone, he also advised Webster not to "dishearten the artist—show him where he has improved, rather than where he has failed, & punch him up to improve more."[8]

His delicate handling of the artists did not wane over time. In 1889, to inspire the artist working on his *A Yankee in King Arthur's Court*, he wrote Fred J. Hall, by then managing Webster & Company, "Upon reflection—thus: tell Beard to obey his *own* inspiration, and when he sees a picture in his mind put *that* picture on paper, be it humorous or be it serious. I want his genius to be wholly unhampered, I shan't have fears as to the result. They will be better pictures than if I mixed in and tried to give him points on his own trade."[9] Despite how opinionated he was, in dealing with the artists Clemens was demonstrating the characteristics of great leadership by wanting to unlock their genius.

Clemens Understands That Only Intense Marketing and Sales Will Insure the Success of Huck Finn

One of Webster's primary tasks at the publishing house was to hire sales agents across the country who, in turn, would hire canvassers to sell subscriptions to *Huck Finn*. Because the novel was a follow-up to *Tom Sawyer*, Clemens thought it was a no-brainer to sell both together, the customer given a small discount if purchasing both.[10] There was one problem, however: American Publishing controlled *Tom Sawyer*, and the "swines" refused to offer terms that would make selling it profitable for Clemens.

During the ongoing negotiations with the despised firm, Clemens explained to Webster that he could not be trusted to help because "I have no diplomacy in my own nature, & you don't suggest any to me. Try to remember that I fly off the handle altogether too easily, & that you want to think twice before you send me irritating news."[11] To purge his angers and frustrations, he would often scribble his tirades in his notebooks or in letters to the objects of his ire, but then destroy those letters. Here again demonstrating savvy leadership, he knew he had to control himself.

As the sales effort for *Huck Finn* geared up, Clemens exhorted Webster: "Get at your canvassing early, and drive it with all your might, with the intent and purpose of issuing on the 10th (or 15th) of next December (the best time in the year to tumble a big pile into the trade)—but if we haven't 40,000 orders then, we simply postpone publication until we've *got* them."[12] The next month he reiterated the message. Clemens made it very clear that the book *must* succeed. It made perfect sense to come out fast and strong to achieve economies of scale and thus reduce per-book publishing costs.

To motivate the sales agents, Clemens supported the idea of offering prizes to the top sellers, which he had done when Osgood published *Life on the Mississippi*. Once again, in managing the process, he was willing to delegate: "As to the prizes," he wrote to Webster, "you can think that out and decide upon it much better than I can. It is not my function to help arrive at conclusions in business matters. The thing should not be submitted to me except in a completed and determined form—

then my function comes in: and it is merely and solely to *approve* or *disapprove*."[13]

To insure timely book reviews in newspapers and magazines, Clemens insisted on sending out press copies. When there was a delay in getting copies to the *Century* and *Atlantic* magazines, he considered it an "irreparable blunder."[14] But then *Huck Finn* received an unexpected boon in publicity when the book was banned by the Concord, Massachusetts public library. As they say, any publicity is good publicity. In reporting on the Concord library's actions, the March 19, 1885, edition of the *New York Times* ran the simple headline of "TRASHY AND VICIOUS." What followed was a reprint from the perversely pious *Springfield Republican*:

> The Concord public library committee deserve well of the public by their action in banishing Mark Twain's new book, "Huckleberry Finn," on the ground that it is trashy and vicious. It is time that this influential pseudonym should cease to carry into homes and libraries unworthy productions. Mr. Clemens is a genuine and powerful humorist, and with a bitter vein of satire on the weaknesses of humanity which is sometimes wholesome, sometimes only grotesque, but in certain of his works degenerates into a gross trifling with every fine feeling. The trouble with Mr. Clemens is that he has no reliable sense of propriety. . . . The advertising samples of this book, which have disfigured the Century magazine, are enough to tell any reader how offensive the whole thing must be.[15]

While the initial printing for *Huck Finn* was only 30,000, another 10,000 were printed by March 1885, and more than 20 million copies would be printed in the coming decades and centuries. In his autobiography, Clemens reflected:

> Webster was successful with Huckleberry Finn and a year later handed me the firm's check for fifty-four thousand five hundred dollars, which included the fifteen thousand dollars capital which I had originally handed to him.

Once more I experienced a new birth. I have been born more times than anybody except Krishna, I suppose.

Webster conceived the idea that he had discovered me to the world but he was reasonably modest about it. He did much less cackling over his egg than Webb and Bliss had done.[16]

While Webster & Company had been created to publish his own books, Clemens immediately set his sights on other authors of distinction. As they looked around for projects, in July 1884 he wrote to Webster: "When you strike something which you want to *recommend* that we tackle, go ahead & recommend it & give your reasons. But a mere blind conundrum, without either recommendations or reasons, is a sort of thing which I don't want the bother of trying to answer."[17] In the first years of operation, Clemens offered sound management advice; however, in his somewhat revisionist autobiography, Clemens recalled this branching out a little differently: "It had never been my intention to publish anybody's books but my own. An accident diverted me from this wise purpose. That was General Grant's memorable book."

Clemens Gives Advice to Ulysses S. Grant, Which He Likens to Columbus's Cook Giving Advice on Navigating

In November 1884, Clemens heard rumors that General Ulysses S. Grant—Civil War hero, former U.S. president, and national treasure—was about to sign a contract to publish his memoirs. Over the years they had encountered each other several times at various receptions and banquets, so they were on friendly terms, friendly enough that Clemens decided to visit with Grant at his East 66th Street New York City home to reconnoiter the situation. As it turned out, the 62-year-old general was indeed about to sign a contract with *Century* magazine, which, Clemens pointed out to Grant, was foolish because while the magazine knew everything about magazine publishing, its editors knew nothing about books. After looking over the proposed contract, which included a 10 percent royalty rate, Clemens determined that the terms would never do: "That was the most colossal bit of cheek the 19th Century can show," he jotted in his notebook.[17] Instead of just a 10 percent royalty rate, he insisted the general demand 75 percent.

"The idea distressed General Grant," Clemens recalled. "He thought it placed him in the attitude of robber—robber of a publisher. I said that if he regarded that as a crime it was because his education was limited. I said it was not a crime and was always rewarded in heaven with two halos." Because the *Century* had been publishing articles he had written, Grant felt as thought he owed them: "He was now most loath to desert these benefactors of his. To his military mind and training it seemed disloyalty."[19] It was a case of letting misguided emotion rule over decision making.

Then Clemens made a bold proposition to the general: Sign a contract with Webster & Company. Even though numbers made Clemens dizzy, in this case he took the time to analyze the financial figures proposed by the *Century* and compared them to what he could offer. Although he carefully explained how much more money the general stood to earn if he went with Webster & Company, the general still demurred and negotiations dragged on into the next year. On February 14, 1885, an anxious Webster wrote to Clemens: "There's big money for us both in that book and on the terms indicated in my note to the General we can make it pay *big*."[20]

A week later Clemens again met with Grant, who, suffering from throat cancer, was thin and frail looking. At that meeting the venerable general came to terms with Clemens, and on February 27, Grant signed a contract with Webster & Company, with the general to receive an astounding 70 percent of the profits. Realistically, Grant couldn't pass on this far more lucrative offer: The May 1884 failure of the brokerage firm, Grant and Ward, in which he was a partner, had left him effectively impoverished.

The general's dire financial situation was so apparent to Clemens that he generously offered to pay the family $500 a month until the first book advance was paid to them.[21]

News of the contract made quite a splash in the newspapers, and, Clemens recounted, made quite an impact on Webster:

> The news went forth that General Grant was going to write his memoirs and that the firm of Charles L. Webster & Co. would publish them. The announcement produced a vast sensation throughout the country. The nation was glad and this feeling poured itself heartily out in all the newspapers. On the one day, young Webster was as unknown as the unborn babe. The next day he was a notoriety. His name was in every paper in the United States. He was young, he was human, he naturally mistook this transient notoriety for fame, and by consequence he had to get his hat enlarged. His juvenile joy in his new grandeur was a pretty and pleasant spectacle to see. The first thing he did was to move out of his modest quarters and secure quarters better suited to his new importance as the most distinguished publisher in the country.[22]

So much for the idea of modesty being the best policy; however, Clemens was more concerned about secrecy. Namely, he wanted absolute secrecy around the Grant book so no pirate could snatch portions of the manuscript and cut into their profits. In the spring of 1885, he warned Webster: "Stop leaving those proofs on your table—keep them always in your safe. . . . No book ever stood in such peril before as this one." A paranoid Clemens also demanded that no request for preview copy be granted without his personal approval and ordered Webster to buy insurance in case the book was pirated and sales lost.[23]

During the actual writing of the book, Clemens learned a valuable lesson about the value of compliments and encouragement. To begin, there was a certain urgency to the project: Grant was dying of throat cancer and he knew his days were numbered. While he worked at his home on 66th Street, and then, when his health declined dramatically, at a resort outside Saratoga Springs, New York, Clemens visited him regularly. By May he was forced to dictate passages, assisted by his son Fred and former military aide and author Adam Badeau, both men jogging his memory, assisting with the detailed reconstruction of events, and tracking down documents. Clemens was impressed that over one two-day period, the general, with his neck wrapped in a shawl and a knit cap on his head, managed 50 pages, covering the Wilderness and Appomattox campaigns.[24]

Later, Clemens recounted Grant's last heroics to Henry Ward Beecher:

He [Grant] was under sentence of death last spring; he sat thinking, musing, several days—nobody knows what about; then he pulled himself together and set to work to finish that book, a colossal task for a dying man. Presently his hand gave out; fate seemed to have got him checkmated. Dictation was suggested. No, he never could do that; had never tried it; too old to learn, now. By and by—if he could only do Appomattox well.

So he sent for a stenographer, and dictated 9,000 words at a single sitting!—never pausing, never hesitating for a word, never repeating—and in the written-out copy he made hardly a correction. He dictated again, every two or three days—the intervals were intervals of exhaustion and slow recuperation—and at last he was able to tell me that he had written more matter than could be got into the book. I then enlarged the book—had to. Then he lost his voice. He was not quite done yet, however:—there was no end of little plums and spices to be stuck in, here and there; and this work he patiently continued, a few lines a day, with pad and pencil, till far into July, at Mt. McGregor.

One day he put his pencil aside, and said he was done—there was nothing more to do. If I had been there I could have foretold the shock that struck the world three days later.[25]

Grant died July 23, 1885.

At the same time that the general pressed resolutely forward, he was yearning for feedback from Clemens, who was subsequently surprised to learn of the tough old bird's desire:

> Whenever galley proofs or revises went to General Grant a set came also to me. General Grant was aware of this. Sometimes I referred to the proofs casually but entered into no particulars concerning them. By and by I learned through a member of the household that he was disturbed and disappointed because I had never expressed an opinion as to the literary quality of the memoirs. It was also suggested that a word of encouragement from me would be a help to him. I was as much surprised as Columbus's cook would have been to learn that Columbus wanted his opinion as to how Columbus was doing his navigating. It could not have occurred to me that General Grant could have any use for anybody's assistance or encouragement in any work which he might undertake to do. He was the most modest of men and this was another instance of it. He was venturing upon a new trade, an uncharted sea, and stood in need of the encouraging word, just like any creature of common clay. It was a great compliment that he should care for my opinion and should desire it and I took the earliest opportunity to diplomatically turn the conversation in that direction and furnish it without seeming to lug it in by the ears.[26]

In learning the nuances of being a great business manager and leader, Clemens now comprehended the critical role compliments played when it came to inspiring others. In his autobiography, he would write one of his oft-quoted maxims: "The happy phrasing of a compliment is one of the rarest of human gifts and the happy delivery of it another."

Proving Himself a Marketing Innovator, Clemens Insists on Progressive Sales Techniques

The sales and marketing of Grant's two-volume memoirs was carried out in a brilliant campaign that was militaristic in its own right. But before launching the campaign, Clemens had to settle the debate concerning whether to package the two-book set together at once or to sell the volumes separately. Initially, Clemens wanted to print and sell both at once to usurp any possible pirates trying to get their hands on the second volume and to prevent bookstores from promising to sell the second volume at a discount, thus undercutting subscription sales. Unfortunately, because the project was so big and the sales ultimately so huge, no printer could handle both volumes at once and the two had to be sold separately.

Clemens concerns were justified as Philadelphia-based retail tycoon John Wannamaker did indeed sell the memoirs at a discount. Born in 1838 and considered the father of the department store, in 1875 Wannamaker had purchased an abandoned railroad depot that he converted into a massive store. As an innovative advertiser, discounting was integral to his strategy. In spite of the fact that Wannamaker was a civic and political force, an incensed Clemens wanted the discounting to end immediately and wrote to Webster, "See that you go for Wannamaker—otherwise I will go down there and rise up in his Sunday School & give him hell, in front of his whole 3000 pupils. I certainly will."[27] In fact, Clemens took Wannamaker to court, but lost. Discounting books was an issue that would continue to be argued over by publishers and booksellers into the twenty-first century.

The real success of Grant's memoirs hinged on the army of salesmen being assembled, the largest ever. To weed out undesirable subscription agents, Webster often did background checks. No drinkers or ill-mannered men were hired, and if a man already had too much on his plate, he was turned away. In a brilliant decision, Clemens ordered Webster to hire as many war veterans as possible and to instruct those men to wear their Grand Army badges—who could turn them away? To accommodate his larger staff—now overseeing 16 general sales agents and 10,000 canvassers—Webster had to move into bigger New

York City offices at 3 East 14th Street. Subsequently, he boasted to his brother-in-law that the company had "the finest sub-scription publishing office in the world."[28] This would not sit well with Clemens, who had once requested that Bliss secure more modest offices for the American Publishing Company because the overhead ate into the author's royalties.

When the agents started taking orders in March 1885, while Grant was still writing, Clemens insisted that the prime sales districts in ripe New York City be given to the best salesmen after they proved themselves in outlying areas. He instructed Webster: "Canvassers must be given streets or portions of streets in New York—all outlying districts to be canvassed first—then the cream of the city to be given to those canvassers who have done the best." It was great motivation for canvassers eager to prove themselves.

Clemens also advocated a sales script, writing to Webster, "Furnish canvassers a list of truthful and sensible things to say—not rot."[29] Subsequently, a 37-page manual was devel-oped—"How to Introduce the Personal Memoirs of U. S. Grant"—that instructed salesman on who to target, how to use flattery, and even the proper etiquette for entering and exiting homes, among other skills. In approaching potential customers, personal, one-to-one contact was best. "Avoid men in groups as you would poison," the manual instructed. "It is better to lie still and do nothing than to go into a group of men to can-vass."[30] When leaving a house, the salesman was never to turn his back on the customer. He was supposed to exit the house sideways, keeping an eye on the prospect.

Not unlike today, it was a three-step sales process: Gain a hearing, create desire, and take the order. The sales pitch itself opened with the salesman stating that he was going to give the prospective client a chance to see Grant's memoirs, which had been so much talked about in the newspapers. No one could turn down a sneak preview. However, the best hook was flattery, that is, a little buttering up: "One of the strongest arguments that can be used to get a man's order is by telling him of his influence," the sales manual stated, "and other means of flattery, or rather compliments, which should always be used in such quantities as will take well, and to be successfully done you must thoroughly inform yourself about the man before calling on him."[31] Confidence and enthusiasm were key characteristics to achieving success, especially considering that, depending on the binding and other options available, the memoirs retailed for anywhere from $3 to over $12, the latter amounting to over $200 today—no cheap proposition.

A confident Clemens predicted that the first volume would sell an enormous, record-breaking 250,000 copies. But there were stumbling blocks, which included Grant having his enemies. Not far into the campaign, Clemens heard of bogus canvassers stealing from unwitting would-be customers, so he ordered Webster to hire detectives to entrap the "head-devils."[32] He would show no mercy.

Potentially far more damaging was an April 1885 article in the popular *World* magazine claiming that Grant had not written a word of his memoirs; the *World* charged that it was entirely ghost written by General Adam Badeau, Grant's former aide, military historian, and author. As charges and countercharges flew through the air, Clemens warned Webster to write nothing in his correspondence that "you would not mind seeing in print." No one was to be trusted. They decided to take the high road and not sue the newspaper for slander, although Clemens was also swayed by the fact that he didn't want to bring any more undue attention to the rag: "I recognize the fact that for General Grant to sue the *World* would be an enormously valuable advertisement for that daily issue of unmedicated closet-paper," he wrote to Webster.[33] Yes, any PR was good PR.

A Record-Setting Sales Campaign Will Be Textbook Material over 100 Years Later

By May 1885—hardly two months into the sales campaign—60,000 two-volume sets had been ordered. Ten days after Clemens's 50th birthday, on November 30, 1885, the first volume of Grant's memoirs was published, and three months later Julia Grant received a record-shattering royalty payment of $200,000 (almost $4 million today). By early 1886 total sales reached 325,000, and she would take in almost $450,000 (just over $8 million today) while Clemens would pocket about $200,000.[34]

Throughout the sales campaign, Clemens remained hands-on. On December 2, 1885, he wrote Howells:

> I've got the first volume launched safely; consequently, half of the suspense is over, and I am that much nearer the goal. We've bound and shipped 200,000 books; and by the 10th shall finish and ship the remaining 125,000 of the first edition. I got nervous and came down to help hump-up the binderies; and I mean to stay here pretty much all the time till the first days of March, when the second volume will issue. Shan't have so much trouble, this time, though, if we get to press pretty soon, because we can get more binderies then than are to be had in front of the holidays. One lives and learns. I find it takes 7 binderies four months to bind 325,000 books.
>
> This is a good book to publish. I heard a canvasser say, yesterday, that while delivering eleven books he took 7 new subscriptions. But we shall be in a hell of a fix if that goes on—it will "ball up" the binderies again.[35]

By July 1886, Clemens was hungry to extract some of the prodigious profits from the firm. He had his lavish lifestyle to support and was funding the Paige typesetter, the latter eating up hundreds of dollars a month in expenses. In good humor, he wrote to Webster & Company's bookkeeper, Fred Hall:

> The supply of money on hand must begetting perilously large by this time.

I can take care of twenty or thirty thousand dollars myself whenever you think it will relieve your bank burdens.

At the time, Clemens's share of the profits was $63,142.87 of the $200,000 he would eventually realize.[36] His strategy and success in selling Grant's memoirs were significant enough that Walter Friedman, a professor at Harvard Business School, included a chapter covering the episode in his 2004 book, *Birth of a Salesman*. Specifically, Friedman extolled Clemens for his ability to organize and motivate such a large sales army and for incorporating innovative elements like the manual into the sales campaign.

Business Success Results in Dangerous Ego Issues

On the heels of their success, Clemens perceived a change in Webster, namely, his head swelled to such proportions that he couldn't fit it "into a barrel," according to Clemens:

> He loved to descant upon the wonders of the book. He liked to go into the statistics. He liked to tell that it took thirteen miles of gold leaf to print the gilt titles on the book backs; he liked to tell how many thousand tons the three hundred thousand sets weighed. Of course that same old natural thing happened: Webster thought it was he that sold the book. He thought that General Grant's great name helped but he regarded himself as the main reason of the book's prodigious success. This shows that Webster was merely human and merely a publisher. All publishers are Columbuses. The successful author is their America.[37]

But Webster wasn't the only one changing. Clemens was so enraptured with his windfall from the Grant book that his motivation to write evaporated. On February 12, 1886, his distraught daughter Susy wrote: "Mamma and I have both been very much troubled of late because papa, since he has been

Pictured on the porch of their Hartford home, Clemens adored his family. Left to right: Clara, Livy, Jean, Sam with cigar, Suzy, and Hash the dog. (COURTESY OF THE MARK TWAIN HOUSE & MUSEUM, HARTFORD, CT)

publishing Gen Grant's book, has seemed to forget his own books and work entirely."[38] In fact, after *Huck Finn* in 1885 there would be nothing more until *A Yankee in King Arthur's Court* in 1889. In Clemens's mind there was simply no pressing need to generate more income. As of July 1886, the firm had $248,000 in the U.S. National and Mount Morris banks and $186,000 in accounts receivable.[39]

Clemens was actually uncomfortable about all that money deposited in just two banks; after all, financial panics, including the recent one in 1884, often resulted in disastrous runs on banks. And the Federal Deposit Insurance Corporation would not be created by Congress until 1933. His concern was justified, but for another reason: In March 1887 they discovered that their bookkeeper, Frank M. Scott, had embezzled $25,000.

Clemens ordered Webster to hire a detective in order to forcefully recover some of the money, and, once the culprit was apprehended, he wanted no less than five years in a state prison for the thief. To exorcise his anger toward Webster, whom he blamed, Clemens wrote in his notebook: "When you imagined that Scott had stolen $4,000 from you, albeit you could produce no evidence of it, you handsomely called on me to make up the loss by an advance in wages—which I did; being an ass."[40] Scott was apprehended and they recovered $8,000. In 1890, showing some mercy, Clemens did not oppose Scott being allowed to go free to support his wife and three children.[41]

It was time to impose stricter controls on fast-growing Webster & Company. Feeling as though they were so awash in money that no one was paying careful attention to the accounting, Clemens demanded better and more regular reports on sales and profits and wanted all of the firm's records to be easily accessible. In addition, he was concerned that Webster had insisted on holding $100,000 of Clemens's money to capitalize the firm; Clemens, who wanted to leave only $50,000 of his own money in the firm, needed to better understand what factors drove his partner's decision making.

However, when it came to communicating these requests, rather than working directly with Webster, Clemens used his attorney, Dan Whitford, as a go-between, to essentially play the heavy and come down on Webster. Disturbed that Clemens was working through Whitford, Webster wrote: "I cannot deal with my partner in business through the intervention of an agent. . . . No business can succeed where partners deal with each other at arms length." Recognizing his folly, Clemens made plans for a face-to-face meeting in New York.[42] Regardless, their relationship would begin to disintegrate as the two differed in their views concerning the direction the firm should take and personality conflicts emerged.

QUIRKY HABITS AND BRAZEN PHILOSOPHY

Smoking Inspires Brainstorming and Problem Solving

*"To cease smoking is the easiest thing, I ought to know.
I've done it a thousand times."*

For Clemens, cigar smoking inspired his thinking; it was "the best of all inspirations," he said. Not one to waste time, he started smoking at age eight. In adulthood, he smoked anywhere from 22 to 40 cigars a day, and declared, "If smoking is not allowed in heaven, I shall not go." For him, it was akin to a religion, his fervor apparent in a letter he wrote to friend Reverend Joe Twichell, who had involuntarily kicked the habit:

> Smoke? I always smoke from 3 till 5 Sunday afternoons—and in New York the other day I smoked a week, day and night. . . . It seems a pity that you quit, for Mrs. T. didn't mind it if I remember rightly. Ah, it is turning one's back upon a kindly Providence to spurn away from us the good creature he sent to make the breath of life a luxury as well as a necessity, enjoyable as well as useful, to go and quit smoking when there ain't any sufficient excuse for it! Why, my old boy, when they use to tell me I would shorten my life ten years by smoking, they little knew the devotee they were wasting their puerile word upon—they little knew how trivial and valueless I would regard a decade that had no smoking in it! But I won't persuade you, Twichell—I won't until I see you again—but then we'll smoke for a week together.[43]

Clemens's smoking was infamous among his friends. "Clemens was a great walker," Howells wrote. "As he walked of course he talked, and of course he smoked. Whenever he had been a few days with us, the whole house had to be aired, for he smoked all over it from breakfast to bedtime. He always went to bed with a cigar in his mouth, and sometimes, mindful of my fire insurance, I went up and took it away, still burning, after he had fallen asleep. I do not know how much a man may smoke and live, but apparently he smoked as much as a man could, for he smoked incessantly."

Of course, Clemens didn't think he overindulged, declaring, "I smoke in moderation. Only one cigar at a time." There were periods in his life when he tried to quit or cut back but with disastrous results. Once, when he attempted to smoke just one cigar a day, he ended up wasting his days by obsessing on finding the largest cigar possible: "But desire persecuted me every day and all day long. I found myself hunting for larger cigars . . . within the month my cigar had grown to such proportions that I could have used it as a crutch."[44]

Whenever he attempted to stop smoking, the absence of tobacco literally brought his writing to a screeching halt, which inspired the following essay.

Smoking as Inspiration

I have not had a large experience in the matter of alcoholic drinks. I find that about two glasses of champagne are an admirable stimulant to the tongue, and is, perhaps, the happiest inspiration for an after dinner speech which can be found; but, as far as my experience goes, wine is a clog to the pen, not an inspiration. I have never seen the time when I could write to my satisfaction after drinking even one glass of wine.

(Continued)

Smoking Inspires Brainstorming and Problem Solving *(Continued)*

As regards to smoking, my testimony is of the opposite character. I am forty-six years old, and I have smoked immoderately during thirty-eight years, with the exception of a few intervals, which I will speak of presently. During the first seven years of my life I had no health—I may almost say that I lived on allopathic medicine, but since that period I have hardly known what sickness is. My health has been excellent, and remains so. As I have already said, I began to smoke immoderately when I was eight years old; that is, I began with one hundred cigars a month, and by the time I was twenty I had increased my allowance to two hundred a month. Before I was thirty, I had increased it to three hundred a month. I think I do not smoke more than that now; I am quite sure I never smoke less. Once, when I was fifteen, I ceased from smoking for three months, but I do not remember whether the effect resulting was good or evil. I repeated this experiment when I was twenty-two; again I do not remember what the result was. I repeated the experiment once more, when I was thirty-four, and ceased from smoking during a year and a half. My health did not improve, because it was not possible to improve health which was already perfect. As I never permitted myself to regret this abstinence, I experienced no sort of inconvenience from it. I wrote nothing but occasional magazine articles during pastime, and as I never wrote one except under strong impulse, I observed no lapse of facility. But by and by I sat down with a contract behind me to write a book of five or six hundred pages—the book called "Roughing It"and then I found myself most seriously obstructed. I was three weeks writing six chapters. Then I gave up the fight, resumed my three hundred cigars, burned the six chapters, and wrote the book in three months, without any bother or difficulty. I find cigar smoking to be the best of all inspirations for the pen, and, in my particular case, no sort of detriment to the health.

During eight months of the year I am at home, and that period is my holiday. In it I do nothing but very occasional miscellaneous work; therefore, three hundred cigars a month is a sufficient amount to keep my constitution on a firm basis. During the family's summer vacation, which we spend elsewhere, I work five hours every day, and five days in every week, and allow no interruption under any pretext. I allow myself the fullest possible marvel of inspiration; consequently, I ordinarily smoke fifteen cigars during my five hours' labours, and if my interest reaches the enthusiastic point, I smoke more. I smoke with all my might, and allow no intervals.[45]

chapter eight

A SHAKESPEAREAN BUSINESS TALE: HOW BLIND LOVE IN BUSINESS TURNS TO TRAGEDY

"At 50 a man can be an ass without being an optimist but not an optimist without being an ass."

In 1885 Clemens was still funding the development of the Paige typesetter and creating a company to manufacture the machine. Over the next five years he sought investors to back him, but by 1888 trouble arose because the inventor was a consummate tinkerer, resulting in delay after delay. In 1889 Clemens cut off funding, but continued to look for new investors. His publishing firm also struggled as Webster was overwhelmed by the number of projects they had taken on. It was difficult for Clemens to hide his bitterness, but he learned that using sarcasm with employees was counterproductive. By 1889 Webster became too ill to remain at the helm and was replaced by the firm's bookkeeper, Fred J. Hall. In the early 1890s, the firm was further hurt by a multivolume book project, the Library of American Literature, *which was undercapitalized and forced Clemens to borrow money for the first time.*

In the second half of the 1880s, Clemens was consumed by two business ventures: his growing involvement in the Paige typesetter and the boomingly successful Webster & Company. Over this period, his adoring public would be rewarded with but one book: *A Yankee in King Arthur's Court*, published in 1889. There would be no other major works until 1892.

Although his typesetting machine was to have been perfected as long ago as 1881, the nitpicking Paige continued to tinker and, finally, in April 1885, once again declared it finished. Clemens crowed to Webster, "It is in perfect working order (the machine is) & stands ready & willing to submit itself to any test an expert chooses to apply." He immediately started counting his chickens. He estimated that the machines, which would include eight different size models, would sell for about $5,000 each. He wrote Webster that he intended to induce 100 newspapers in various cities to lease a machine, and then do the same in England: "Three years from now I calculate to have about 1000 of those machines hired out in this country at $2,500,000." He still believed it was "a greater machine than you imagine." He calculated that the capital for the new company should be doubled to $2 million, with him and his partner Hamersley, the Hartford lawyer, taking $250,000 each in stock. Clemens's job was to sell the remainder of the stock to investors.[1] There remained one obstacle: the machine had to stand up to rigorous testing.

Confident it would pass any test, he told Webster to invite their potential customers and investors to visit Paige's shop, located in Pratt & Whitney's Hartford factory complex, and "sleep with the machine & watch it day & night as long as they please, at my expense."[2] Webster did organize a group visit, but then, under more extensive testing, the machine failed. And Paige went back to tinkering to repair the flaws.

Undaunted, the next year Clemens signed a contract with Paige to pay the inventor an annual salary of $7,000 until the profits of the machine yielded at least that amount. Even though his friend Franklin G. Whitmore, a billiards partner and business adviser who was keeping tabs on Paige, warned him that it was not prudent to keep throwing money at Paige, that it could lead to his bankruptcy, Clemens continued to assume the responsibility for raising the capital to manufacture the machine. In his notebook during this period, he made pages of detailed calculations, such as the cost of the typesetter per thousand letters set to justify the machine's price, how many typesetters various cities should require based on their population, and his strategy for raising capital. Delays in bringing the machine to market continued to frustrate him, prompting him to also note, "profanity given up—on account of fatigue."[3]

When It Came to the Typesetter, Perhaps Patience Was Not the Best Policy

Toward the end of 1887, the project's monthly expenses had ballooned to $3,000—this on top of the $50,000 in capital Clemens had already contributed. No doubt the venture capitalist was becoming ever more incensed with the inventor because Paige had originally promised that only $20,000 investment was needed to refine the typesetter.[4] The machine was not only draining his wallet, but his energy to write. In December 1887, he wrote to his sister:

> Dear Pamela,—will you take this $15 and buy some candy or some other trifle for yourself and Sam and his wife to remember that we remember you, by?
> If we weren't a little crowded this year by the typesetter, I'd send a check large enough to buy a family Bible or some other useful thing like that. However we go on and on, but the type-setter goes on forever—at $3,000 a month; which is much more satisfactory than was the case the first seventeen months, when the bill only averaged $2,000, and promised to take a thousand years. We'll be through, now, in 3 or 4 months, I reckon, and then the strain will let up and we can breathe freely once more, whether success ensues or failure.[5]

In October 1888, Clemens wrote to his brother Orion that the machine should be done within a couple of months. The situation was definitely beginning to smack of throwing lots of good money after bad. Finally, in November 1888, Clemens attempted to cut his ties with Paige by issuing a warning to the inventor: "Since the spring of '86, the thing has gone straight downhill toward sure destruction. It must be brought to an end Feb. 1 at all hazards. This is final." Unfortunately, the warning spurred Paige onward and he had the machine working that December. His faith restored, Clemens had Paige print the following message to Livy: "The machine is finished, and this is the first work done on it."[6] Well, not quite.

While the machine did not booze it up like human typesetters were prone to do, as Clemens once remarked glibly, it was certainly temperamental, and through 1889 Paige had to continue to make refinements; meanwhile, somehow, the hypnotic inventor managed to placate Clemens, who was now demanding daily reports. In November 1889, Clemens invited Albany businessman and friend Dean Sage to Hartford to view the typesetter. Clemens had offered to sell him a 1/45th interest, but Sage was very skeptical. In particular, he was astounded that Clemens was talking about capitalizing the company at $2 million—before any machines were actually sold and proving themselves. "You have either got a great bonanza or nothing," he wrote Clemens, "and until you have a good number of the machines actually turning out successfully the work they are expected to do this is a question. . . . To tell the truth I feel anxious about you—as I understand it, you are the man who will have to furnish the capital, so large amount that a failure in the business might sweep away all you have, or very seriously embarrass you."[7]

The promises of riches had something to do with the author's insane patience and rose-colored view. But the story was beginning to take on an absurdly comic nature that could only end like a Shakespearean tragedy. Meanwhile, Paige had no financial risk—a mistake, the same mistake Clemens was making with his nephew Webster, who reaped only benefits at the publishing firm but shared none of the risk.

Webster & Co. Fails to Adapt to a Changing Marketplace

While Clemens had Herculean patience with Paige, it was anything but with Webster; he took a more acrimonious attitude toward him as the publishing business became more complicated and they endured a series of misfortunate events. To begin with, they and their firm were simply too popular. With the success of Grant, other authors approached Clemens and Webster in droves and they were inundated with unwanted projects. For those books they didn't want Clemens wisely insisted they decline them promptly and courteously. An easy, inoffensive excuse he suggested to Webster was to say that "our already overcrowded decks" make it impossible.[8]

Webster & Company did take on memoirs by Civil War Generals William T. Sherman, P. H. Sheridan, and George McClellan. Three other projects they were banking on were a biography of Pope Leo XIII, which Clemens predicted would sell 100,000 copies; Henry Ward Beecher's autobiography; and Beecher's recounting of the life of Christ. Unfortunately and rather inconveniently for Clemens, Beecher died on March 8, 1887, so he wasn't around to promote his *Life of Christ*, and what was going to be an autobiography became a lame duck biography completed by his family. Sales of both were flat. And apparently the Pope was also not a bestseller in the Gilded Age as sales of the biography were anemic. In 1888 another book Clemens had pinned high hopes on was the memoirs of General William T. Sherman, but it, too, proved unprofitable, so much so that Clemens demanded that terms with the general be renegotiated. "Demand a reconstruction of contract placing power in my hands where it belongs," he jotted in his notebook. "Refused? Go into court. Second: Demand dissolution. Go into court."[9] Clemens loved his lawyers—for now.

The firm truly appeared cursed when it was struck yet another blow: Webster fell ill and soon would be unable to manage the business on a daily basis. Realizing that his manager was under duress, in February 1887 Clemens advised Webster to take some rest from work. Two months later the sympathetic author also faulted himself for not taking some of the burden off his lieutenant's shoulders: "Everything is on the pleasantest possible basis, now, and is going to stay so. I blame myself for not looking in on you oftener in the past—that would have prevented all trouble. I mean to stand by my duty better, now."[10]

Despite the ease in responsibilities, that summer Webster was visibly suffering from neuralgia. The company's finances mirrored his failing health. In August 1887, Clemens, who had been expecting to clear $100,000, wrote Webster: "I have to confess that to me our outlook is disturbing. I suppose the Pope's book and the McClellan book together will not more than pay expenses of the last year and a half—you will correct me if I am wrong."[11]

In addition to the firm's bad luck, there were market forces at work that they failed to adapt to. In the 1880s America was rapidly becoming more urbanized as people gravitated to the cities in search of work. Bookstores were gaining traction and the subscription method for selling books was on the decline. Even as the subscription market was weakening, in the fall of 1887 Webster & Company had at least eight books planned. To issue so many books in one sales campaign flew in the face of what Clemens had advised Bliss 10 years earlier: to publish no more than one or two books a year when relying on subscription sales. In an 1876 letter to Bliss, he had explained, "I think we publish books so fast that canvassers are likely to merely skim the cream of a district and then 'lay' for the next book. This is only human nature, and they are not to be blamed for it."[12] Now he and Webster were falling victim to their human nature.

Clemens Learns That Explosive Growth Requires Very Disciplined Management

In September 1887, Clemens's patience with Webster cracked. In a letter to Orion he unleashed the first of many blistering criticisms:

I woke up 6 weeks ago, to find that there was no more system in the office than there is in a nursery without a nurse. But I have spent a good deal of time there since, and reduced everything to exact order and system—insomuch that even Webster can run it now—and in most particulars he is a mere jackass. I could never interfere before; the former contract was so ingeniously contrived that for two years I have had no more say in the concern than the errand-boy; and to ask a question was to invoke contemptuous silence, and to make a suggestion was to have it coolly ignored. During two years I couldn't get the shadow of a statement as to the condition of the business. If Webster wanted the contract changed (for his advantage) he demanded the change—never asked for it; and I had to comply; but he made one grab too many, last April, and turned the tables on himself. He knew I had been spending $5,000 a month here for a year on a project of mine, and that this was to continue for another year; so he got frightened and demanded and required that I put up a permanent cash capital of $75,000 for the publishing-house to save it from destruction in case I ruined myself. (Formerly I had to furnish limitless capital and be responsible for everything.) It was offering me my emancipation-papers, and I did not lose any time in signing the document.

Up to that time he had been all insolence; but he is the gentlest spirit in this region since—perfectly tame and civil. And stands criticism like a pupil; stands being reminded of the numerous ways in which he has betrayed the fact that he is not the miracle of a publisher he supposed he was, but a blundering, ignorant apprentice.[13]

With a razor-sharp tongue and indulgent pleasure, the humorist proceeded to shred the man's dignity. "Webster had immense pride but he was short of other talents," he wrote scathingly in his autobiography.[14] Incidentally, Webster was hardly the first to fall victim to Clemens's pen. Anyone who fell from his grace suffered vicious, sarcastic attacks, the victims including, in part, Elisha Bliss, fellow author (and former friend) Bret Harte, sundry newspaper and magazine editors such as Whitelaw Reid, and even potential suitors such as the publishing house Houghton, Mifflin, which Clemens referred to as Houghton Syphillis & Co.

In dealing with Webster, Clemens certainly learned how to (or how not to) manage people, the bitter experience resulting in an unjustifiably long and damning diatribe in his autobiography:

It was a mistake to deal in sarcasms with Webster. They cut deep into his vanity. He hadn't a single intellectual weapon in his armory and could not fight back. It was unchivalrous in me to attack with mental weapons this mentally weaponless man and I tried to refrain from it but couldn't. I ought to have been large enough to endure his vanities but I wasn't. I am not always large enough to endure my own. He had one defect which particularly exasperated me, because I didn't have it myself. When a matter was mentioned of which he was ignorant, he not only would not protect himself by remarking that he was not acquainted with the matter, but he had not even discretion enough to keep his tongue still. He would say something intended to deceive the hearers into the notion that he knew something about that subject himself—a most unlikely condition, since his ignorance covered the whole earth like a blanket and there was hardly a hole in it anywhere. Once in a drawing-room company some talk sprang up about George Eliot and her literature, I saw Webster getting ready to contribute. There was

no way to hit him with a brick or a Bible or something and reduce him to unconsciousness and save him, because it would
have attracted attention. . . .[15]

In his autobiography, Clemens actually stated that he felt it
was his duty to damn Webster.[16]

In spite of the gloomy outlook, over six months ending
September 1, 1887, the company cleared about $20,000 after
all expenses had been paid.[17] On the heels of the nine books
published in 1887, just six more were planned for 1888. Nevertheless, Webster, who had been largely absent since September, was finished. On February 16, 1888, Clemens took out
his notebook and jotted down: "On the 13th we at last got
Webster to retire from business, from all authority, and from
the city, till April 1, 1889, and try to get back his health. How
long he has been a lunatic I do not know; but several facts
suggest that it began in the summer or very early in the fall of
'85—while the 1st vol of the Grant Memoirs was in preparation and the vast canvass."[18] Webster's understudy, Fred J. Hall,
who had been serving as the firm's bookkeeper, bought Webster's share of the firm for a measly $12,000 and now took the
hot seat as manager.

As the company's cash on hand fell to $2,000 or less at some
points over the ensuing months, Clemens quickly came to
blame Webster for all their troubles.[19] Webster fired back, writing to the author's confidant Daniel Whitford that "Mr.
Clemens now complains of a clause (placing all business in my
hands) which has appeared in every contract he ever made
with me. . . . I only hope that when Fred is engaged in some
great, or even fairly profitable, enterprise, I do hope Mr.
Clemens won't want him to drop it or neglect it to revive that
'patent baby clamp' business, to prevent lively infants from
kicking off the bed clothes and catching cold."[20] Apparently,
Webster was as equally adept at using sarcasm as his uncle-in-
law. He also railed about how he had sold out for far less than

he thought his share worth. Both sides were rapidly becoming bitter.

In July 1889, Clemens wrote to his sister Pamela, "My feeling against Webster—who is not a man but a hog—is so bitter that I could not even endure the idea of addressing a letter" to his niece Annie, knowing Webster might see it.[21] The Clemens family also accused Webster of taking a servant to Washington, D.C., for a little vacation treat and giving her $500 as a Christmas gift. Whether there was infidelity or not didn't matter—it just didn't look good.[22] Partly due to the relentless pounding he took from Clemens, Webster died on April 22, 1891, at the age of 39. Cause of death was listed as inflammation of the bowels—a fitting end, no doubt, as far as Clemens was concerned.

Unwilling to Listen to Nay-Sayers, Clemens Continues to Gamble on the Typesetter

Intertwined with the struggles of Webster & Company was the great white elephant, otherwise known as the Paige typesetter. After eight years, this sordid love affair appeared to know no boundaries as the still enthusiastic Clemens wrote in a January 1889 letter to Orion:

> At 12:20 this afternoon a line of movable types was spaced and justified by machinery, for the first time in the history of the world! And I was there to see. It was done automatically—instantly—perfectly. This is indeed the first line of movable types that ever was perfectly spaced and perfectly justified on this earth. . . .
>
> All the witnesses made written record of the immense historical birth—the first justification of a line of movable type by machinery—and also set down the hour and the minute. Nobody had drank anything, and yet everybody seemed drunk. Well-dizzy, stupefied, stunned.[23]

While it truly appeared Clemens was about to realize his dream of riches, there were yet again further delays thanks to Paige's incessant tinkering. So, seven months after writing his brother, Clemens was writing a similarly buoyant note to his friend Howells: "After patiently & contentedly spending more than $3,000 a month for 44 consecutive months, I've got it at last, & it's a daisy! . . . Come & see this sublime magician of iron & steel work his enchantments. . . . Come!"[24] In *The Gilded Age*, Clemens had written, "If you get into anybody far enough you've got yourself a partner." This appeared to be the case now as he was out over $132,000 in operating expenses over a 44-month period alone.

A month after his letter to Howells, in November 1889, Clemens, now determined to take sole control of Paige's patents, signed an agreement with the inventor in which he offered Paige $160,000 up front, plus $25,000 a year for the life of the patents. There was just one catch: Clemens was going to have to raise the cash to fund this buyout, which he was convinced he could do.[25] Once in control of the patents, he could then find a reliable manufacturer to bring the amazing typesetter to life.

That fall he assigned old friend Joe Goodman the task of raising $100,000, paying him a 10 percent commission. In particular, he wanted Goodman to target their mutual friend, the wealthy Senator Jones. Like Jones, he had met Goodman out west when Goodman was the editor of the Virginia City *Territorial Enterprise*, for which Clemens had gone to work in 1862. Meanwhile, Clemens was able to convince potential customers such as the New York *Sun, Herald, Times*, and *World*; Harper Brothers; and the Boston *Globe*, to wait for a demonstration before committing to the leading competitor, the Mergenthaler typesetter, which was being developed in a Brooklyn shop.

Clemens's exhortations became more urgent as time and

money were finally running out. In March 1890, he wrote to Goodman:

> I have talked with the madam, and here is the result. I will go down to the factory and notify Paige that I will scrape together $6,000 to meet the March and April expenses, and will retire on the 30th of April and return the assignment to him if in the meantime I have not found financial relief. . . .

> There's an improved Mergenthaler in New York; Paige and Davis and I watched it two whole afternoons.

In spite of the improved Mergenthaler, three months later he extolled the Paige typesetter in another letter to Goodman: "This machine is totally without a rival. Rivalry with it is impossible. . . . It makes me cheerful to sit by the machine: come up with Mrs. Goodman and refresh yourself with a draught of the same."[26]

The Mergenthaler typesetter was indeed a slower and simpler machine, but it was also less expensive and more reliable. To avoid any debilitating competition and to insure financial success for both, the Mergenthaler people offered to trade stock for stock with the Paige company. Still convinced he was backing the ultimate winner, Clemens declined their offer. It would cost him millions, according to his official biographer, Albert Bigelow Paine. In fact, contrary to raising anything close to $100,000, in July 1890 Goodman reported that he was "going round hat in hand and begging pennies!"[27] The less than warm reception should have raised yet another red flag that financial backing for the Paige machine was slipping away—but not for Clemens, who was determined to prove everyone wrong.

The year of 1890 was challenging on multiple levels: Charles L. Webster & Company was returning little profit; Clemens's mother had died in Keokuk at the end of October; his mother-in-law died in Elmira a month later; and between the high living and funding the Paige typesetter, Clemens was financially strapped. To reimburse Paige for expenses in March 1890, he was forced to borrow money from his partner William Hamersley, who told him that this was the last of the money he would front for the venture. It was also made as a personal loan to Clemens that had to be paid back by July 1. He would miss the deadline.[28]

Then it appeared Clemens's luck had finally changed when it looked like Goodman hit pay dirt: Senator Jones expressed real interest in investing. Subsequently, Jones backed out, explaining in a February 11, 1891, letter that on investigation he discovered that Paige had no credibility. Outraged, Clemens declared that Jones was "a penny-worshipping humbug and shuffler."[29] However, four days earlier, a torn Clemens had jotted in his notebook, "Wrote a note to Paige saying I now hold myself as released from any further effort or expense in behalf of the machine."[30] And he lashed out at the inventor, scribbling, "Paige the Microbe." He never did pay the inventor another penny. Still the machine would continue to own him, as he would frantically look for a way both to cut his staggering losses and to lure in new investors.

Clemens Becomes the Target of a Lawsuit and Accusations Fly

As the Paige typesetter project crumbled around his feet, Clemens also struggled to hold together his publishing house. Even though Webster had been replaced by Hall, internal strife—including personnel conflicts and lawsuits—continued to roil the company.

Hall immediately came into conflict with the firm's bookkeeper, A. H. Wright, who had been hired after Scott's swindle. Apparently, Wright had a very disagreeable personality, so Hall decided to discharge him. Wright subsequently appealed to Clemens, who gave him a hearing. After mulling over the situation, Clemens concluded that Wright could be of value and thought it proper to let Hall know, but was not going to force the man upon him: "If he is personally disagreeable to you, that is another matter. I told him a man can't have a subordinate around him who is personally disagreeable and unconquerably so. He thought he could make himself agreeable to you. I told him I could not make a request of you in his favor—I could only undertake to acquiesce in what you should decide; he must plead his cause himself. I could not do it for him or interfere in the matter."[31] Hall elected to terminate Wright as their bookkeeper, but then hired him as a salesman, a position in which he would prove successful.

In January 1889, Clemens was pleased with the direction of his publishing company: "The substitution of brains for guesswork was accomplished when you took Webster's place last February," he wrote to Hall. Clemens approved of Hall's plans, which included, for example, hiring a corps of women to sell a cookbook that Charles Webster had agreed to publish before his departure. While the cookbook was a success, there were other Webster legacies that required cleaning up. The next year found the firm in court: J. J. Little and Company, a printer, was suing them for breech of contract.

Webster & Company had contracted with J. J. Little and Company to print Grant's memoirs exclusively, but halfway through they were running so far behind on orders that Webster hired other printers. Little filed suit for breech of contract and won—and it cost Clemens's firm $2,900 plus lawyers fees. More internal strife, accusations, and counter-accusations concerning this case ensued. Why? Because before Webster had quit the business, Little offered a compromise settlement of $800, but Webster refused it. So, when Clemens blamed his lawyer, Whitford, for losing the case, Whitford, in turn, blamed Webster for not settling. In a spiteful December 27, 1890, letter to Hall, Clemens ranted:

> I don't believe Whitford. Webster was too big a coward to bring a suit when advised against it. The real mistake was in trusting law

business to an ignorant, blethering gas-pipe like Whitford. I am not saying this in hatred, for I do not dislike Whitford. He is simply a damned fool—in Court—& will infallibly lose every suit you put into his hands. If you are going to have any lawsuits with Gill, I beg that you will either compromise or have some other law conduct the thing.

I am mighty sorry for you, but this result was to be expected. If I were you I would ask Whitford to present a modified bill—or better still, present it to the parties he won the case for.

Merry Xmas to you!—& I wish to God I could have one myself before I die.[32]

Ultimately, lawyers left a very bad taste in Clemens's mouth, even though he had always been quick to hire their services. In a speech he admitted, "I believe you keep a lawyer. I have always kept a lawyer, too, though I have never made anything out of him. It is a service to an author to have a lawyer. There is something so disagreeable in having a personal contact with a publisher. So it is better to work through a lawyer—and lose your case." And one of his quotables cut to the bone: "Lawyers are like other people—fools on the average; but it is easier for an ass to succeed in that trade than any other."[33]

A Successful Project That Is Undercapitalized Could Kill the Company

While Clemens had always been the one doling out money, now it was he who took his first loan. With 13 books planned for 1891 and a spike of 32 planned for 1892, Webster & Company was committed to publishing more books and making more advances to said authors than it could handle financially, so the company was forced to establish a line of credit of $30,000 from the Mount Morris Bank. To keep the firm solvent, Hall would have to dip into their credit line from time to time in the coming years. In addition, in late 1890, to further capitalize the firm Livy loaned it $10,000 at 6 percent; and income from Clemens's books was poured back into the company.[34] But all of this money just seemed to disappear.

The culprit behind the financial drain was not the advances due authors, but a very ambitious project Clemens had agreed to take on: the *Library of American Literature* (L.A.L.), a multivolume extravaganza, a collection of America's best literature, from the earliest settlement to the present time. It would number 10 volumes and contain over 1,700 selections by over 500 authors. It was the brainchild of Edmund Clarence Stedman, a notable New York literary critic, who originally sold it to publisher W. E. Dibble, who, in turn, sold the plates for it to Webster for $8,000. "I think well of the Stedman book," a hesitant Clemens wrote Webster in 1887, "but I can't somehow bring myself to think *very* well of it."[35] Nevertheless, Webster bought it and started issuing it in early 1888. Despite Clemens's misgivings, the L.A.L. sold well—that was the problem.

The books had to be produced and distributed before money could be collected from customers, so right off the bat cash flow was an issue. Further hampering cash flow, customers could pay on an installment plan while contracts with printers and sales agents had to be honored immediately. Hall quickly realized that the firm was woefully undercapitalized and could not fund the venture even though the long-term revenue would make it quite profitable. Consider that in 1889 the cash flow for the *Library* was a negative $22,000.[36] It was snowballing into a financial avalanche that could not be stopped because, as perverse as the logic was, the project was a success, with orders selling briskly.

Further compounding the brewing troubles, Clemens became an absentee owner in June 1891, when he took his family to Europe, where he calculated he could live much more cheaply. It was a critical time when Webster & Company needed him, but he had another major consideration weighing on his mind: Livy's health was suffering and he hoped to find doctors who could nurse her strength back. Even as he grappled with these personal troubles, in an April 1891 letter to Hall he shows great sensitivity and loyalty to his coachman:

> Dear Mr. Hall,—Privately—keep it to yourself—as you are already aware, we are going to Europe in June, for an indefinite stay. We shall sell the horses and shut up the house. We wish to provide a place for our coachman, who has been with us 21 years, and is sober, active, diligent, and unusually bright and capable. You spoke of hiring a colored man as engineer and helper in the packing room. Patrick would soon learn that trade and be very valuable. We will cease to need him by the middle or end of June. Have you made irrevocable arrangements with the colored man, or would you prefer to have Patrick, if he thinks he would like to try?
>
> I have not said anything to him about it yet.[37]

On June 6, 1891, the Clemenses left for Europe. The mansion in Hartford was closed up and they would never live there again.

While residing in Berlin for the winter, Clemens received clean, succinct business reports from Hall that elicited encouraging responses. On September 15, 1891, Clemens wrote to Hall to say that he was pleased with the state of business. And two months later, while in Geneva, Switzerland, he wrote to Hall:

> Keep it up. Don't let it fall into desuetude.
>
> Everything looks so fine and handsome with the business, now, that I feel a great let-up from depression. The rewards of your long and patient industry are on their way, and their arrival safe in port, presently, seems assured.
>
> By George, I shall be glad when the ship comes in![38]

Meanwhile, contrary to Clemens positive assessment, Webster & Company had dipped into the Mount Morris Bank three times and now owed the bank $25,000. Although always averse to owing money, there was little Clemens could do to repay the bank in the short term. He himself had capital in the company of over $74,000; in addition, all of his royalties for 1891, almost $10,000, and his share of the profits for the year, over $11,000, went back into the company. Even so, Hall now estimated that a $100,000 cash infusion was needed to stay afloat.[39]

Clemens seemed to be in self-denial concerning their precarious money predicament, but not Livy, who was financially savvy from growing up in a capitalist's house. Her thoughts were focused on their family's financial well-being and the desperate need to protect their money. In a letter to Hall, she stated that she was "anxious" that her husband take $16,000 due him from writing projects and "invest it elsewhere because it surely is very bad to have all ones eggs in one basket so I think it will be well for him now to make small investments when he can outside of Webster & Co." Following his wife's lead, Clemens used Noah Wetmore Halsey, of N.W. Harris & Co., at 15 Wall Street, to make some investments, and then instructed Hall to put the securities into a safety deposit vault and "keep a list of them for reference."[40]

By December 1892 the picture was so grim as the L.A.L. project continued to siphon away money that Clemens was fishing for investors to inject cash into Webster & Company. On December 26 Clemens wrote to Hall: "Suppose that you get acquainted with *Carnegie* and ask him to lend us money enough at 6 or 8 per cent to run the *L.A.L.* up to 1,000 sets per month. . . . If he won't, then ask him to put his financial head on the problem and tell us how and where to raise the money." If they could achieve economies of scale then they would cut their short-term losses on the book. Unfamiliar with high finance and uncomfortable with approaching such a tycoon as Carnegie, Hall resisted.

On December 28 Clemens again pushed Hall to look for investors. This time his scheme was to find someone to buy a fourth interest in the L.A.L. project for $200,000, and again he suggested Carnegie. Another option was to sell a fourth interest for $250,000 and create an independent stock company. Growing desperate for any relief, less than a week later Clemens lowered his sights to an investor with $100,000, and exclaimed to Hall: "You have done magnificently with the business, and we *must* raise the money somehow, to enable you to reap the reward of all that labor."[41]

No one wanted to invest in a company already in hock to the bank. Not until it appeared to be too late did Clemens, who was vacationing in Switzerland, realize just how deep in the proverbial hole his publishing firm was. In his autobiography, he reflected:

> At last I found that additions had been made to the borrowings, without my knowledge or consent. I began to feel troubled. I wrote Mr. Hall about it and said I would like to have an exhaustive report of the condition of the business. The next mail brought that exhaustive report, whereby it appeared that the concern's assets exceeded its liabilities by ninety-two thousand dollars. Then I felt better. But there was no occasion to feel better, for the report ought to have read the other way. Poor Hall soon wrote to say that we needed more money and must have it right away or the concern would fail.[42]

If he had to declare bankruptcy, he understood that it would forever tarnish his literary reputation. Equally torturous to him, bankruptcy would be a repeat of his father's complete and utter failure, the antithesis of what Clemens had dreamed for himself. For Clemens, life had always been a merciless, manic, emotional roller coaster, his days alternately filled with genuine euphoria, delusional delights, gloom, and foreboding visions of the future. In the 1890s, all of these emotions would be amplified as he fought to save his business and his reputation.

QUIRKY HABITS AND BRAZEN PHILOSOPHY

Image Is Everything,
But Interviews Are Twaddle

"Many a small thing has been made large
by the right kind of advertising."

From the day in Nevada Territory that he instructed Orion to find a posh office, Clemens was acutely aware of public image. Office, dress, behavior, language—all of it was consequential. As an author, early in his career, he enjoyed attacking the tycoons of his age, using their sordid public image as a weapon. He was particularly disgusted with Cornelius Vanderbilt, who made millions operating a line of steamships and railroads. In 1869 Clemens wrote the robber baron an open and rather brazen letter (excerpted here) that was published in the newspapers. While the tone is playful, Clemens hits upon some serious issues: glorifying money, public image, wealth and responsibility, and simply setting a good example—words of wisdom for today's gluttonous executives.

How my heart goes out in sympathy to you! How I do pity you, Commodore Vanderbilt! Most men have at least a few friends, whose devotion is a comfort and a solace to them, but you seem to be the idol of only a crawling swarm of small souls, who love to glorify your most flagrant unworthinesses in print; or praise your vast possessions worshippingly; or sing of your unimportant private habits and sayings and doings, as if your millions gave them dignity; friends who applaud your superhuman stinginess with the same gusto that they do your most magnificent displays of commercial genius and daring, and likewise your most lawless violations of commercial honor—for these infatuated worshippers of dollars not their own seem to make no distinctions, but swing their hats and shout hallelujah every time you do anything, no matter what it is. I do pity you. I would pity any man with such friends as these. I should think you would hate the sight of a newspaper. I should think you would not dare to glance at one, for fear you would find in it one of these distressing eulogies of something you had been doing, which was either infinitely trivial or else a matter you ought to be ashamed of. . . .

All I wish to urge upon you now is, that you crush out your native instincts and go and do something worthy of praise—go and do something you need not blush to see in print—do something that may rouse one solitary good impulse in the breasts of your horde of worshippers; prove one solitary good example to the thousands of young men who emulate your energy and your industry; shine as one solitary grain of pure gold upon the heaped rubbish of your life. . . .

And in parting, I say that, surely, standing as you do upon the pinnacle of moneyed magnificence in America you must certainly feel a vague desire in you sometimes to do some splendid deed in the interest of commercial probity, or of human charity, or of manly honor and dignity, that shall flash into instant celebrity over the whole nation, and be rehearsed to ambitious boys by their mothers a century after you are dead.[43]

As for his own image, Clemens always had to work at it because, at heart, he was a crude fellow who relished telling dirty jokes. In the Victorian Age, a refined author simply didn't even use words like *hell* or *damn* in a vain manner—words he used with impunity—so Livy and Howells were forever editing any offending language from his manuscripts. Well aware that he must present a much different public image than what was true of his own character, in his autobiography he wrote:

(Continued)

Image Is Everything, But Interviews Are Twaddle (*Continued*)

I said I had been revealing to her my private sentiments, not my public ones; that I, like all the other human beings, expose to the world only my trimmed and perfumed and carefully barbered public opinions and conceal carefully, cautiously, wisely, my private ones.

I explained that what I meant by that phrase "public opinions" was published opinions, opinions spread broadcast in print. I said I was in the common habit, in private conversation with friends, of revealing every private opinion I possessed relating to religion, politics and men, but that I should never dream of printing one of them, because they are individually and collectively at war with almost everybody's public opinion while at the same time they are in happy agreement with almost everybody's private opinion.[44]

In cultivating his image, Clemens was very sensitive about interviews, which he rarely found satisfactory. Such was the case when Edward W. Bok interviewed Clemens and then sent the author a copy of his article for review before it went to press. It was a mistake. Instead of returning the article with any corrections, Clemens sent a letter, critiquing interviews in general:

My Dear Mr. Bok,—

No, no. It is like most interviews, pure twaddle and valueless.

For several quite plain and simple reasons, an "interview" must, as a rule, be an absurdity, and chiefly for this reason—It is an attempt to use a boat on land or a wagon on water, to speak figuratively. Spoken speech is one thing, written speech is quite another. Print is the proper vehicle for the latter, but it isn't for the former. The moment "talk" is put into print you recognize that it is not what it was when you heard it;

you perceive that an immense something has disappeared from it. That is its soul. You have nothing but a dead carcass left on your hands. Color, play of feature, the varying modulations of the voice, the laugh, the smile, the informing inflections, everything that gave that body warmth, grace, friendliness and charm and commended it to your affections—or, at least, to your tolerance—is gone and nothing is left but a pallid, stiff and repulsive cadaver.

Such is "talk" almost invariably, as you see it lying in state in an "interview." The interviewer seldom tries to tell one how a thing was said; he merely puts in the naked remark and stops there. When one writes for print his methods are very different. He follows forms which have but little resemblance to conversation, but they make the reader understand what the writer is trying to convey. . . .

Now, in your interview, you have certainly been most accurate; you have set down the sentences I uttered as I said them. But you have not a word of explanation; what my manner was at several points is not indicated. Therefore, no reader can possibly know where I was in earnest and where I was joking; or whether I was joking altogether or in earnest altogether. Such a report of a conversation has no value. It can convey many meanings to the reader, but never the right one. To add interpretations which would convey the right meaning is a something which would require—what? An art so high and fine and difficult that no possessor of it would ever be allowed to waste it on interviews.

No; spare the reader, and spare me; leave the whole interview out; it is rubbish. I wouldn't talk in my sleep if I couldn't talk better than that.

If you wish to print anything print this letter; it may have some value, for it may explain to a reader here and there why it is that in interviews, as a rule, men seem to talk like anybody but themselves.

Very sincerely yours,
Mark Twain[45]

ENDURING FINANCIAL CRISIS AND ADVERSITY: A ROCKEFELLER CRONY COMES TO THE RESCUE

"A banker is a fellow who lends you his umbrella when the sun is shining and wants it back the minute it begins to rain."

One of the worst financial panics in history hit the United States in 1893 and resulted in a prolonged depression, which hurt Clemens's publishing firm and his personal portfolio. The Library of American Literature remained undercapitalized, which resulted in a net loss even though it was enjoying successful sales. To fund the project, Clemens sought investors, such as Andrew Carnegie. He also had to create and personally fund an emergency bank account to cover daily expenses at Webster & Company. In 1893 and 1894, Clemens considered selling the firm in an attempt to cut further losses. At the same time, he had to manage his firm's debt so that creditors could not go after his highly valued books.

The worst financial panic in U.S. history up to that time hit the country in 1893 and precipitated what was then called the Great Depression, which would last into 1896. This national disaster began on May 5, 1893, when the stock market tumbled and an initial panic swept the country. Less than two months later, on June 27, a far more precipitous stock market crash hit

Wall Street. There was a run on gold, draining the reserves. The Philadelphia & Reading Railroad went bankrupt, followed by the Northern Pacific Railway, the Union Pacific Railroad, and the Atchison, Topeka & Santa Fe Railroad. A series of bank failures followed, which triggered the bankruptcy of numerous other companies. A total of over 15,000 companies and 500 banks failed and unemployment reached about 18 percent.[1] The financial condition of Webster & Company quickly hit a critical point and Clemens was faced with a bankruptcy that could destroy him personally. But a man depicted as a Standard Oil fiend and nicknamed "Hell Hound" would come to his rescue.

In the months leading up to the great crash, an increasingly astute Clemens finally became acutely alarmed by both his personal financial situation and that of Webster & Company, which were, to put it mildly, hemorrhaging. He continued to believe that if they could sell off the *Library of American Literature* all would be saved, so he pressed Hall on the matter. Clemens also hoped that Hall could facilitate the sale prior to firing their sales agents—whose commissions were devouring any money on hand—because he wisely considered the agents "a valuable part of the property." In a postscript to a letter, Clemens wrote, "I feel panicky."[2] Hard words for a proud man to utter.

The financial difficulties now caused friction between Clemens and Livy, who were living in a Florence, Italy, villa at the time. "Mrs. Clemens is deeply distressed, for she thinks I have been blaming you or finding fault with you about something," he wrote to Hall in January 1893. "But most surely that cannot be. I tell her that although I am prone to write hasty and regrettable things to other people, I am not a bit likely to write such things to you. I can't believe I have done anything so ungrateful. If I have, pile coals of fire on my head, for I deserve it! . . . You have done magnificently with the business, and we must raise the money somehow, to enable you to reap the reward of all that labor."[3] If the L.A.L. could not be sold, Clemens stated, he once again proposed that they raise $100,000 to capitalize the project.

Clemens Searches for an Angel Investor, But Must Face the Grim Reality of Finding No One

Just hanging on in late January 1893, Clemens had to renew loans from the Mount Morris bank, but the new line of credit did not cover expenses. Cash flow was also being strangled because there was more than $62,000 in uncollected L.A.L. installments. Increasingly desperate for funding, a potentially delusional Clemens still dreamed of luring steel tycoon Andrew Carnegie into investing. Convinced that the Scotsman, who stood at 5 foot 3 inches and had a severe Napolean complex, could be his white knight, he wrote yet another letter pushing Hall to contact Carnegie:

> I want to throw out a suggestion and see what you think of it. We have a good start, and solid ground under us; we have a valuable reputation; our business organization is practical, sound and well-devised; our publications are of a respect-worthy character and of a money-breeding species. Now then I think that the association with us of some one of great name and with capital would give our business a prodigious impetus—that phrase is not too strong.
>
> As I look at it, it is not money merely that is needed; if that were all, the firm has friends enough who would take an interest in a paying venture; we need some one who has made his life a success not only from a business standpoint, but with that achievement back of him, has been great enough to make his power felt as a thinker and a literary man. It is a pretty usual thing for publishers to have this sort of partners. Now you see what a power Carnegie is, and how far his voice reaches in the several lines I speak of. Do you know him? You do by correspondence or purely business talks about his books—but personally, I mean? so that it would not be an intrusion for you to speak to him about this desire of mine—for I would like you to put it before him, and if you fail to interest him in it, you will probably get at least some valuable suggestions from him. I'll enclose a note of introduction—you needn't use it if you don't need to. . . . Do your best with Carnegie.[4]

Becoming manic, in a second letter written on January 28, Clemens again offered to send Hall a letter of introduction, which he did a week later. He also suggested a Plan B, which was for himself to put $20,000 toward the L.A.L. project; a rich banker friend named Matthias Arnot to put in $45,000; other Webster & Company people, including Hall, to put in $35,000; and then go to Carnegie for a mere $100,000.[5] Clemens was clearly very desperate, yet he remained in Europe for now, rather than returning to Hartford to provide forceful leadership.

Clemens Proposes a Series of Plans for Exiting the Publishing Business

By the end of February 1893, while in Florence, Clemens finally realized he had to return to the United States to deal with his bleak business affairs, so in late March 1893 he left his family and sailed for New York. An immediate task involved setting up an emergency bank account to cover daily expenses because the firm's ready cash was nearly tapped out. Ideally, Hall wanted $30,000 in it, but that amount would not be enough.[6] To raise some funds quickly, Clemens had to ask sister-in-law Susan Langdon Crane to buy a 1/500 share in the company. And when a bill of $6,000 came due he was forced to turn to brother-in-law Charles Langdon for a loan, but Charles refused to help. Fortunately, $15,000 due to Livy from the Langdon family's coal company arrived in the nick of time to cover expenses. It was merely a band-aid.

If men like Carnegie, who loved literature, and Charles Langdon, part of the family circle, didn't want to invest, Clemens was in trouble. In fact, the situation only grew worse. By late May, several weeks after the initial stock market collapse, Clemens wanted to throw in the towel. Between Paige's unfilled promises that resulted in no riches, Webster & Company bleeding red ink, and creditors like the Mount Morris Bank breathing down his neck, he was at wit's end. Back in Florence, growing desperate and depressed, he wrote to Hall with a vague plan to extricate himself from business all together:

> I have been looking over the past year's letters and statements and am depressed still more.
>
> I am terribly tired of business. I am by nature and disposition unfitted for it and I want to get out of it. I am standing on the Mount Morris volcano with help from the machine a long way off—doubtless a long way further off than the Connecticut Co. imagines.
>
> Now here is my idea for getting out.

According to Clemens, the firm owed him and his wife upwards of $175,000, but he calculated that the business was about $250,000 above indebtedness; so he proposed to Hall that they attempt to sell Clemens's two-thirds interest in the firm to publishers Harper, Appleton or to Putnam for $200,000. The buyer would be responsible for all debts except money owed Clemens and Livy. Looking to simply get out, Clemens was willing to be paid the $200,000 over three years. He concluded the letter with a plea for help:

> Such a deal would make it easy for a big firm to pour in a big cash capital and jump L. A. L. up to enormous prosperity. Then your one-third would be a fortune—and I hope to see that day! . . .
>
> Get me out of business!
>
> And I will be yours forever gratefully,
>
> S. L. Clemens.[7]

Hall was less than enthusiastic because the plan left him with his one-third interest in the wounded publishing house that could be worthless without Clemens, especially if the author took his books with him. If Clemens left, he wanted to leave too. In addition, he calculated that the Clemenses' interest in the firm was less: a total of just over $140,000, not $175,000. Not exactly the bearer of good news, Hall also informed Clemens that the Mount Morris Bank had called in a loan of $10,000, but there was not enough money in the coffers to pay it.[8] With Webster & Company owing sundry creditors about $96,000, they were faced with an imminent public relations disaster.

Yet again, Clemens fired off a letter instructing Hall to sell the firm, for "the worry of it makes me old, and robs life of its zest. I wish you were able to buy me out yourself and reap the fruits of your hard work and excellent management." However, with the country's financial situation deteriorating rapidly, any potential investors with deep pockets were going to be hard to come by. At the same time, Clemens was holding out hope that the Paige machine, which was still kicking even though he had cut off funding, would pull through and save the day.[9]

As Clemens became more irritable and lost sleep, Livy felt moved to get involved. While her husband was in Berlin with their daughter Clara, on the very day the stock market crashed, June 27, 1893, she wrote an apologetic letter to Hall:

> Mr. Clemens did not realize what trouble you would be in when his letter should reach you or he would not have sent it just then. I hope you will not worry any more than you can help. Do not let our interests weigh on you too heavily. We both know you will, as you always have, look in every way to the best interests of all.
>
> I think Mr. Clemens is right in feeling that he should get out of business, that he is not fitted for it; it worries him too much.
>
> But he need be in no haste about it, and of course, it would be the very farthest from his desire to imperil, in the slightest degree, your interests in order to save his own. . . .
>
> We can draw on Mr. Langdon for money for a few weeks until things are a little easier with you. . . .
>
> Hoping you will see a change for the better and begin to reap the fruit of your long and hard labor.[10]

Of course, the screws only tightened on the heels of the crash and reaping any fruit seemed more distant. Meanwhile, at the same time that they were dealing with these relentless business aggravations, Livy was quite ill and in late June Clemens took her to Munich, Germany, to consult with medical specialists.

Clemens had no choice but to push Hall to sell out, which he continued to do but now with a new twist on an old idea. He proposed just selling the L.A.L. outright instead of seeking an investor:

> The firm is in debt, but L. A. L. is free—and not only free but has large money owing to it. A proposition to sell that by itself to a big house could be made without embarrassment we merely confess that we cannot spare capital from the rest of the business to run it on the huge scale necessary to make it an opulent success.
>
> It will be selling a good thing—for somebody; and it will be getting rid of a load which we are clearly not able to carry. Whoever buys will have a noble good opening—a complete equipment, a well organized business, a capable and experienced manager, an enterprise not experimental but under full sail, and immediately able to pay 50 per cent a year on every dollar the publisher shall actually invest in it—I mean in making and selling the books.
>
> I am miserably sorry to be adding bothers and torments to the over-supply which you already have in these hideous times, but I feel so troubled, myself, considering the dreary fact that we are getting deeper and deeper in debt and the L. A. L. getting to be a heavier and heavier burden all the time, that I must bestir myself and seek a way of relief.[11]

As Hall put it in a July letter to Clemens, the L.A.L. project was "the one great mistake we have made . . ." According to his estimates, it had required $200,000 in capital to swing, which they had failed to provide. Hall now shut down sales of the L.A.L. but kept a skeleton crew to keep it alive and hopefully attractive to prospective buyers.[12] Also, as the Mount Morris bank pressed harder for their money, Clemens encouraged his lawyer, Daniel Whitford, who was also on the bank's board, to attempt to hold them off. There was little Whitford could accomplish, however, because several companies that owed the bank money had failed so the bank itself was feeling squeezed.

On July 18, Clemens wrote to Hall:

> . . . I have never felt so desperate in all my life—and good reason, for I haven't got a penny to my name, and Mrs. Clemens hasn't enough laid up with Langdon to keep us two months.
>
> It makes me quake to think that if Whitford should have to withdraw his protection, even my royalties might be seized before we got the Mount Morris bill paid. Yet if the firm can be kept alive a while longer no doubt you can save yourself and me too by selling L.A.L.

To keep food on the table, Clemens cranked out a series of humorous articles for *Cosmopolitan* magazine—although it was mighty difficult to find something to laugh about. There would be no more books until 1894, and his most recent, the 1892 *An American Claimant*, a comedy that reintroduces Colonel Sellers as a mad scientist, had sold poorly. On July 26 Clemens wrote Hall, who had just "cut the help down in all departments to one-quarter what it was," that he hoped the Paige machine would finally be finished and save the day.[13] Delusion had taken over. Just four days later, he wrote to Hall, "Do your best for me, for I do not sleep, these nights, for visions of the poorhouse. . . . Everything does look so blue, so dismally blue!" In another letter he wrote, "Great Scott but it's a long year—for you and me! I never knew the almanac to drag so."[14]

Clemens Understands He Must Protect His Books at all Costs As the Financial Panic of 1893 Grips the Country

Newspaper accounts of the dismal U.S. economy kept Clemens in an alarmed state of mind, and, fearing bankruptcy, he advised Hall to use any and all income to pay down debt to creditors. "What I am mainly hoping for, is to save my royalties," he explained. He absolutely did not want creditors like Mount Morris Bank to attempt to seize control of his book royalties. If there was any indication they would try to do so, Clemens wanted Hall to wire him and he would then return to the United States immediately. At the moment he was focused on Livy's health—she suffered from rheumatism and diphtheria.[15]

In spite of the current troubles, in July 1893, Clemens, a hopeless optimist, expressed interest in starting a magazine: "Dear Mr. Hall,— . . . I may be able to run over about mid-October. Then if I find you relieved of L. A. L. we will start a magazine—*inexpensive*, and of an entirely unique sort. . . . But we cannot undertake it until L. A. L. is out of the way. With our hands free and some capital to spare, we could make it hum." In this letter, he also stated that he thought Paige would have his typesetter "finished this month."[16]

At the same time, Hall attempted to cheer Clemens with some positive news, but Clemens still dreaded the thought of losing his books to creditors and wisely continued to insist all revenue go toward paying down debt:

> Dear Mr. Hall,—I am very glad indeed if you and Mr. Langdon are able to see any daylight ahead. To me none is visible. I strongly advise that every penny that comes in shall be applied to paying off debts. I may be in error about this, but it seems to me that we have no other course open. We can pay a part of the debts owing to outsiders—none to the Clemenses. In very prosperous times we might regard our stock and copyrights as assets sufficient, with the money owing to us, to square up and quit even, but I suppose we may not hope for such luck in the present condition of things.
>
> What I am mainly hoping for, is to save my royalties. If they come into danger I hope you will cable me, so that I can come over and try to save them, for if they go I am a beggar.[17]

Even though Livy's health remained tenuous, Clemens decided to return to the United States without his family to see what holes in the proverbial dike could be plugged. On arrival on September 7, he was immediately confronted with the news that the Mount Morris Bank would no longer extend any credit to Webster & Company. Fortunately, Charley Langdon stepped in and endorsed notes totaling $21,000. Meanwhile, Clemens and Hall scrambled to search for money among friends and banks alike. "I looked around to see where we could borrow money," he reflected. "There wasn't any place. This was in the midst of the fearful panic of '93." On September 17, Clemens wrote to Livy, "When I fell on the bed at 8 that evening, ruin seemed inevitable, but I was physically so exhausted that mental misery had no chance & I was asleep in a moment."[18] To keep Webster & Company afloat, he took $24,000 from personal savings—all he could afford.

A Mutual Friend Sets Up a Meeting with a Tycoon Who Is Either a Hell Hound or an Angel

After taking up residence in the plush Players Club in New York City, the 58-year-old Clemens, who still sported a head of thick, wildly curly hair, albeit gray, continued to socialize, which would yield unexpected but spectacular benefits. One night in early September, at the Murray Hill Hotel, his friend and literary colleague Dr. Clarence C. Rice introduced Clemens to Henry H. Rogers, an incredibly wealthy financier and a top officer in the Standard Oil behemoth. Five years Clemens's junior, the multimillionaire was born in Massachusetts, worked as a grocery clerk, and then sought fortune in Pennsylvania's oil fields. In 1872 Rogers attempted to stand up to John D. Rockefeller, but his business was ultimately absorbed. Nevertheless, he had so impressed Rockefeller that the relentless oil monger made him a junior partner. Thanks to his own forceful tactics, Rogers acquired the nickname "Hell Hound" as he rose through the ranks and accumulated wealth beyond imagination.

Standard Oil executive and multimillionaire, Henry "Hell Hound" Rogers, became Clemens's business mentor and friend. (COURTESY OF THE MARK TWAIN HOUSE & MUSEUM, HARTFORD, CT)

Taking Rogers aside, Rice asked him to look into Clemens's troubled business affairs. Without hesitation, Rogers agreed to meet Clemens on September 16, a Saturday, at his executive office at 26 Broadway. As Clemens took the elevator to the 11th floor and was then ushered into the mahogany-trimmed office with a view of the Statue of Liberty, he no doubt wondered what price Rogers might exact from him for his assistance. With graying hair meticulously parted in the middle and a full white mustache, the lithe Rogers was attractive and regal in bearing. His impeccable manners in greeting Clemens disguised the brutal businessman underneath.

Yet, as the two chatted, it was obvious that they shared certain qualities, namely that there were two sides to both of them.

There was Twain the humorous raconteur and Clemens the obsessive businessman. There was Henry Rogers the civic-minded socialite and "Hell Hound" who would squash any business obstacle. Both were charming, enjoyed off-color jokes, and relished travel as well as their leisure time. Most importantly, Clemens was not blind to Rogers's tough business side: "He's a pirate all right, but he owns up to it and enjoys being a pirate. That's the reason I like him."[19] The fact that Rogers was forthright earned Clemens's respect; the oilman was not a hypocrite.

After listening to Clemens's financial travails, Rogers agreed to help him sort through the sordid Paige typesetter affair to see what might be salvaged, and he loaned Webster & Company $4,000 to meet immediate needs—he never did ask for the money back. In addition, without fully understanding the firm's financial predicament, in mid-October Rogers arranged for his son-in-law, William Evarts Benjamin, to purchase the languishing *Library of American Literature* for $50,000. "This will insure our safety for several months to come," Hall informed Clemens.[20] So the sale of the L.A.L. was not the panacea Clemens had hoped it would be. Nevertheless, on the same day that Hall wrote to Clemens, a relieved and ecstatic Clemens wrote an effusive letter to Livy:

Dear, Dear Sweetheart,—

Apparently everything is at last settled as to the giveaway of L. A. L., and the papers will be signed and the transfer made tomorrow morning.

Meantime I have got the best and wisest man in the whole Standard Oil group of multi-millionaires a good deal interested in looking into the type-setter (this is private, don't mention it.) He has been searching into that thing for three weeks, and yesterday he said to me, "I find the machine to be all you represented it—I have here exhaustive reports from my own experts, and I know every detail of its capacity, its immense value, its construction, cost, history, and all about its inventor's character. I know that the New York Co. and the

Chicago Co. are both stupid, and that they are unbusinesslike people, destitute of money and in a hopeless boggle."

After being cut off by Clemens, inventor James Paige had run off to Chicago, where he had found new investors to keep his dream alive. The only issue now was that his New York area backers like Clemens and Hamersley (New York Co.) were fighting with the new Chicago contingent (Chicago Co.) over control and future spoils. Astoundingly, a dozen years after the machine was supposed to have been perfected, "Hell Hound" Rogers intended to settle the dispute by creating a completely new organization in which he would have a sizable stake.[21]

QUIRKY HABITS & BRAZEN PHILOSOPHY

Are Ethics for Fools?

"Good friends, good books and a sleepy conscience:
this is the ideal life."

"Honesty is the best policy—when there is money in it."

Talk of ethics is ubiquitous and wearisome in this age of billion-dollar corporate scandals and executive excess. So it was in Clemens's time during the Industrial Revolution and the Gilded Age when the robber barons established the rules to meet their needs. With fewer laws governing business back then, swindling was rampant; of course, so it is today but simply more sophisticated.

(Continued)

Are Ethics for Fools? *(Continued)*

As Clemens surveyed the business landscape, the cynic in him was inspired to say, "Honesty is the best policy—when there is money in it." On another occasion, he declared, "There are people who think that honesty is always the best policy. This is a superstition. There are times when the appearance of it is worth six of it." Yes, image was and is everything. However, Clemens took his morals and ethics relatively seriously for a satirist. At his 70th birthday party, mixing earnestness with flippancy, he told the crowd:

> I have lived a severely moral life. But it would be a mistake for other people to try that, or for me to recommend it. Very few would succeed: you have to have a perfectly colossal stock of morals; and you can't get them on a margin; you have to have the whole thing, and put them in your box. Morals are an acquirement—like music, like a foreign language, like piety, poker, paralysis—no man is born with them. I wasn't myself, I started poor. I hadn't a single moral. There is hardly a man in this house that is poorer than I was then. Yes, I started like that—the world before me, not a moral in the slot. Not even an insurance moral.

Being an upstanding citizen isn't easy, warned Clemens, who found it quite annoying:

> If I had the remaking of man, he wouldn't have any conscience. It is one of the most disagreeable things connected with a person; and although it certainly does a great deal of good, it cannot be said to pay, in the long run; it would be much better to have less good and more comfort. Still, this is only my opinion, and I am only one man; others, with less

experience, may think differently. They have a right to their view. I only stand to this: I have noticed my conscience for many years, and I know it is more trouble and bother to me than anything else I started with. I suppose that in the beginning I prized it, because we prize anything that is ours; and yet how foolish it was to think so. If we look at it in another way, we see how absurd it is: if I had an anvil in me would I prize it? Of course not. And yet when you come to think, there is no real difference between a conscience and an anvil—I mean for comfort.

Rather than contend with morals, Clemens the humorist concluded it was best to give them away: "It's my opinion that everyone I know has morals, though I wouldn't like to ask. I know I have. But I'd rather teach them than practice them any day. 'Give them to others'— that's my motto."[22]

chapter ten

SALVAGING A CAREER
AND DIGNITY

"The proper office of a friend is to side with you
when you are in the wrong. Nearly anybody
will side with you when you are in the right."

*I*n the fall of 1893, Clemens became friendly with Henry "Hell Hound" Rogers, a very wealthy partner of John D. Rockefeller and a potential financial angel. In the winter of 1893–1894, Rogers assisted Clemens in hard negotiations as they reorganized the typesetter business into a new entity. Later in 1894, Clemens's emotional attachment to the project had to be set aside as they were finally forced to shutter the business. In 1894 Rogers also assisted with Webster & Company, which went bankrupt in April. Negotiations with creditors would last for several years as Clemens protected his family and reorganized his finances. To pay off all debts, he launched a worldwide lecture tour in 1895. All debts were fully paid in 1898, and that year his income was $200,000, or more than $3.5 million in today's dollars.

Before linking up with Rogers, Clemens had traveled to Chicago to meet with Paige, who was as upbeat as ever and intent on producing as many 50 machines. The inventor's infectious optimism prompted the author to conclude that "he could persuade a fish to come out and take a walk with him. When he is present I always believe him: I can't help it. When he is gone away all the belief evaporates. He is a most daring and majestic liar." With a tinge of vindictiveness, he also jotted in his notebook, "Paige and I always meet on effusively affectionate terms, and yet he knows, perfectly well, that if I had him in a steel trap I would shut out all human succor and watch that trap, until he died."

On another occasion, after speaking with Paige on the telephone, Clemens wrote in his notebook: "I asked him if his conscience troubled him any about the way he had treated me. . . . He said it broke his heart when I left him."[1] Yet they remained cordial as Clemens continued to dream of the promised land.

Clemens's biographer Paine pointed out that Paige must have been a hypnotist. Possibly so, for equally mesmerized was Henry "Hell Hound" Rogers, who traveled to Chicago to investigate and subsequently wrote to Clemens, "Certainly it was a marvelous invention. It was the nearest approach to a human being in the wonderful things it could do of any machine I have ever known. But that was just the trouble: it was too much of a human being and not enough of a machine." Nevertheless, he invested $78,000.[2] Perhaps Clemens hadn't been delusional all these years when it came to Paige's typesetter.

Business Negotiations Concerning the Paige Typesetter Take On a Tough Tone, Not Unlike Taking Scalps

Rogers not only gave Clemens hope, but the humorist stopped suffering from indigestion, which had plagued him for years; he was able to eat raw oysters, sausage, corned beef and cabbage, and custard. One for action, in December Rogers took him to Chicago aboard his private rail car, Clemens reported to Livy, who was in Paris. "On the way out Mr. Rogers would plan out the campaign while I walked the floor and smoked and assented," he wrote. "Then he would close it up with a snap and drop it and we would totally change the subject and take up the scenery, etc." The rich food was delightful too: "The colored waiter knew his business, and the colored cook was a finished artist. Breakfasts: coffee with real cream; beefsteaks, sausage, bacon, chops, eggs in various ways, potatoes in various—yes, and quite wonderful baked potatoes, and hot as fire. Dinners—all manner of things, including canvas-back duck, apollinaris, claret, champagne, etc."[3]

The two remained in Chicago a mere 25 hours while Rogers forged a new company—the Paige Compositor Manufacturing Company, capitalized by both the Chicago and New York interests—that would either pay Clemens $240,000 in cash or $500,000 in stock. Paige didn't want to give away so much and threatened to walk away, but the seasoned Rogers was hardened against such threats and stood his ground. "Mr. Paige must accept *our* terms," he told Clemens, who in turn told Livy that observing Rogers was "better than a circus."[4]

Rogers cut to the marrow of the matter. As Clemens explained to Livy, "It was beautiful to see Mr. Rogers apply his probe & his bung-starter & remorselessly let out the wind & the water from the so-called 'assets' of these companies. And he did it so sweetly & courteously—but he stripped away all the rubbish & laid bare the fact that their whole gaudy property consisted of just $276,000 & no more! Then he said, 'Now we know where we stand, gentlemen. I am prepared to listen to a proposition from you to furnish capital.' " For Clemens, the negotiations were like taking "scalps" and "games in a long tournament."[5]

On January 15, 1894, Paige blinked and effectively agreed to Rogers's terms, which included giving Clemens control of the patents and a possible windfall of $500,000. "I came up to my room and began to undress," Clemens wrote to Livy, "and then, suddenly and without warning the realization burst upon me and overwhelmed me: I and mine, who were paupers an hour ago, are rich now and our troubles are over!"[6] Two weeks later he wrote another effusive letter to her, although his expectation to exit business was indeed premature:

When the anchor is down, then I shall say:
    'Farewell—a long farewell—to business! I will never touch it again!'

I will live in literature, I will wallow in it, revel in it, I will swim in ink! . . . but this is premature; the anchor is not down yet.[7]

To Rogers, Clemens expressed undying thanks: "You have saved me and my family from ruin and humiliation. You have been the best friend that ever a man had, and yet you have never by any word made me feel the weight of this deep obligation." But to his friend Arthur Hardy, Clemens admitted, "I am so tuckered out with 5 months of daily and nightly fussing with business, that I shall not feel any interest in literature or anything else until I have had a half-year of rest and idleness to compensate that account."[8]

After six emotionally roiling months in the United States, Clemens made plans to return to his family in Paris, and, although midnight was fast approaching on February 15, he wrote to Livy joyfully:

When I arrived in September, lord how black the prospect was— how desperate, how incurably desperate! Webster and Co had to have a small sum of money or go under at once. I flew to Hartford—to my friends—but they were not moved, not strongly interested, and I was ashamed that I went. It was from Mr. Rogers, a stranger, that I got the money and was by it saved. And then— while still a stranger—he set himself the task of saving my financial life without putting upon me (in his native delicacy) any sense that I was the recipient of a charity, a benevolence—and he has accomplished that task; accomplished it at a cost of three months of wearing and difficult labor. He gave that time to me—time which could not be bought by any man at a hundred thousand dollars a month—no, nor for three times the money.[9]

Ultimately, It Takes a Hard Heart to Rule the Business World

Now that Rogers was supporting him, Clemens actually renewed his efforts to find more investors for the typesetter, including Bram Stoker, the renowned Irish author who would pen *Dracula*; and Henry Irving, renowned actor, theater producer, and man of letters. In the spring of 1894 reports from Chicago indicated—yet again—that the new machine was close to perfection. And, as promised, in June, Paige, whom Clemens considered "a lineal descendent of Judas Iscariot," signed over control of his patents. "I am glad Paige has signed," a bellicose Clemens wrote to Rogers. "I wish it was his death-warrant. Well, maybe it is."[10] All seemed rosy in July when Paige tested the machine for the Chicago *Herald* and it actually worked. "It affects me like Columbus sighting land," Clemens wrote to Rogers melodramatically.[11] Clearly, he was writing to the "Hell Hound" more frequently than he had ever written to his mother (over 50 letters in 1894 alone).[12]

But then the machine failed and, ensconced in Paris, Clemens sensed that Armageddon was upon him—he knew Rogers did not have the patience he had displayed over the last 12 plus years. At the same time, Livy again fell ill and was receiving an "electric treatment" to help restore her health.[13] In a long, rambling December 22 letter to Rogers that reflected his agitated mind, Clemens found it difficult to accept that the end was nigh:

> It hit me like a thunder-clap. It knocked every rag of sense out of my head, and I went flying here and there and yonder, not knowing what I was doing, and only one clearly defined thought standing up visible and substantial out of the crazy storm-drift that my dream of ten years was in desperate peril, and out of the 60,000 or 90,000 projects for its rescue that came floating through my skull, not one would hold still long enough for me to examine it and size it up. Have you ever been like that? Not so much so, I reckon.
>
> There was another clearly defined idea—I must be there and see it die. That is, if it must die; and maybe if I were there we might hatch up some next-to-impossible way to make it take up its bed and take a walk.

. . . I cabled you, and said to myself that I would take the French steamer tomorrow (which will be Sunday).

By bedtime Mrs. Clemens had reasoned me into a fairly rational and contented state of mind; but of course it didn't last long. So I went on thinking—mixing it with a smoke in the dressing room once an hour—until dawn this morning. Result—a sane resolution; no matter what your answer to my cable might be, I would hold still and not sail until I should get an answer to this present letter which I am now writing, or a cable answer from you saying "Come" or "Remain."[14]

It was as if the typesetter had become a beloved, living thing to Clemens, and he wanted to be at its side when it passed away. It was more foolish melodrama, of course.

A hardened businessman, Rogers took a detached approach, and on December 21 he shut down the Paige Compositor Manufacturing Company. His explanation to Clemens was contrite and consoling as he blamed his own "old and hard" heart for the decision and truly regretted the pain it would cause Clemens.

From the beautiful studio home of the artist Pomroy on the Rue de l'Universite, two days after Christmas Clemens struggled to write a coherent letter to Rogers: "I shall keep your regard while we two live—that I know; for I shall always remember what you have done for me, and that will insure me against ever doing anything that could forfeit it or impair it. I am 59 years old; yet I never had a friend before who put out a hand and tried to pull me ashore when he found me in deep waters." His thoughts turned to Stoker and Irving, whom he had lured into the enterprise; he wanted to make sure they were refunded their money, but he was too ashamed to do it himself. "Madam says No," he continued, "I must face the music." Aware that belt-tightening must occur immediately, he confessed to Rogers that they had "to find a tenant for our Hartford house; not an easy matter, for it costs heavily to live in. We can never live in it again; though it would break the family's hearts if they could believe it." At the conclusion of the letter, he alluded to his true emotional state: "Nothing daunts Mrs. Clemens or makes the world look black to her—which is the reason I haven't drowned myself."[15]

Clemens Learns That Being Lucky Only Carries You So Far

Clemens had wholeheartedly always believed that the typesetting machine would eventually bring him riches; he was steadfast in this belief for one reason: his horoscope, as silly as it may sound. "There's one thing which makes it difficult for me to soberly realize that my ten year dream is actually dissolved;" he wrote to Rogers on January 2, "and that is, that it reveries my horoscope. The proverb says, 'Born lucky, always lucky,' and I am very superstitious." Clemens explained how as a boy he had survived near drowning nine times, and how he had not been aboard the riverboat *Pennsylvania* when it blew up, killing his younger brother and 60 others.

> I am so superstitious that I have always been afraid to have business dealings with certain relatives and friends of mine because they were unlucky people. All my life I have stumbled upon lucky chances of large size, and whenever they were wasted it was because of my own stupidity and carelessness. And so I have felt entirely certain that that machine would turn up trumps eventually. It disappointed me lots of times, but I couldn't shake off the confidence of a life-time in my luck.
>
> Well, whatever I get out of the wreckage will be due to good luck—the good luck of getting you into the scheme—for, but for that, there wouldn't be any wreckage; it would be total loss.[16]

Truthfully, there was nothing to salvage: Clemens's total losses have been estimated to be between $170,000 and $300,000—or between $3.3 million and $4.9 million in today's dollars.[17]

In his autobiography there is not one mention of his epic relationship with Paige. When Clemens did reflect on Paige, the same bitterness that he felt toward Webster would surface. "I have, as you say, been interested in patents and patentees," he wrote in a letter to a fellow author. "If your books tell how to exterminate inventors send me nine editions. Send them by express."[18] It is safe to assume that Paige was on his mind. It probably would have been little comfort to Clemens to know that Paige would die penniless in 1917 and be buried in a potter's field outside Chicago.

Bankruptcy Is Not Worth Killing Yourself Over

Henry Rogers's work on behalf of Clemens had only just begun. In mid-February 1894, while they were dealing with Paige, over a late-night game of billiards Clemens confessed to the tycoon that Webster & Company was still in trouble despite the sale of the L.A.L. As he admitted to his sister Pamela: "It was insanely managed from the day it got the Grant book till now. That terrible book! Which made money for everyone concerned but me. *Privately*, I will confide to you that I am trying to wind up that hated concern. It owes me a hundred and ten thousand dollars, it owes Livy about sixty thousand, and it owes banks and printers eighty-three thousand—and has assets which I *hope* are marketable for sixty thousand, but I sort of doubt it."[19] According to Clemens, that would be some $253,000 in liabilities and only $60,000 in assets. A grim picture of Webster & Company—the glory days of the Grant book long removed.

That March found Fred Hall tightening the belt another notch as he scrambled to reduce overhead by leasing office space and cutting heating. On April 16, Clemens, who had rushed back to the United States, reported to Livy that Rogers felt Webster & Company could "pull through alive" and suggested paying all creditors "a hundred cents on the dollar and

finally closing the concern without any stain upon its name."
But later that very day, Hall reported that the Mount Morris
Bank refused to renew two absolutely needed $5,000 notes and
Whitford could not stop them from taking legal action against
Webster & Company.[20] It was not a huge sum of money, but all
it took was one disgruntled creditor to bring the house of cards
tumbling down.

Bankruptcy was declared April, 18, 1894, pursuant to Henry
Rogers's grim instructions. Hall was close to tears, an emotional display that prompted Clemens to lash out at him in a
letter to Livy: "I half thought he would go off and drown himself. . . . In all my days I have never seen so dull a fool." Like
Bliss, Webster, Paige, and numerous others, Hall would now fall
victim to Clemens's bitter tongue. Clemens himself refused to
show weakness even though the failure made a great stir in the
press. "As I hadn't done anything to be ashamed of, I wasn't
ashamed;" he explained to Livy, "so I didn't avoid anybody, but
talked with everybody I knew . . ." Livy was ashamed, however; she declared to a friend that she felt as though her entire
life was a failure and at times she wanted to die. Between their
dire financial situation and her failing health, there were days
when she was overwhelmed. But she too would steel herself.[21]

In his autobiography, Clemens sketched out the ugly after-
math as they sifted through the remains:

The panic had stopped Mrs. Clemens's income. It had stopped my
income from my books. We had but nine thousand dollars in the
bank. We hadn't a penny wherewith to pay the Webster creditors.
Henry Robinson said, "Hand over everything belonging to Webster and Company to the creditors and ask them to accept that in
liquidation of the debts. They'll do it. You'll see that they'll do it.
They are aware that you are not individually responsible for those
debts, that the responsibility rests upon the firm as a firm."

I didn't think much of that way out of the difficulty and when
I made my report to Mrs. Clemens she wouldn't hear of it at all.

She said, "This is my house. The creditors shall have it. Your books are your property—turn them over to the creditors. Reduce the indebtedness in every way you can think of—then get to work and earn the rest of the indebtedness, if our life is spared. And don't be afraid. We shall pay a hundred cents on the dollar yet."

It was sound prophecy. Mr. Rogers stepped in about this time and preached to the creditors. He said they could not have Mrs. Clemen's house—that she must be a preferred creditor and would give up the Webster notes for sixty-five thousand dollars, money borrowed of her. He said they could not have my books, that they were not an asset of Webster and Company, that the creditors could have everything that belonged to Webster and Company, that I would wipe from the slate the sixty thousand dollars I had lent to the Company, and that I would now make it my task to earn the rest of the Webster indebtedness, if I could, and pay a hundred cents on the dollar—but that this must not be regarded as a promise.[22]

While Rogers held the creditors at bay and reorganized Clemens's finances, the most important element the author took away from the tragedy was the critical importance of protecting his copyrights, his books, which he now considered selling to raise money. There was no need to panic, Rogers reassured him; the books would earn him money on a continuous basis, especially once the depression ended. To fully protect the books, Rogers listed Livy as the preferred creditor because she was owed $65,000; therefore, she would be given control of the copyrights and associated future proceeds until paid off. It was great foresight to hang on to the copyrights because once the depression ended, the stream did indeed flow freely again and the Clemenses would reap upwards of $200,000 a year in royalties (over $3.5 million in today's dollars). Rogers's decision was "a service which saved me and my family from want and assured us permanent comfort and prosperity," wrote Clemens, who, after protecting his books and then being willing to sell the rights, now fully realized his intellectual capital was priceless.

At the End of the Day, Clemens Realizes His Reputation Is Everything and It Must Be Saved

On April 22 Clemens wrote a letter to Livy in which he acknowledged that the court had appointed a receiver to manage Webster & Company and to insure Mount Morris was paid. Putting a positive spin on the situation, he hoped that "the assignee will put things on a stringent basis and we shall have no more of Mr. Hall's stupid and extravagant mismanagement."[23] Yes, he had definitely turned on Hall.

Mount Morris was hardly the only creditor, however. In total, 101 creditors filed claims for a total of $79,704.80, not including Livy Clemens, who was owed $65,000.[24] The toughest creditors were going to be the Mount Morris Bank, owed over $20,000; George Barrow, who had been a personal friend of Webster and whose family was owed over $15,000; and Thomas Russell & Son, a printer and bookbinder firm, owed over $5,000.

Now came a grueling debate between Clemens, Rogers, and Livy as to whether the creditors should be paid in full. "I was morally bound for the debts," he wrote in his autobiography, "though not legally. The panic was on, business houses were falling to ruin everywhere, creditors were taking the assets—when there were any—and letting the rest go. Old business friends of mine said: 'Business is business, sentiment is sentiment—and this is business. Turn the assets over to the creditors and compromise on that; other creditors are not getting 33 per cent.'"[25]

Before negotiations could begin, the creditors tightened their grip by petitioning the court successfully to shut down Webster & Company. Clemens had hoped that the creditors would allow the business to keep operating, but they wanted what assets there were now as they, too, were pressed. Livy took the news hard, so, from 3,000 miles away, Clemens did his best to bolster her: "You only seem to see rout, retreat, and dishonored colors dragging in the dirt—whereas none of these things exist. There is temporary defeat, but no dishonor—and we will march again."[26] Although he put on a brave face, Clemens detailed this angst-ridden period in his autobiography, which included one particularly painful exchange of words he overheard:

> One day I got a shock—a shock which disturbed me a good deal. I overheard a brief conversation between Mr. Rogers and a couple of other seasoned men of affairs.
>
> First Man of Affairs: "How old is Clemens?"
>
> Mr. Rogers: "Fifty-eight."
>
> First Man of Affairs: "Ninety-five per cent of the men who fail at fifty-eight never get up again."
>
> Second Man of Affairs: "You can make it ninety-eight per cent and be nearer right."
>
> Those sayings haunted me for several days, troubling me with melancholy forebodings, and would not be reasoned away by me.[27]

Then real tragedy struck on May 21, 1894, when Rogers's wife Abbie died, a reminder to them all as to what was really important in life: their families and their health. But marching resolutely onward, within 10 days Rogers was back at work on Clemens's behalf, arranging a meeting with creditors: "I will attend the meeting and try and catch the temper."[28] Gauging their mood was critical because Clemens was not anxious to pay the creditors in full and Rogers intended to aggressively negotiate for only 50 cents on the dollar. There was just one other hurdle: Livy, who acted as their collective conscience. She wouldn't allow for less than full payment; on July 31 she wrote her husband: "Oh my darling we want those debts paid and we want to treat them all not only honestly but we want to help them in every possible way. . . .You know my darling, now is the time for you to add to or mar the good name that you have made. Do not for one moment let your sense of our need of money get advantage of your sense of justice & generosity."[29]

Rogers estimated that to pay all of the creditors in full would take Clemens seven years, while Livy calculated a more optimistic four years. Negotiations dragged on and by September 1894 Clemens was on edge. Back in Paris, he couldn't sleep because he was "all nerves and over-wrought and spiritually raw to the touch." At one point a thunderstorm annoyed him beyond reason, and on another occasion a ticking clock in his Paris hotel room wreaked havoc on his mental state.[30] In November he contracted a nasty cough and would not be able to smoke for three whole days, which intensified his agitated state. Finally, all but a few creditors agreed Clemens could take his time in paying off his debts. "He won them over," Clemens wrote of Rogers. "There was clarity about his reasonings and a charm about his manner, his voice and the kindness and sincerity that looked out of his eyes that could win anybody that had brains in his head and a heart in his body."[31]

In Evaluating His Personal Finances, Clemens Realizes He Must Embark on a Grueling But Lucrative Worldwide Tour

In a January 1895 letter to Rogers, Clemens evaluated his family's bleak personal finances, including Livy's share of the Langdon family's coal business and sundry investments: "Of the rags left of Mrs. Clemens's Elmira interests she may count upon $3,000 a year for herself and $1,000 for the children. Then there is about $1,500 a year from the Hartford books and $2,000 from the London publisher—total $7,500. To that I must add $5,000 a year by work, and that will keep the tribe alive."[32] His once bountiful stock and bond portfolio of over $100,000 had dwindled to almost nothing. He was also still trying to rent the Hartford house, and the Clemens family would remain in Europe, where it was cheaper to live. As for adding the $5,000 a year and the paying of his creditors, one solution became painfully clear: a worldwide lecture tour, which could earn him tens of thousands of dollars but be excruciatingly painful. In February 1895, he told Rogers, "Apparently I've got to mount the platform next fall or starve; therefore I am examining into this thing seriously."[33]

By the end of February he was deep into the logistics of a worldwide lecture tour to begin in July and was already counting the dollars; he hoped to make $25,000 or $30,000 on speaking engagements in the United States alone. After traveling across the country, he planned to sail to Hawaii, Fiji, Australia, India, South Africa, and Britain, among many other places.[34] Despite this surefire revenue boon, in June an impatient Thomas Russell served Clemens with papers to appear in court in a move to recoup his loan immediately. Shortly thereafter, the judge ruled in Russell's favor, which made the newspapers, of course. It was also reported in the papers that on the eve of his world tour Clemens's health was suffering and a nurse had come from Elmira to attend to him.

In actuality, Livy was far more distressed by the public press than her husband, and she wrote to Rogers surreptitiously to tell him that she was willing to sacrifice $30,000 of her family's money to reach a settlement with Russell and the other creditors pushing them. She could not, however, hide her anguish from Clemens. "I found Mrs. Clemens in the deeps of despair and misery when I arrived," he then wrote to Rogers, "because my name had gotten into the papers in connection with the examination . . . So I have formally instructed Sterne & Rushmore to settle or pay in full, and draw on Mr. Langdon for the money."

Although it was against Rogers's better judgment and even though the consensus was that Russell was behaving in an "outrageous" manner, Rogers agreed they should make the $5,000 settlement immediately.[35]

Clemens vented to Rogers: "It is incredible, the worry and anger that that Russell business has cost me since the day my idiot lawyers allowed me to be dragged to New York by a court which had no more authority over me than the Mikado of

Japan. There was no 'technicality' in the matter, and no 'quibble.' My personal liberty was invaded without due process of law—wholly without right or reason—and those lawyers did not know it."[36]

It was during this period that Clemens came to wholly despise lawyers: They were idiots and jackrabbits, making blunder after blunder while he was flogged mercilessly by creditors, judges, and newspaper editors. He also harbored a deep bitterness against Mount Morris Bank and Barrow: "It was the Bank's criminal stupidity that caused my destruction, and I never greatly liked Barrow. I don't want to pay those two anything until all the others have been paid in full—if that day ever comes."[37] How it was the bank's fault, one could only guess. Not until Clemens fully accepted responsibility would he achieve some inner peace.

On the heels of the Russell lawsuit, which fueled sordid rumors about his personal financial condition, a month into his lecture tour Clemens decided to issue a public statement that clarified his situation and summarized his plan for paying off his debts:

> It has been reported that I sacrificed, for the benefit of the creditors, the property of the publishing firm whose financial backer I was, and that I am now lecturing for my own benefit. This is an error. I intend the lectures, as well as the property, for the creditors. The law recognizes no mortgage on a man's brain, and a merchant who has given up all he has may take advantage of the rules of insolvency and start free again for himself; but I am not a business man; and honor is a harder master than the law. It cannot compromise for less than a hundred cents on the dollar, and its debts never outlaw. . . .
>
> The present situation is that the wreckage of the firm, together with what money I can scrape together with my wife's aid, will enable me to pay the other creditors about 50 per cent of their claims. It is my intention to ask them to accept that as a legal discharge, and trust to my honor to pay the other 50 per cent as fast

as I can earn it. From my reception thus far on my lecturing tour, I am confident that, if I live I can pay off the last debt within four years, after which, at the age of sixty-four, I can make a fresh and unincumbered start in life.

I do not enjoy the hard travel and broken rest inseparable from lecturing, and, if it had not been for the imperious moral necessity of paying these debts, which I never contracted but which were accumulated on the faith of my name by those who had a presumptive right to use it, I should never have taken to the road at my time of life. I could have supported myself comfortably by writing, but writing is too slow for the demands that I have to meet.[38]

Clemens slyly excused himself from being culpable, which meant he was placing the blame squarely on Hall and Webster, but nevertheless was taking charge of paying off the debts he was *not responsible for.*

The tour immediately proved a success and by the time Clemens, who was accompanied by his wife and his 21-year-old daughter Clara, reached the west coast he had netted $5,000. On August 23, 1895, they sailed from Vancouver for Hawaii. Over the next 12 months he took in almost $25,000. In his autobiography, he provided a brief summary:

Mrs. Clemens and Clara and I started, on the 15th of July, 1895, on our lecturing raid around the world. We lectured and robbed and raided for thirteen months. I wrote a book and published it. I sent the book money and lecture money to Mr. Rogers as fast as we captured it. He banked it and saved it up for the creditors. We implored him to pay off the smaller creditors straightway, for they needed the money, but he wouldn't do it. He said that when I had milked the world dry we would take the result and distribute it pro rata among the Webster people.[39]

It was wise of Rogers to hold off paying the creditors until all could be paid at once because playing favorites would have only stirred up more trouble.

As well as lecturing in his nasally drawl, Clemens sat for many interviews as he attempted to bolster his public image. Almost 60 years of age, he had long unkempt hair and a ferocious mustache, but gray, gentle eyes that peered out over a thin beaked nose. His nervous energy was apparent as he could hardly sit still for 15 minutes and fiddled incessantly with his pipe.

All was going according to plan, but then, more than a year into his tour, in August 1896, the world came crashing down yet again. It seemed the man who was allegedly born lucky could not escape the black cloud hanging over him. On August 18, 1896, his 24-year-old daughter Susy, who, along with her sister Jean, had been living with an aunt, passed away. Even though she died from spinal meningitis, in his twisted way Clemens blamed Charles Webster for not only his debts but her death: "I am not able to think of him without cursing him & cursing him & cursing the day I opposed your better judgment of the lousy scoundrel & thief & sided with Annie in her desire to marry him," he wrote to his sister Pamela. "The thought of the treacherous cur can wake me out of my sleep. . . . He was all dog. And he put me where I am, & Susy where she is."[40] Clemens reasoned that if they had been home, rather than on the tour, Susy could have been saved.

Henry Rogers attempted to bolster his friend's fragile emotional state, support that Clemens appreciated. "I have just read the sheaf of letters brought from you by my wife," he wrote to Rogers in September, "and it makes my bones ache to think of the work and thought and persistency and patience they represent."[41] It was a lesson for Clemens, even though he was a ripe 61 years old. The manner in which Rogers aided him was also commendable: "By no sign, no hint, no word did he ever betray any consciousness that I was under obligations to him," wrote Clemens, who considered this attribute to be one of the loftiest. "This is a world where you get nothing for nothing; where you pay value for everything you get and 50 percent over; and when it is gratitude you owe, you have to pay a thousand. In fact, gratitude is a debt which usually goes on accumulating, like blackmail; the more you pay, the more is exacted. In time you are made to realize that the kindness done you is become a curse and you wish it had not happened."[42]

Overzealous Friends Bring Bad Publicity That Hurts Clemens's Image

Despair again gripped Clemens in October when, while still lecturing, he learned that his portion of Webster & Company debt owed to creditors was not $40,000 as he initially thought, but almost $80,000. It was more than he thought he could ever manage to pay off.[43] With the public kept painfully aware of his financial troubles thanks to an overzealous media, in the summer of 1897 the New York *Herald* decided to start a fund-raising effort to help Clemens out of debt. While the effort quickly raised a few thousand dollars, it would spark a series of editorials not all together kind to Clemens.

Initially, Clemens was pleased and impressed by the success of the charity fund, but he kept it a secret from his family because he was afraid Livy would not let him accept the money. He was right, of course. His close friends weren't too keen on the idea, either, so he asked the *Herald* to cease and desist.

In a July 15, 1897 editorial, the *Chap-Book* magazine hit the nail on the head: "For years there has been more or less sniveling in the press about Mark Twain's poverty and his debts. We have never believed that this lachrymose sentimentality was at all pleasing to Mr. Clemens. To be sure, his misfortunes were to be regretted, but we have understood that they were legitimate business losses, due largely to the fact that Mr. Clemens could not force himself to be content with one trade only—that of author." The editorial went on to severely criticize his apparent willingness to accept the *Herald* fund money if it had carried on and wondered if Clemens had lost his grip on reality.

On reflection, Clemens wrote to Rogers, "Their proposition convinced me that I had friends; the failure of the present scheme does not prove that they have ceased to exist, but only that they do not approve this method. . . . I have many personal friends, and only crimes could alienate them, not blunders. I commit twenty-four blunders a day, and they always expect that. I have not kept up my average for a while back, but that was because I was busy. I can make it up now."[44]

Paying Off Debts Brings Peace of Mind

Income from his lectures, books, and articles slowly accumulated. By August 1897 Clemens regained his financial footings, and Livy had $39,000 in the bank, almost enough to wipe out the remainder of the Webster & Company debt. While vacationing in Lucerne, Switzerland, in the fall, Clemens announced to Rogers:

> I throw up the sponge. I pull down the flag. Let us begin on the debts. I cannot bear the weight any longer. It totally unfits me for work. I have lost three entire months now. In that time I have begun twenty magazine articles and books—and flung every one of them aside in turn. The debts interfered every time, and took the spirit out of any work. And yet I have worked like a bond slave and wasted no time and spared no effort. . . . A man can't possibly write the kind of stuff that is required of me unless he have an unharassed mind. . . . Peace of mind is easily attainable—and let's go for it.

Clemens was tired of the wolves howling at his door.

The month and year his brother Orion died, December 1897, he started paying the smaller creditors, which inspired elated comments to Rogers: "Land we are glad to see those debts diminishing. For the first time in my life I am getting more pleasure out of paying money out than pulling it in." And: "Since we have begun to pay off the debts I have abundant peace of mind again—no sense of burden. Work has become a pleasure again—it is not labor any longer."[45] In accepting and fulfilling his responsibilities, Clemens was achieving the peace of mind he had been yearning for.

As of February 11, 1898, Clemens would have all debt paid off except the bank, Barrow, and almost $1,500 owed to Grant's widow. According to Rogers's executive assistant, Miss Katherine Harrison, the bank was still owed over $21,000 and Barrow just over $11,000.[46] Both Clemens and Livy expressed a desire to pay off George Barrow as soon as possible because his claim was clear-cut and legitimate, but that didn't stop Clemens from spewing venom once it was paid off in August: "I was so cussed tired of the name of Barrow! Now he can go hang himself as soon as he wants to; I have no further use for him."[47] By 1898 all claims against Webster & Company were paid—paid in full, or, as Clemens liked to say, a hundred cents on the dollar. "Mrs. Clemens has been reading the creditors' letters over and over again and thanks you deeply for sending them," Clemens wrote to Rogers, "and says it is the only really happy day she has had since Susy died."[48]

There was one more loose end: What to do with Clemens's books, all those titles by Mark Twain, which Webster & Company, as well as American Publishing, had been printing? In a first step, Rogers readily took on the task of extracting Clemens from agreements made with the Bliss family of the American Publishing Company. To do so he had to bully Frank Bliss, who was quite adept at talking his way around most every issue. "They talk longer and cover a wider range than anybody I know," Rogers reported to Clemens. "The only mistake those fellows made was in going into the Publishing business instead of the preaching business."[49] Nevertheless, Rogers succeeded in transferring the rights to Harper & Brothers, and they laid plans to publish a uniform edition of all his books.

Before 1898 was out, Clemens was able to crow to his old friend Howells: "We own a house & furniture in Hartford . . .

my English & American copyrights pay an income which rep-
resents $200,000; & . . . we have $107,000 cash in the bank."[50]
After having made and lost a fortune, he was once again a very
wealthy man, earning more than $3.5 million annually in to-
day's dollars. Yet, after all the madcap adventures, he was still addicted to speculation, and before long the 63-year-old Clemens
would be knee-deep in new ventures.

QUIRKY HABITS AND BRAZEN PHILOSOPHY

"Avoid My Example"

*"One of the strong points about my business life
was that I never gave up."*

Among the rich and famous with whom Clemens enjoyed
cavorting, the author was just as renowned for his business
successes and blunders as he was for his writing and humor.
He made and lost and then made again millions in today's
dollars. At a 1901 banquet, in a speech before a group of
businessmen, Clemens thoroughly enjoyed poking fun at
not only the world of business but his own roller-coaster
career. And at age 65, when most men would consider re-
tirement, he still envisioned himself a businessman looking
for the next big thing. It was remarkable that Clemens still
had a zest for the game of business after weathering numerous financial panics and the bankruptcy.

While often flip, his remarks are thought provoking and at
times earnest as he offered some basic business principles.
The president of the Fourth National Bank and established
financier, Mr. James G. Cannon, introduced Clemens, who
then took the podium.

(Continued)

"Avoid My Example" *(Continued)*

Business

I took exception to the introducing of Mr. Cannon as a great financier, as if he were the only great financier present. I am a financier. But my methods are not the same as Mr. Cannon's.

I cannot say that I have turned out the great business man that I thought I was when I began life. But I am comparatively young yet, and may learn. I am rather inclined to believe that what troubled me was that I got the big-head early in the game. I want to explain to you a few points of difference between the principles of business as I see them and those that Mr. Cannon believes in.

He says that the primary rule of business success is loyalty to your employer. That's all right—as a theory. What is the matter with loyalty to yourself? As nearly as I can understand Mr. Cannon's methods, there is one great drawback to them. He wants you to work a great deal. Diligence is a good thing, but taking things easy is much more-restful. My idea is that the employer should be the busy man, and the employee the idle one. The employer should be the worried man, and the employee the happy one. And why not? He gets the salary. My plan is to get another man to do the work for me. In that there's more repose. What I want is repose first, last, and all the time.

Mr. Cannon says that there are three cardinal rules of business success; they are diligence, honesty, and truthfulness. Well, diligence is all right. Let it go as a theory. Honesty is the best policy—when there is money in it. But truthfulness is one of the most dangerous—why, this man is misleading you.

I want to tell you of some of my experiences in business, and then I will be in a position to lay down one general rule for the guidance of those who want to succeed in business. My first effort was about twenty-five years ago. I took hold of an invention—I don't know now what it was all about, but some one came to me and told me it was a good thing, and that there was lots of money in it. He persuaded me to invest $15,000, and I lived up to my beliefs by engaging a man to develop it. To make a long story short, I sunk $40,000 in it.

Then I took up the publication of a book. I called in a publisher and said to him: "I want you to publish this book along lines which I shall lay down. I am the employer, and you are the employee. I am going to show them some new kinks in the publishing business. And I want you to draw on me for money as you go along," which he did. He drew on me for $56,000. Then I asked him to take the book and call it off. But he refused to do that.

My next venture was with a machine for doing something or other. I knew less about that than I did about the invention. But I sunk $170,000 in the business, and I can't for the life of me recollect what it was the machine was to do.

I was still undismayed. You see, one of the strong points about my business life was that I never gave up. . . . My axiom is, to succeed in business: avoid my example.[51]

chapter eleven

BACK IN THE SADDLE: PLAYING THE INSIDER'S GAME

"It is good to obey all the rules when you're young, so you'll have the strength to break them when you're old."

*U*nable to sit idle on the sidelines, in 1898 Clemens again began to invest. Relying on Rogers's advice, he put his money in blue chip stocks, such as Federal Steel, a virtual monopoly created by J. Pierpont Morgan. That year he also discovered a carpet-weaving machine in Austria and considered buying the rights to the patents, but fortunately he had learned from the Paige typesetter ordeal and refrained. In 1900 he did become an equity investor in Plasmon, a food additive, purchasing a large enough interest to acquire a seat on the firm's board. Again, learning from the past, he did not overcommit himself. In the early 1900s, Clemens continued to view himself as a businessman and built a sizable portfolio, preferring to invest in monopolies organized by Rogers's cronies.

The bankruptcy of Webster & Company was a torturous event in Clemens's life, not a story he liked to rehash. In his autobiography, he concluded the episode with both a bold flourish and a painful admission:

> At the end of '98 or the beginning of '99 Mr. Rogers cabled me, at Vienna, "the creditors have all been paid a hundred cents on the dollar. There is eighteen thousand five hundred dollars left. What shall I do with it?"

I answered, "Put it in Federal Steel"—which he did, all except a thousand dollars, and took it out again in two months with a profit of a hundred and twenty-five per cent.

There—Thanks be! A hundred times I have tried to tell this intolerable story with a pen but I never could do it. It always made me sick before I got halfway to the middle of it. But this time I have held my grip and walked to the floor and emptied it all out of my system, and I hope to never hear of it again.[1]

In a further display of remorse, he even admitted to Rogers, "I robbed the family to feed my speculations."[2] Yet, as painful as his experience with Webster & Company, as well as his wayward investments, had been, Clemens was eager to hop into the Wall Street cauldron. With Rogers and men like J. Pierpont Morgan behind the formation of the conglomerate Federal Steel and intent on controlling the market, this particular investment was a safe bet.

Clemens Grasps the Wonders of Investing in Monopolies

While in Austria, in September 1898, he had first heard of the steel trust and wrote to Rogers, "The papers are telling about the vast steel trust, and they add that you are in it. I hope you have remembered to insert me into it too on the ground floor." Sure enough, Rogers bought Clemens preferred shares at steep discounts that cost him just over $17,000 but were worth $50,000 par. After receiving the good news, Clemens replied, "I would rather have that stock than be free of sin." An incorrigible optimist and risk taker, Clemens even considered mortgaging his Hartford house in order to buy another $25,000 worth.[3]

A month later, Clemens was basking in the Federal Steel steal. "If I could afford it I would be like this all the time;" he wrote to Rogers, "merely lie around and manage the Steel Company and never do any work."[4] In December Rogers sold the preferred stock for a profit of over $5,000 and immediately bought common stock in Federal that netted a profit of more than $4,500 in two weeks. By late January 1899 Clemens would pocket $16,000—almost doubling his investment—and he was feeling very flush: "I am gradually getting over the disorganizing effects of sudden wealth," he wrote to Rogers, "steadying down and resuming normalcy."[5] Yes, Clemens was fast on his way to winning another fortune, with a little help from a filthy rich friend.

Incidentally, after cranking out two books in 1894, *Pudd'nhead Wilson* and *Tom Sawyer Abroad*, and a book each in 1896 and 1897, *Personal Recollections of Joan of Arc* and *Following the Equator*, the revenue from which went a long way toward paying off his debts, not until 1906 would another appear. So, as we had witnessed after the success of the Grant book, Clemens, while certainly still writing in the interim years, was clearly not feeling pressed to work. He was far more interested in enjoying the fruits of his new investment vehicle: Henry "Hell Hound" Rogers, who, at the moment, had over $50,000 of Clemens's money to invest.[6]

On the heels of the successful steel monopoly investment, in May 1899 Clemens heard about a great copper combination— the Amalgamated Copper Company—which had none other than Rogers on its board of directors. He urged Rogers to invest some of his money "for you know how to make a copper hen lay a golden egg." Rogers did indeed make an investment for Clemens.[7] The latter 1890s witnessed an astounding number of such amalgamations or mergers of companies within many industries as financiers like Morgan sought to impose order on the U.S. economy—for their own profit, of course. Clemens unabashedly shared in the excitement of being an insider who stood to reap big rewards. "I wonder what it is you've got your financial eye on now—for I guessed from a remark you made that you are watching another combination," he wrote to Rogers in late 1899. "Don't leave me out; I want to be in, with the other capitalists."[8] Yes, Clemens had always wanted to be a capitalist, regardless of how much he enjoyed writing.

A Carpet–Weaving Machine Captures Clemens's Imagination

After all the wild speculating, it appeared that in his fast-approaching twilight years Clemens was displaying a more conservative side; at one point he instructed Rogers to put money "into a safe thing which stands a chance to rise in value."[9] He was willing to let investments lie "undisturbed"— such as the Brooklyn Gas Company, which had been bought at $75 and was now worth $155—until Rogers decreed that the harvest should be "raked in."[10] Well, he hadn't quite changed.

Clemens couldn't help himself; he was a chronic speculator. While vacationing in Vienna, in March 1898, he heard about a young Austrian, Jan Szczepanik, who had invented an incredibly advanced carpet-weaving machine. Clemens immediately told a literary colleague, "I would like to have the opportunity to raise capital & introduce it in America."[11] The very next day after hearing of the invention, Clemens researched weaving machines and textile factories, and that night he had a meeting with Szczepanik. Another inventor and invention had him hypnotized.

"I've landed a big fish to-day," an excited Clemens wrote to Rogers on March 17, 1898. "He is a costly one, but he is worth the money. . . . He is going to be the European Edison, I suppose." In this letter that ran for more than a few pages, he explained how he had met with Szczepanik and immediately negotiated for the North American rights to his invention. "I couldn't beat him down any from his price— $1,500,000;" Clemens explained, "he is well in cash, now, and knows the value of the invention nearly as well as I do. He said he would dearly like the fame of being associated in business with me, but that *I* knew he was not asking a high price."[12] Yes, it sounded like another Paige debacle in the making.

Nevertheless, over the coming weeks Clemens wrote one long letter after another concerning his great find in the Austrian inventor, who had a substantial laboratory in Vienna that further impressed Clemens. In another March letter to Rogers, at least he opened with a self-deprecating comment: "I feel like Col. Sellers," the colorful character in his 1873 satire *The Gilded Age*. Clemens certainly echoed Sellers as he related his conversation with Szczepanik's business agent, Ludwig Kleinberg, and expounded on the textile market, of which he knew little only days before but now considered himself an expert.

According to Clemens, he advised Kleinberg on a strategy for selling the rights to the patents: "I suggest that you stop those negotiations and put those people off two or three months. They are anxious now, they will not be less anxious then—just the reverse; people always want a thing that is denied them." The author-tycoon then estimated the potential market penetration Szczepanik might enjoy in the United States, and what savings a typical textile might realize if they used his highly automated weaving machine. Clemens concluded that if a company were formed to control the Szczepanik patents it would "collar $50,000,000 of that, as its share. Possibly more." Clearly, Clemens had been bitten by the monopoly bug gripping the American business landscape. In relating his conversation to Rogers, he even sounded like the controlling banker Morgan, who was creating a number of monopolies:

> Competition would be at an end in the Jacquard business, on this planet. Price-cutting would end. Fluctuations in values would cease. The business would be the safest and surest in the world; commercial panics could not seriously affect it; its stock would be as choice an investment as Government bonds. When the patents died the Company would be so powerful that it could still keep the whole business in its hands. Would you like to grant me the

privilege of placing the whole jacquard business of the world in the grip of a single Company? And don't you think that the business would grow—grow like a weed?

Kleinberg's response to Clemens's grand vision was tepid: "Ach, America—it is the country of the big! Let me get my breath—then we will talk."

Their conversation continued late into the night, and ended with Clemens boldly requesting an option for the patents that would "cover the world." Secrecy was paramount, he believed, and he did not want his name attached to Szczepanik. "And we will now keep the invention itself out of print as well as we can," he told Rogers. "Descriptions of it have been granted to the 'Dry Goods Economist' (New York) and to a syndicate of American papers. I have asked Mr. Kleinberg to suppress these, and he feels pretty sure he can do it."[13]

The secrecy and talk of big numbers did not impress Rogers, who did a little investigation of his own and hired a textile expert, William Whitman, to evaluate the machine's potential. He quickly put the kibosh on Clemens's high-flying, Morganesque dreams by forwarding Whitman's report. "I do not feel that it would be of any value to us in our mills," the textile expert wrote bluntly, "and the number of jacquard looms in America is so limited that I am of the opinion that there is no field for a company to develop the invention here. A cursory examination of the pamphlet leads me to place no very high value upon the invention, from a practical standpoint."[14] Clemens wisely listened and dropped his pursuit of the miracle carpet-weaving machine.

Addicted to Speculation, Clemens Gets into the Food Additive Business

Clemens once wrote, "Few of us can stand prosperity. Another man's I mean." But obviously he couldn't stand his own prosperity either, as he delved into yet another suspicious scheme. Undeterred in his pursuit of tycoondom, in March 1900 Clemens wrote to Rogers that "it was about time to look around & buy something. So I looked around and bought."[15]

What he bought was an interest in a futuristic-sounding product called Plasmon. Developed in Vienna and now being made by a Berlin-based firm, Plasmon was a food additive, a powder made from albumin, which is the waste milk from dairies. According to alleged experts, a pound of this by-product equated to 16 pounds of beef in terms of nutrition. A true believer, Clemens wrote to an acquaintance, "I take it in cold milk—all lumpy—not half dissolved. It has completely cured my ancient curse of indigestion."[16] And to colleague John MacAlister, who was also an investor in Plasmon, he wrote gleefully, "The scientific testimonials are strong enough to float Gibraltar."[17]

In this case, at least Clemens wasn't just diving in; he had been tracking the product for a couple of years—although this period as observer was no fault of his own. "I tried to get a chance in Plasmon when it was invented in Vienna two years ago, but failed;" he explained to Rogers, "but I have been keeping track of it since, and I got in here, through finding out that a special friend of mine was in it."[18] Naturally, he tried to entice Rogers: "I think it would be well" to "buy control of the company."[19] Rogers declined. He was involved in far bigger business deals, such as Federal Steel and Amalgamated Copper, that were reshaping America's economic landscape.

Clemens elected to invest $25,000 cash, for which he was given a one-sixth interest in the British syndicate that controlled the sales and distribution rights in Great Britain and was given a seat on the board. Wisely, he understood that he should invest enough to have a significant voice in the company; on the other hand, he would have to be careful to not overextend himself unnecessarily as he had with Paige. In 1901 the company was shipping seven to eight tons a month, and he was soon earning over $1,500 in quarterly dividends, which was more than Paige ever paid. (Of course, anything was more than nothing.) Clemens was convinced that he and MacAlister would eventually "clear £20,000 a month"—which equated to $100,000.[20]

Ever the optimist, Clemens became more deeply involved by investing more than $30,000 in the syndicate created to control Plasmon in the United States, and, convinced Plasmon would dominate the market if capital could be raised to produce and market it, he started promoting the stock. A sophisticated marketer, Clemens knew the name behind the brand sometimes counted as much as the product itself, so he took it upon himself to solicit funds from Andrew Carnegie—just as he had when Webster & Company was struggling.

In May 1900 he actually wrote Carnegie's three-year old daughter Margaret in a bid to soften up the tight-fisted Scotsman. Knowing full well Carnegie would be reading the letter, he instructed Margaret to give her daddy "five or six fingers of Scotch, and then talk. This will mellow him up and enlarge his views, and before he solidifies again you will *have* him. That is to say, you will have his cheque for £500, drawn to order of 'Plasmon Syndicate, Ltd.' which you will send to me, and you and I will be personally responsible that the money is back in his hands in six months, and along with it 500 shares in the Plasmon Company, all paid up."[21] Clemens's charm again failed to convince Carnegie, who lived by the motto: "Put all your eggs in one basket and watch that basket." In other words, Carnegie stuck to steel.

While the British Plasmon syndicate continued to pay relatively decent returns, the U.S. syndicate did not, and in early 1903 Clemens suspected foul play. In 1904 his suspicions were confirmed when the company's treasurer, Ralph W. Ashcroft, informed him that he had not been given bonus shares he deserved. Within two years, Clemens would find himself swindled by two "rascals" who formed a new U.S. syndicate that did not include Clemens and he would find himself out $50,000. "If I had kept out of American Plasmon I would now be a good business man;" he lamented to Rogers, "but as it is, I am only half a good business man."[22]

A Few Investment Temptations Are Resisted

Clemens did learn to stop throwing good money after bad. In late 1901, a Wall Street broker, Charles Fairchild, enticed Clemens to invest $16,000 in the American Mechanical Cashier Company, which was to manufacture an automatic money-changing and registering machine. It was hardly a sure bet because there was serious competition. For one, a patent for a mechanical cash register had been issued to James Ritty almost 20 years earlier, and his successful machine was now the property of steely John H. Patterson, who ran the National Cash Register Company with an iron fist. Regardless, with glowing assurance, Fairchild claimed that Clemens's $16,000 would soon be worth $40,000. After a series of production delays, eight months later found Fairchild telling Clemens, "The machine is as yet one of promise rather than performance."[23] It was Paige all over again. Fortunately, Clemens walked away.

And the chronic speculator continued to soak up Rogers's prudent wisdom. In August 1902 Clemens informed Rogers that he had a wonderful opportunity to buy $50,000 worth of bonds in the Kansas City, Mexico and Orient Railroad. Rogers replied with admirable patience: "In the first place, it would seem quite natural to inquire as to the Kansas City, Mexico & Orient Railroad. In view of the fact that Poor's Manual makes no reference to the railroad, it is reasonably fair to assume that it is not of any great prominence. I certainly would never undertake to enter into the arrangement for myself. . . . Do be careful. It is much easier to keep out of trouble than it is to get out. You and I know that of old."[24]

The firm had just laid its first rail in 1901 and would grow until 1911, when, building a line through Mexico, its tracks and equipment would come under attack by revolutionary Pancho Villa. In a delicious twist of fate, Villa had been one of the railroad's contractors. Already overextended, the Kansas City, Mexico and Orient Railroad would declare bankruptcy in 1911, but reorganize. While Clemens may have realized a profit prior to colorful 1911, he did not invest. Rogers's advice was well taken: Once in trouble, it was much more difficult to extract oneself than it would have been to show restraint from the start.

Great Riches Cannot Stop the Greatest Swindle

While Clemens still had his perverse need to speculate, he fortunately continued to rely on Rogers to manage his investments. In June 1901 he asked Rogers to invest in a railroad combination that was being orchestrated by Morgan and financier E. H. Harriman: "Put me in deep, in the Monoline combination—and do me a line and tell me about it when you've accomplished the cinch." There was also a $20,000 investment in Union Pacific, as well as an investment in the Chicago & Alton Railroad. And he held stock in the latest and greatest steel amalgamation, U.S. Steel, which would soon yield a 27 percent return.[25]

As of May 1904, Clemens was receiving dividends from the following investments: U.S. Steel preferred stock, Brooklyn Union Gas, Borden's Condensed Milk, Chicago & Alton preferred, Union Pacific preferred, and the Jewell Pin Company. In addition, he owned Amalgamated Copper stock; had 500 shares of Utah Consolidated Mining Company stock, which he would sell in January 1906 for $34,700; owned 400 shares of the Anaconda Company, another copper giant whose name stated its intention; and Rogers put him into International Navigation, a shipping combine financed by yet another Morgan syndicate.[26] Adding to their bountiful swag, Livy's stock in the Langdon family's coal company was worth $100,000 and she owned $75,000 worth of other stock that her brother had purchased for her.[27] When not hobnobbing in Europe's magnificent cities, the family resided in a stone mansion at 21 Fifth Avenue, New York City, which Clemens had leased for a mere $3,000 a year for three years.

However, all of his wealth could not help Clemens when he was faced with the greatest crisis in his life. It was what he called the greatest swindle: the death of Livy at the age of 57. After years of frail health, she passed away on June 5, 1905, at their rented villa in Florence, Italy. The death was sudden— one moment she was cheerful and happy, the next gone. A day later he wrote to his old friend Howells, "I am tired & old; I wish I were with Livy." Two weeks later, a deeply wounded Clemens jotted in his notebook, "Ah, this odious swindle, human life."[28]

A year after Livy's death, Clemens wrote to Rogers, "Nothing agrees with me. If I drink coffee it gives me dyspepsia; if I drink wine it gives me the gout; if I go to church it gives me dysentery. A vacation seems necessary."[29] He and Rogers, who would die in 1909, would vacation together in Bermuda on a number of occasions, or cruise the northeast coast aboard Rogers's 227-foot yacht. Together, this unlikely pair of widowers played poker, smoked cigars, and entertained each other with outrageous stories only old men can get away with.

In the coming years, Clemens essentially put himself out to pasture by building a house in bucolic Redding, Connecticut, but the home was not to be filled with happy memories of grandchildren running about. Here his 29-year-old daughter Jean died from a seizure the night of December 23, 1909. With only Clara, who had married Ossip Gabrilowitsch, remaining of his immediate family, mercifully, Clemens died on April 21, 1910, and was buried next to Livy in the family plot in Elmira, New York. Four months later, Clara gave birth to a baby girl,

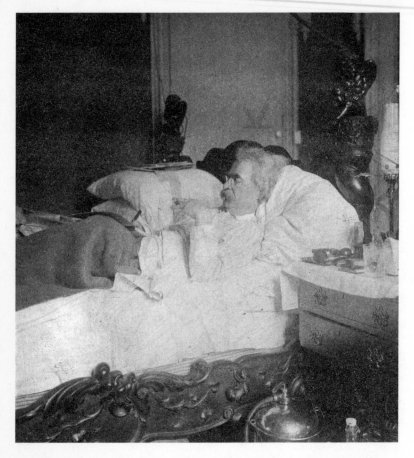

In 1906, at age 71, Clemens preferred to use his bedroom as his office.
(COURTESY OF THE MARK TWAIN HOUSE & MUSEUM, HARTFORD, CT)

Nina, who would be Clemens's last direct descendent. At the
time of Nina's death in 1966, she was living off the Clemens
estate, which was then valued at two million dollars.[30] Fortunately, Mark Twain lives on.

No real estate is permanently valuable but the grave.

—Sam Clemens, 1898

QUIRKY HABITS AND BRAZEN PHILOSOPHY

How to Live a Long, Successful Life

*"As for drinking, I have no rule about that.
When the others drink I like to help."*

Clemens always enjoyed a good party and his 70th birthday bash in December 1905 did not disappoint him. His friends hosted him at New York City's most venerable steakhouse: Delmonico's. He was expected to tantalize the crowd with his humor, and so he did. In his speech, he revealed his personal habits for achieving longevity and personal success. Naturally, smoking cigars, drinking, and exercise (actually, a lack of exercise) were critical elements.

The Seventieth Birthday Address

I have achieved my seventy years in the usual way: by sticking strictly to a scheme of life which would kill anybody else. It sounds like an exaggeration, but that is really the common rule for attaining to old age. When we examine the programme of any of these garrulous old people we always find that the habits which have preserved them would have decayed us; that the way of life which enabled them to live upon the property of their heirs so long, as Mr. Choate says, would have put us out of commission ahead of time. I will offer here, as a sound maxim, this: That we can't reach old age by another man's road.

I will now teach, offering my way of life to whomsoever desires to commit suicide by the scheme which has enabled me to beat the doctor and the hangman for seventy years. Some of the details may sound untrue, but they are not. I am not here to deceive; I am here to teach.

(Continued)

How to Live a Long, Successful Life *(Continued)*

We have no permanent habits until we are forty. Then they begin to harden, presently they petrify, then business begins. Since forty I have been regular about going to bed and getting up—and that is one of the main things. I have made it a rule to go to bed when there wasn't anybody left to sit up with; and I have made it a rule to get up when I had to. This has resulted in an unswerving regularity of irregularity. It has saved me sound, but it would injure another person.

In the matter of diet—which is another main thing—I have been persistently strict in sticking to the things which didn't agree with me until one or the other of us got the best of it. Until lately I got the best of it myself. But last spring I stopped frolicking with mince-pie after midnight; up to then I had always believed it wasn't loaded. For thirty years I have taken coffee and bread at eight in the morning, and no bite nor sup until seven-thirty in the evening. Eleven hours. That is all right for me, and is wholesome, because I have never had a headache in my life, but headachy people would not reach seventy comfortably by that road, and they would be foolish to try it. And I wish to urge upon you this—which I think is wisdom—that if you find you can't make seventy by any but an uncomfortable road, don't you go. When they take off the Pullman and retire you to the rancid smoker, put on your things, count your checks, and get out at the first way station where there's a cemetery.

I have made it a rule never to smoke more than one cigar at a time. I have no other restriction as regards smoking. I do not know just when I began to smoke, I only know that it was in my father's lifetime, and that I was discreet. He passed from this life early in 1847, when I was a shade past eleven; ever since then I have smoked publicly. As an example to others, and not that I care for moderation myself, it has always been my rule never to smoke when asleep, and never to refrain when awake. It is a good rule. I mean, for me; but some of you know quite well that it wouldn't answer for everybody that's trying to get to be seventy.

I smoke in bed until I have to go to sleep; I wake up in the night, sometimes once, sometimes twice; sometimes three times, and I never waste any of these opportunities to smoke. This habit is so old and dear and precious to me that I would feel as you, sir, would feel if you should lose the only moral you've got—meaning the chairman—if you've got one: I am making no charges: I will grant, here, that I have stopped smoking now and then, for a few months at a time, but it was not on principle, it was only to show off; it was to pulverize those critics who said I was a slave to my habits and couldn't break my bonds. . . .

As for drinking, I have no rule about that. When the others drink I like to help; otherwise I remain dry, by habit and preference. This dryness does not hurt me, but it could easily hurt you, because you are different. You let it alone. . . .

I have never taken any exercise, except sleeping and resting, and I never intend to take any. Exercise is loathsome. And it cannot be any benefit when you are tired; and I was always tired. But let another person try my way, and see where he will come out. I desire now to repeat and emphasise that maxim: We can't reach old age by another man's road. My habits protect my life, but they would assassinate you.[31]

SELECTED
MARK TWAIN MAXIMS

ADVERSITY

By trying we can easily learn to endure adversity—another man's I mean.

ADVERTISING

Many a small thing has been made large by the right kind of advertising.

AUDIENCES

When an audience do not complain, it is a compliment, & when they do it is a compliment, too, if unaccompanied by violence.

BANKERS

A banker is a fellow who lends you his umbrella when the sun is shining and wants it back the minute it begins to rain.

BANQUETS

A banquet is probably the most fatiguing thing in the world except ditchdigging. It is the insanest of all recreations. The inventor of it overlooked no detail that could furnish weariness, distress, harassment, and acute and long-sustained misery of mind and body.

BOLDNESS

The timid man yearns for full value and demands a tenth. The bold man strikes for double value and compromises on par.

BUSINESS

Let your sympathies and your compassion be always with the under dog in the fight—this is magnanimity; but bet on the other one—this is business.

The primary rule of business success is loyalty to your employer. That's all right—as a theory. What is the matter with loyalty to yourself?

CHARACTER

One must keep one's character. Earn a character first if you can, and if you can't, then assume one. From the code of morals I have been following and revising and revising for 72 years I remember one detail. All my life I have been honest—comparatively honest. I could never use money I had not made honestly—I could only lend it.

There is no character, howsoever good and fine, but it can be destroyed by ridicule, howsoever poor and witless. Observe the ass, for instance: his character is about perfect, he is the choicest spirit among all the humbler animals, yet see what ridicule has brought him to. Instead of feeling complimented when we are called an ass, we are left in doubt.

COMPLIMENTS

An occasional compliment is necessary to keep up one's self-respect. . . . When you can't get a compliment any other way, pay yourself one.

I have been complimented many times and they always embarrass me; I always feel that they have not said enough.

The happy phrasing of a compliment is one of the rarest of human gifts and the happy delivery of it another.

None but an ass pays a compliment and asks a favor at the same time. There are many asses.

Conformity

We are discreet sheep; we wait to see how the drove is going, and then go with the drove.

Conformity—the natural instinct to passively yield to that vague something recognized as authority.

Diligence

Diligence is a good thing, but taking things easy is much more restful.

Dressing for Success

Clothes make the man. Naked people have little or no influence in society.

Strip the human race, absolutely naked, and it would be a real democracy. But the introduction of even a rag of tiger skin, or a cowtail, could make a badge of distinction and be the beginning of a monarchy.

Modesty died when clothes were born.

Duty

Do something every day that you don't want to do; this is the golden rule for acquiring the habit of doing your duty without pain.

Do your duty and repent tomorrow.

A man's first duty is to his own conscience and honor; the party and country come second to that, and never first.

Hardship

It is poison—rank poison to knuckle down to care and hardships. They must come to us all, albeit in different shapes—and we may not escape them—it is not possible—but we may swindle them out of half of their puissance with a stiff upper lip.

HONESTY

Honesty is the best policy—when there is money in it.

There are people who think that honesty is always the best policy. This is a superstition. There are times when the appearance of it is worth six of it.

Yes, even I am dishonest. Not in many ways, but in some. Forty-one, I think it is.

IDEAS

The man with a new idea is a Crank until the idea succeeds.

The fact is the human race is not only slow about borrowing valuable ideas—it sometimes persists in not borrowing them at all.

There is no such thing as a new idea. It is impossible. We simply take a lot of old ideas and put them into a sort of mental kaleidoscope. We give them a turn and they make new and curious combinations. We keep on turning and making new combinations indefinitely; but they are the same old pieces of colored glass that have been in use through all the ages.

INSTINCT

For all the talk you hear about knowledge being such a wonderful thing, instinct is worth forty of it for real unerringness.

INVENTION

Name the greatest of all inventors. Accidents.

A man invents a thing which could revolutionize the arts, produce mountains of money, and bless the earth, and who will bother with it or show any interest in it?—and so you are just as poor as you were before. But you invent some worthless thing to amuse yourself with, and would throw it away if let alone, and all of a sudden the whole world makes a snatch for it and out crops a fortune.

It takes a thousand men to invent a telegraph, or a steam engine, or a phonograph, or a photograph, or a telephone, or any other Important thing—and the last man gets the credit and we forget the others. He added his little mite—that is all he did.

INVESTING

Prosperity is the best protector of principle.

October: This is one of the peculiarly dangerous months to speculate in stocks in. The other are July, January, September, April, November, May, March, June, December, August, and February.

MERIT

Merit alone should constitute the one title to eminence, and we Americans can afford to look down and spit upon miserable titled nonentities.

I am prouder to have climbed up to where I am just by sheer natural merit than I would be to ride the very sun in the zenith and have to reflect that I was nothing but a poor little accident, and got shot up there out of somebody else's catapult. To me, merit is everything—in fact, the only thing. All else is dross.

MONEY

The lack of money is the root of all evil.

Some men worship rank, some worship heroes, some worship power, some worship God, & over these ideals they dispute & cannot unite—but they all worship money.

OPPORTUNITY

I was seldom able to see an opportunity until it had ceased to be one.

POVERTY

Honest poverty is a gem that even a King might be proud to call his own, but I wish to sell out. I have sported that kind of jewelry long enough.

It is good to begin life poor; it is good to begin life rich—these are wholesome; but to begin it poor and prospectively rich! The man who has not experienced it cannot imagine the curse of it.

PROBLEM SOLVING

Plain question and plain answer make the shortest road out of most perplexities.

PROSPERITY

Prosperity is the surest breeder of insolence I know.

When you ascend the hill of prosperity, may you not meet a friend.

Few of us can stand prosperity. Another man's I mean.

The offspring of riches: Pride, vanity, ostentation, arrogance, tyranny.

RULES

It is good to obey all the rules when you're young, so you'll have the strength to break them when you're old.

SMOKING

As an example to others, and not that I care for moderation myself, it has always been my rule never to smoke when asleep and never to refrain when awake.

SPECULATION

There are two times in a man's life when he should not speculate: when he can't afford it, and when he can.

SUCCESS

It is strange the way the ignorant and inexperienced so often and so undeservedly succeed when the informed and the experienced fail.

Human nature is the same everywhere; it deifies success, it has nothing but scorn for defeat.

All you need in this life is ignorance and confidence, and then Success is sure.

WEALTH

How unfortunate and how narrowing a thing it is for a man to have wealth who makes a god of it instead of a servant.

What is the chief end of man?—to get rich. In what way?—dishonestly if we can; honestly if we must. Who is God, the one only and true? Money is God. God and Greenbacks and Stock—father, son, and the ghost of same—three persons in one; these are the true and only God, mighty and supreme.

NOTES

Today, much of what Samuel L. Clemens wrote is not only in the public domain but available on the Internet. A particularly key resource is Project Gutenberg, which can be accessed via http://onlinebooks.library.upenn.edu/lists.html and or via http://www.gutenberg.org/browse/authors/. This material includes his books, speeches, essays, and letters.

Chapter One   Early Hard Knocks on the Road to Riches and Fame

1. Ron Powers, *Mark Twain: A Life* (New York: Free Press, 2005), 9.
2. Mark Twain, *The Autobiography of Mark Twain* (New York: Harper & Brothers, 1917), 18–19. A two-volume set can be accessed online at http://gutenberg.net.au/ebooks02/0200551h.html.
3. Ibid, 22–23.
4. Ibid, 24–25.
5. Ibid, 218.
6. Ibid, 24–25.
7. Ibid, 87–88.
8. Samuel L. Clemens (SLC) to Henry Clemens (HC), 5 August 1856, vol. I, http://onlinebooks.library.upenn.edu/webbin/gutbook/lookup?num=3199. Except where noted otherwise, all letters referenced in this book are from the six volumes on this web site and are hereafter referred to as "Letters" with date and volume number only.
9. Powers, *Mark Twain: A Life*, 46.

10. Samuel Charles Webster, *Mark Twain, Businessman* (Boston: Little, Brown and Company, 1946), 20.
11. Twain, *Autobiography*, 83.
12. Ibid, 85.
13. Edwin G. Burrows and Mike Wallace, *Gotham: A History of New York City to 1898* (New York: Oxford University Press, 1999), 737.
14. Ibid., 748.
15. SLC to Jane Clemens (JC), 31 August 1853. Mark Twain's Letters. Vol. I, 1853–1866, edited by Edward Marquess Branch, et al. (Berkeley: University of California Press, 1988.)
16. SLC to Orion Clemens (OC), 28 November 1853, Letters, vol. I.
17. SLC to Mrs. Moffett, 5 December 1853, Letters, vol I.
18. SLC to JC, 10 June 1856, Letters, vol. I.

How to Outwit Your Superiors

19. Mark Twain, "Advice to Youth," http://pintday.org/funny/advicetoyouth.

Chapter Two   How to Quit a Good Job and Then Lose a Million Dollars

1. Twain, *Autobiography*, 98.
2. Mark Twain, *Life on the Mississippi* (New York: Penguin, 1984), 64.
3. Webster, *Mark Twain, Businessman*, 33.
4. Twain, *Life on the Mississippi*, 51.
5. Twain, *Autobiography*, 98.
6. Twain, *Life on the Mississippi*, 72–73.
7. Ibid., 76.
8. Ibid., 86.
9. Ibid., 94.
10. Ibid., 118–119.
11. Ibid., 155.

12. Ibid., 122.
13. Ibid., 79–80.
14. Ibid., 117.
15. Ibid., 152.
16. Twain, *Autobiography*, 102.
17. Mark Twain, *Roughing It* (New York: Viking Press, 1984), 1:1–2.
18. Ibid., 5.
19. SLC to JC, date not given but September or October 1861, Letters, vol. I.
20. Twain, *Roughing It*, 1:183–184.
21. SLC to Pamela Moffett , 25 October 1861, Letters, vol. 1.
22. Henry Nash Smith, ed., *Mark Twain of the Enterprise* (Berkeley: University of California Press, 1957), 119–121.
23. Twain, *Roughing It*, 1:186.
24. Ibid., 191.
25. Ibid., 199.
26. Ibid., 205.
27. SLC to OC, 10, 13, 17, and 19 April 1862, quoted in Powers, *Mark Twain*, 108
28. SLC to OC, Summer 1862, Webster, *Mark Twain, Businessman*, 70–71.
29. SLC to OC, undated fragment, 1862, Letters, vol. I.
30. Twain, *Roughing It*, 1:276.
31. Ibid., 283–284.
32. Ibid., 244.
33. Twain, *Autobiography*, 110.
34. Twain, *Roughing It*, 1:251.
35. Ibid., 2:1.

Even a Crank Knows to Dress for Success

36. Powers, *Mark Twain: A Life*, 178; Webster, *Mark Twain, Businessman*, 92.
37. Twain, *Autobiography*, 149–150.
38. Interview in New York *World*, 8 December 1906.

Chapter Three   Sometimes Necessity Is the Mother of a Career

1. Twain, *Roughing It*, 2:4.
2. Ibid., 5.
3. Ibid., 19.
4. SLC to mother and sister, 16 February 1863, in Webster, *Mark Twain, Businessman*, 77–78.
5. Twain, *Roughing It*, 2:76.
6. SLC to JC and Mrs. Moffett, 19 August 1863, Letters, vol. I.
7. See Powers, *Mark Twain: A Life*, 118-119, for more on the origin of the pseudonym Mark Twain and its meaning.
8. Powers, *Mark Twain: A Life*, 145.
9. SLC to Mrs. Jane Clemens and Mrs. Moffett, 25 September 1864, Letters, vol. I.
10. Twain, *Roughing It*, 2:137.
11. Ibid., 146.
12. SLC to OC, 19 and 29 October 1865, in Powers, *Mark Twain: A Life*, 155–156.
13. SLC to Mrs. Jane Clemens and Mrs. Moffett, 20 January 1866, in Powers, *Mark Twain: A Life*, 159.
14. SLC to Mrs. Jane Clemens and Mrs. Moffett, 24 January 1868, Letters, vol. II.
15. Twain, *Roughing It*, 2:164.
16. Ibid., 251.
17. Ibid., 292.
18. Twain, Autobiography, 143, and Powers, *Mark Twain: A Life*, 163.
19. Ibid., 182.
20. Powers, *Mark Twain: A Life*, 165.
21. SLC to Mrs. Jane Clemens and family, 4 December 1866, Letters, vol. I.
22. Twain *Autobiography*, 173.

Overcoming Stage Fright and Winning the Audience as a Public Speaker

23. Twain, *Autobiography*, 166–167.
24. Twain, *Roughing It*, 292–296.

Chapter Four   Welcome to Corporate America

1. SLC to Mrs. Jane Clemens and family, 7 June 1867, Letters, vol. II.
2. Elisha Bliss (EB) to SLC, 21 November 1867, Letters, vol. II.
3. SLC to EB, 2 December 1867, Letters, vol. II.
4. SLC to Folks, 20 November 1867, in Webster, *Mark Twain, Businessman*, 95.
5. SLC to Mrs. Jane Clemens and Mrs. Moffett, 24 January 1868, Letters, vol. II.
6. Ibid.
7. Twain, *Autobiography*, 154.
8. SLC to Folks, 4 June 1868, Letters, vol. II.
9. Twain, *Autobiography*, 190.
10. SLC to Mary Fairbanks, 13 March 1869, in Powers, *Mark Twain: A Life*, 270.
11. SLC to EB, 22 July 1869, in Powers, *Mark Twain: A Life*, 273.
12. Twain, *Autobiography*, 158–159.
13. SLC to EB, 28 January 1870, Letters, vol. II.
14. Powers, *Mark Twain: A Life*, 277.
15. Ibid., 318 and 322.
16. Ibid., 350.
17. SLC to EB, 15 May 1871, Letters, vol. II.
18. SLC to EB, 28 November 1870; and EB to SLC, 30 November 1870, in Hamlin Hill, ed., *Letters to His Publisher, 1867–1894* (Berkeley: University of California Press, 1967), 42–44 (hereafter "LTHP").
19. Twain, *Autobiography*, 225.

20. Powers, *Mark Twain: A Life*, 322; SLC to Elisha Bliss, LTHP, 71.
21. LTHP, 69.
22. SLC to EB, 24 June 1876; EB to SLC, 18 July 1876; and SLC to EB, 22 July 1876, LTHP, 99–100.
23. SLC to W. D. Howells, 5 July 1875, Letters, vol. II.
24. SLC to James R. Osgood, 17 January 1876, LTHP, 93–94.
25. SLC to W. D. Howells, 25 April 1876, Letters, vol. III.
26. Twain, *Autobiography*, 225–226.
27. Ibid., 227.
28. Twain, *Autobiography*, circa 226.
29. SLC to OC, 24 October 1880, Letters, vol. III.
30. Twain, *Autobiography*, 228.

The Author's Stormy Work Habits
31. Anonymous interviewer, "Mark Twain on His Methods of Work," Bombay (India) *Gazette*, 23 January 1896, reprinted in Louis J. Budd, ed., *Interviews with Samuel L. Clemens 1874–1910* (Arlington: American Literary Realism, 1977).
32. SLC to W. D. Howells, in Boston, no date given, Letters, vol. II.
33. SLC to EB, 15 May 1871, Letters, vol. II.
34. Twain, *Autobiography*, 266.

Chapter Five   Sucked into the Gilded Age
1. Mark Twain and Charles Dudley Warner, *The Gilded Age, A Tale of Today* (New York: Library of America Edition, 2002), 120.
2. Ibid., 356.
3. Ibid., 195–196.
4. Powers, *Mark Twain: A Life*, 287.
5. SLC to Mrs. Jane Clemens and family, 4 June 1868, Letters, vol. II.
6. SLC to W. D. Howells, 4 May 1878, Letters, vol. III.
7. SLC to OC, 1 August 1870, in Powers, *Mark Twain: A Life*, 286.

8. SLC to OC, 9 September 1870, Letters, vol. II.

9. SLC to OC, 1 March 1875, in Powers, *Mark Twain: A Life*, 372.

10. http://www.twainquotes.com/FullerRevisited.html, January 23, 2006.

11. SLC to Mrs. Jane Clemens and family, 4 June 1868, Letters, vol. II.

12. SLC to EB, 12 August 1869, LTHP, 26.

13. Powers, *Mark Twain: A Life*, 274, 282, 297.

14. Ibid., 350, 421.

15. Webster, *Mark Twain, Businessman*, 140.

16. http://www.twainquotes.com/Invention.html, 13 February 2006.

17. Fred Kaplan, *The Singular Mark Twain: A Biography* (New York: Doubleday, 2003), 270–271; and http://www.twainquotes.com/19390312.html, 13 February 2006.

18. SLC to OC, 11 August 1872, Letters, vol. II.

19. Webster, *Mark Twain, Businessman*, 160–161 and 273; and Frederick Anderson, Lin Salamo, and Bernard L. Stein, eds., *Mark Twain's Notebooks and Journals*, vol. II (Berkeley: University of California Press, 1975), 12.

20. Twain, *Autobiography*, 230.

21. http://www.druglibrary.org/SCHAFFER/GENERAL/twins1.htm, February 14, 2006.

22. *Notebooks and Journals*, vol. II, 56.

23. Twain, *Autobiography*, 232.

24. Ibid., 232–233.

25. SLC to My Dear Mother, 17 February 1878, Letters, vol. III.

26. *Notebooks and Journals*, vol. II, 135.

27. SLC to Orion Clemens and family, 22 July 1883, Letters, vol. III.

28. See *Notebooks & Journals*, vol. III, 19–32 as an example of his obsession with the game.

29. SLC to W. D. Howells in Boston, 1883 (no date given), Letters, vol. III; *Notebooks and Journals*, vol. II, 252.

30. See letters in Webster, *Mark Twain, Businessman*, 218–223.

31. SLC to Charles L. Webster (CLW), 1 July 1884, Webster, *Mark Twain, Businessman*, 263.
32. SLC to Fred J. Hall (FJH), 17 February 1891, LTHP, 270.
33. http://www.twainquotes.com/Invention.html, February 13, 2006.
34. SLC to FJH, 8 March 1892, LTHP, 307.
35. SLC to CLW, 31 October 1884, Webster, *Mark Twain, Businessman*, 279–280.
36. CLW to SLC, 19 January 1884, Webster, *Mark Twain, Businessman*, 182.
37. SLC to CLW, 15 January 1885; SLC to CLW, 19 January 1885; CLW to SLC, 10 January 1885; and SLC to CLW, 25 January 1885, Webster, Mark Twain, Businessman, 291, 180, 181, 296.
38. SLC to CLW, June 29, 1883, Webster, *Mark Twain, Businessman*, 216–217.

Managing a Glut of Loathsome Correspondence

39. SLC to My Dear Sister, 12 June 1885, Webster, *Mark Twain, Businessman*, 325.
40. SLC to CLW, 28 October 1885, Webster, *Mark Twain, Businessman*, 334.
41. Mark Twain, "One of Mankind's Bores," http://www.twainquotes.com/Galaxy/187102e.html.

***Chapter Six* Seeing and Seizing Opportunities**

1. Powers, *Mark Twain: A Life*, 362.
2. SLC to unnamed manufacturer, 19 March 1875, Letters, vol. III.
3. SLC to unknown person, 24 April 1883, Powers, *Mark Twain: A Life*, 478.
4. Fred Kaplan, *The Singular Mark Twain: A Biography* (New York: Doubleday, 2003), 428.
5. SLC to Howells, 28 February 1891 and 3 March 1891, in Powers, *Mark Twain: A Life*, 535.

6. SLC to Frank Bliss, 10 June 1879, LTHP, 116.
7. SLC to Pamela Clemens, 28 February 1880, in Powers, *Mark Twain: A Life*, 435.
8. SLC to EB, 20 March 1880, LTHP, 121–122.
9. SLC to OC, 26 February 1880, in Webster, *Mark Twain, Businessman*, 142.
10. SLC to OC, 27 November 1880, in Webster, *Mark Twain, Businessman*, 148.
11. SLC to Howells, 15 February 1887, in Powers, *Mark Twain: A Life*, 449.
12. SLC to Dear Sister, 16 March 1881, in Webster, *Mark Twain, Businessman*, 150; and SLC to Dan Slote, March 1881, in Webster, *Mark Twain, Businessman*, 151.
13. Charles H. Gold, *Hatching Ruin* (Columbia: University of Missouri Press, 2003), 16; and Powers, *Mark Twain: A Life*, 448.
14. SLC to Daniel Slote, 31 March 1881, in Webster, *Mark Twain, Businessman*, 152.
15. SLC to Dear Sister, 16 March 1881, in Webster, *Mark Twain, Businessman*, 150.
16. QSLC to CLW, 29 April 1881.
17. QSLC to CLW, 6 May 1881, in Webster, *Mark Twain, Businessman*, 153–154.
18. SLC to CLW, 6 May and 14 May 1881, Webster, *Mark Twain, Businessman*, 153–155; and CLW to SLC, 18 May 1881, reprinted in Mark Twain, *Notebooks and Journals*, vol. II (Berkeley: University of California Press, 1975–1979), 393.
19. See letters in Webster, *Mark Twain, Businessman*, 155–157.
20. SLC to CLW, 2 October 1882, in Webster, *Mark Twain, Businessman*, 201–203.
21. SLC to CLW, 20 June 1881, in Webster, *Mark Twain, Businessman*, 160.
22. SLC to CLW, 17 August 1881, in Webster, *Mark Twain, Businessman*, 165.
23. http://bancroft.berkeley.edu/MTP/databases.html.

24. SLC to CLW, 22 November 1881, and Webster's response, in Webster, *Mark Twain, Businessman*, 177.
25. SLC to CLW, 24 November 1881, in Webster, *Mark Twain, Businessman*, 178–179.
26. SLC to CLW, 9 August 1882, in Webster, *Mark Twain, Businessman*, 193–194.
27. CLW to SLC, 23 November 1881, in Gold, 34.
28. Twain, *Autobiography*, 229; and Powers, *Mark Twain: A Life*, 452.
29. Pamela Clemens to Orion Clemens, 30 August 1882, in Webster, *Mark Twain, Businessman*, 195.
30. SLC to CLW, September 1882, in Webster, *Mark Twain, Businessman*, 199.
31. Twain, *Autobiography*, 229.
32. Ibid., 230.
33. *Notebooks and Journals*, vol. II, 491. See investment in N.Y. Vaporizing Company that is listed in his portfolio.
34. SLC to Pamela Moffett, 1 March 1881; Fred Kaplan, *Singular Mark Twain*, 365; Twain, *Autobiography*, 230; and *Notebooks and Journals*, vol. II, p. 490.
35. Powers, *Mark Twain: A Life*, 436.
36. CLW to SLC, undated, in Gold, *Hatching Ruin*, 36.
37. Powers, *Mark Twain: A Life*, 490–491.
38. SLC to CLW, undated 1881, in Webster, *Mark Twain, Businessman*, 171.
39. SLC to CLW, 28 October 1881, in Webster, *Mark Twain, Businessman*, 175.
40. SLC to CLW, 11 January 1882, in Webster, *Mark Twain, Businessman*, 182.
41. CLW to SLC, 26 October 1881, in Gold, 29.
42. SLC to CLW, 25 October 1881, in Webster, *Mark Twain, Businessman*, 172.
43. CLW to SLC, 3 and 6 December 1881, in Gold, *Hatching Ruin*, 30.

44. Alexander & Green to SLC, 24 December 1881, in *Hatching Ruin*, Gold, 37.
45. *Notebooks and Journals*, vol. II, 252.
46. Ibid., 302.
47. Fred Kaplan, *Singular Mark Twain*, 360.
48. *Notebooks and Journals*. vol. II, 490–491.
49. Ibid., 416.
50. Frank Fuller to SLC, 23 March 1882, *Notebooks and Journals*, vol. II, 459–460.
51. SLC to CLW, 5 September 1884, Webster, *Mark Twain, Businessman*, 275.
52. Webster, *Mark Twain, Businessman*, 159.
53. SLC to CLW, 31 October 1884, Webster, *Mark Twain, Businessman*, 280.
54. See Peter Krass, *Carnegie* (New York: John Wiley & Sons, 2002).
55. Powers, *Mark Twain: A Life*, 448.
56. SLC to CLW, 19 January 1885, Webster, *Mark Twain, Businessman*, 293.
57. SLC to CLW, 25 April 1884, Webster, *Mark Twain, Businessman*, 250–251.
58. SLC to the Rev. J—, in Baltimore, 2 March 1885, Letters, vol. III.

The Half-Soled Stockbroker
59. Mark Twain, "Daniel In The Lion's Den—And Out Again All Right," *The Californian*, November 5, 1864.

Chapter Seven **Bold Vision and Imagination**
1. SLC to James R. Osgood, 21 December 1883, LTHP, 164–165.
2. SLC to CLW, October 26, 1881, in Webster, *Mark Twain, Businessman*, 174; and SLC to CLW, 24 and 25 June 1884, 261–262.

3. SLC memo, 18 July 1881, in Webster, *Mark Twain, Businessman*, 161.

4. Webster, *Mark Twain, Businessman*, 238.

5. LTHP, 170–171; and Webster, *Mark Twain, Businessman*, 313.

6. Twain, *Autobiography*, 234–235.

7. SLC to CLW, 3 or 4 March 1884; 241; SLC to CLW, 15 January 1885; and SLC to CLW, 19 January 1885, in Webster, *Mark Twain, Businessman*, 241, 291–292, 293.

8. SLC to SCW, May 24, 1884, IBID, pp. 255–256.

9. SLC to FJH, 24 July 1889, LTHP, 253–254.

10. SLC to CLW, 29 February 1884, LTHP, 172.

11. SLC to CLW, 1 September 1884, in Webster, *Mark Twain, Businessman*, 274.

12. SLC to CLW, 14 April 1884, LTHP, 173.

13. SLC to CLW, 1 September 1884, LTHP, 179.

14. SLC to CLW, 8 February 1885, in Webster, *Mark Twain, Businessman*, 299.

15. http://www.twainquotes.com/18850319.html, June 7, 2006.

16. Twain, *Autobiography*, 236.

17. SLC to CLW, 13 July 1884, in Webster, *Mark Twain, Businessman*, 268.

18. Albert Bigelow Paine, ed., *Mark Twain's Notebook* (New York: Harper & Brothers Publishers, 1935), 175.

19. Twain, *Autobiography*, 236–237.

20. CLW to SLC, 14 February 1885, in Webster, *Mark Twain, Businessman*, 302–303.

21. Paine, *Mark Twain's Notebook*, 176.

22. Twain, *Autobiography*, 246.

23. SLC to CLW, 11 April 1885, in Webster, *Mark Twain, Businessman*, 314.

24. SLC to W. D. Howells, 5 May 1885, Letters, vol. III.

25. SLC to Henry Ward Beecher, 11 September 1885, Letters, vol. III.

26. Twain, *Autobiography*, 251–252.

27. SLC to CLW, 11 June 1886, in Webster, *Mark Twain, Businessman*, 361.
28. CLW to Samuel E. Moffett, 24 December 1886, *Notebooks & Journals*, vol. III (1883–1891), 322–323.
29. Walter A. Friedman, *Birth of a Salesman* (Cambridge: Harvard University Press, 2004), 45.
30. Ibid., p. 47.
31. Ibid., p. 46.
32. SLC to Webster, Summer 1885 (no date given), in Webster, *Mark Twain, Businessman*, 332.
33. SLC to CLW, undated 1885, in Webster, *Mark Twain, Businessman*, 323.
34. Friedman, *Birth of a Salesman*, 49; and Powers, *Mark Twain: A Life*, 504.
35. SLC to W. D. Howells, 2 December 1885, Letters, vol. III.
36. SLC to FJH, 12 July 1886, LTHP, 199, 200.
37. Twain, *Autobiography*, 253.
38. Powers, *Mark Twain: A Life*, 505.
39. CLW to SLC, 19 February 1886, in Gold, *Hatching Ruin*, 39; and FJH to SLC, 20 July 1886, LTHP, 201.
40. Powers, *Mark Twain: A Life*, 514.
41. CLW to Your Excellency, 29 November 1890, in Webster, *Mark Twain, Businessman*, 394–395.
42. CLW to SLC, 8 April 1887, and SLC to CLW, 10 April 1887, LTHP, 215–216.

Smoking Inspires Brainstorming and Problem Solving

43. SLC to Reverend Twichell, 19 December 1870, Letters, vol. II.
44. http://www.cigaraficionado.com/Cigar/CA_Profiles/People_Profile/0,2540,43,00.html.
45. Mark Twain, "Smoking as Inspiration," reprinted in Charles Neider, ed., *Life as I Find It* (New York: Harper & Row, 1977), 202–203.

Chapter Eight   **A Shakespearean Business Tale**

1. SLC to CLW, 28 July 1885, and SLC to CLW, 4 April 1885, in Webster, *Mark Twain, Businessman*, 330 and 307–308.
2. SLC to CLW, 6 April 1885, in Webster, *Mark Twain, Businessman*, 310.
3. *Notebooks & Journals*, vol. III (1883–1891), 241; Powers, *Mark Twain: A Life*, 510.
4. Gold, *Hatching Ruin*, 39.
5. SLC to Pamela Moffett, 18 December 1887, Letters, vol. IV.
6. SLC to OC, 3 October 1888, Letters, vol. IV; and Powers, *Mark Twain: A Life*, 526.
7. Dean Sage to SLC, 19 November 1889, *Notebooks & Journals*, vol. III (1883–1891), 527.
8. SLC to CLW, 14 December 1886, LTHP, 211.
9. Paine, *Mark Twain's Notebook*, 203.
10. SLC to CLW, 17 April 1887, Webster, *Mark Twain, Businessman*, 379.
11. SLC to CLW, 3 August 1887, LTHP, 221.
12. SLC to EB, 24 June 1876, LTHP, 99.
13. SLC to OC, 7 September 1887, LTHP, 229–230.
14. Twain, *Autobiography*, 256.
15. Ibid., 246–247.
16. Ibid., 248.
17. SLC to CLW, 28 December 1887, and CLW to SLC, 29 December 1887, LTHP, 241–242.
18. Gold, *Hatching Ruin*, 70.
19. Powers, *Mark Twain: A Life*, 525.
20. CLW to Daniel Whitford, 31 December 1888, in Webster, *Mark Twain, Businessman*, 391.
21. CLW to Pamela A. Moffett, 1 July 1889, in Gold, *Hatching Ruin*, 132-133.
22. Mollie Clemens to SLC, 30 April 1891, in Gold, *Hatching Ruin*, 134.

23. SLC to OC, 5 January 1889, Letters, vol. IV.

24. SLC to Howells, 21 October 1889, in Powers, *Mark Twain: A Life*, 530.

25. Powers, *Mark Twain: A Life*, 531.

26. SLC to Jos. T. Goodman, 31 March and 22 June 1890, Letters, vol. IV.

27. SLC to Joseph T. Goodman, 7 October and 29 November, 1889: and Joe Goodman to SLC, 26 July 1890, in Powers, *Mark Twain: A Life*, 530.

28. Powers, *Mark Twain: A Life*, 531.

29. SLC to Joe Goodman, 22 February 1891, in Powers, *Mark Twain: A Life*, 536.

30. Paine, *Mark Twain's Notebook*, 211.

31. SLC to FJH, 12 November 1888, LTHP, 249–250.

32. SLC to FJH, 27 December 1890, LTHP, 265–266.

33. http://www.twainquotes.com/Lawyer.html, March 13, 2006.

34. SLC to FJH, 11 November 1890, LTHP, 264.

35. SLC to CLW, 1 March 1887, Powers, 525.

36. Gold, *Hatching Ruin*, 132.

37. SLC to FJH, 14 April 1891, Letters, vol. IV.

38. SLC to Mr. Hall, 27 November 1891, Letters, vol. IV.

39. Powers, *Mark Twain: A Life*, 536.

40. Olivia Clemens to FJH, 21 January 1892; and SLC to FJH, 25 January 1892, LTHP, 302 and 304.

41. SLC to FJH, 26 and 28 December 1892 and 1 January 1893, LTHP, 329–332.

42. Twain, *Autobiography*, 257.

Image Is Everything, But Interviews Are Twaddle

43. Twain, *Life As I Find It*, 38-42.

44. Twain, *Autobiography*, 356.

45. SLC to Edward W. Bok, undated but circa 1888, Letters, vol. IV.

Chapter Nine   Enduring Financial Crisis and Adversity

1. http://en.wikipedia.org/wiki/1893, March 26, 2006.
2. SLC to FJH, 8 July 1892, Letters, vol. IV.
3. SLC to FJH, 1 January 1893, Letters, vol. IV.
4. SLC to FJH, 28 January 1893, Letters, vol. IV.
5. SLC to FJH, 3 February 1893, LTHP, 337.
6. SLC to FJH, 8 March 1893, and FJH to SLC, 10 March 1893, LTHP, 340-341.
7. SLC to FJH, 30 May 1893, Letters, vol. IV.
8. SLC to FJH, 2 June 1893, and FJH to SLC, 16 June 1893, LTHP, 343–345.
9. SLC to FJH, 26 June 1893, LTHP, 346–347.
10. Olivia L. Clemens (OLC) to FJH, 27 June 1893, Letters, vol. IV.
11. SLC to FJH, 3 July 1893, Letters, vol. IV.
12. SLC to FJH, 8 July 1893, and FJH to SLC, 23 June and 3 July 1893, LTHP, 349–350.
13. SLC to FJH, 18 and 26 July 1893, LTHP, 351–352.
14. SLC to FJH, 30 July 1893; FJH to SLC, 24 July 1893; and SLC to FJH, 9 August 1893, LTHP, 355, 357, 358.
15. SLC to FJH, 14 August 1893, LTHP, 359–360.
16. SLC to FJH, 26 July 1893, Letters, vol. IV.
17. SLC to FJH, 14 August 1893, LTHP, pp. 358–9.
18. Twain, *Autobiography*, 257; SLC to OC, 17 September 1893, in Powers, *Mark Twain: A Life*, 554.
19. It is an oft quoted line, reprinted at http://www.salwen.com/mtbelle.html.
20. FJH to SLC, 18 October 1893, reprinted in Lewis Leary, ed., *Mark Twain's Correspondence with Henry Huttleston Rogers* (University of California Press, 1969), 11 (hereafter "CHHR").
21. SLC to OLC, 18 October 1893, Letters, vol. IV.

Are Ethics for Fools?

22. Mark Twain's 70th birthday speech, December 5, 1905, http://www.search-engine-lists.com/marktwain/70th-birthday

.html; Mark Twain, "Morals and Memory," reprinted in *Mark Twain's Speeches* (New York: Harper & Brothers, 1910), 225.

Chapter Ten Salvaging a Career and Dignity

1. Powers, *Mark Twain: A Life*, 545; Paine, *Mark Twain's Notebook*, 233, 231.
2. Gold, *Hatching Ruin*, 32, 45; and CHHR, 31.
3. SLC to OLC, 25 December 1893, Letters, vol. IV.
4. SLC to Livy, 9 December 1893, in Powers, *Mark Twain: A Life*, 555.
5. SLC to OLC, 9 December 1893, and SLC to OLC, 13 January 1894, CHHR, 17, 19.
6. SLC to Olivia, 15 January 1894, in Powers, *Mark Twain: A Life*, 559.
7. SLC to OLC, 27–30 January 1894, CHHR, 20.
8. SLC to HHR, 4 March 1894, and SLC to Arthur S. Hardy, 3 February 1894, CHHR, 38, 10.
9. SLC to OLC, 15 February 1894, Letters, vol. IV.
10. SLC to HHR, 16 June 1894. CHHR, p. 66.
11. SLC to HHR, 7 October 1894, in Powers, *Mark Twain: A Life*, 561.
12. According to those letters documented by the Mark Twain Project, he wrote Rogers 51 times in 1894.
13. SLC to HHR, 29–30 November 1894. CHHR, 99–100.
14. SLC to HHR, 22 December 1894, Letters, vol. IV.
15. SLC to HHR, 27 December 1894, Letters, vol. IV.
16. SLC to HHR, 2 January 1895, Letters, vol. IV.
17. Powers, *Mark Twain: A Life*, 561; Webster, *Mark Twain, Businessman*, 171, 311.
18. http://www.twainquotes.com/Invention.html, April 6, 2006.
19. SLC to Pamela Moffett, 25 February 1894, LTHP, 364.
20. SLC to Olivia Clemens, 16 April 1894, LTHP, 364–365.
21. Powers, *Mark Twain: A Life*, 558.
22. Twain, *Autobiography*, 258.

23. SLC to Olivia Clemens, 16 April 1894, LTHP, 365.

24. LTHP, 365.

25. Twain, *Autobiography*, 260-261.

26. SLC to OLC, 22 April 1894, Letters, vol. IV.

27. Twain, *Autobiography*, 260-261

28. HHR to SLC, 1 June 1894, CHHR, 59–60.

29. Olivia Clemens to SLC, 31 July 1894, in Powers, *Mark Twain: A Life*, 559.

30. SLC to HHR, 24 September 1894, CHHR, 77–78.

31. Twain, *Autobiography*, 261.

32. SLC to HHR, 21 January 1895, CHHR, 119.

33. SLC to HHR, 8-9 February 1895, CHHR, 129.

34. SLC to HHR, 20-22 July 1895, CHHR, 172-173; Interview with *New York Times*, August 17, 1895, CHHR, 181–182.

35. SLC to HHR, 25 June 1895; OLC to HHR, 27 June 1895; SLC to HHR, 14 July 1895; and HHR to SLC, 16 July 1895, CHHR, 157, 158–159, 166–167.

36. SLC to HHR, 20–22 July 1895, CHHR, 172.

37. SLC to HHR, 24 July 1895, and SLC to HHR, 20 September 1896, CHHR, 173–174, 236.

38 "Mark Twain's Plan of Settlement," *New York Times*, August 17, 1895.

39. Twain, *Autobiography*, 263–264.

40. SLC to Pamela A. Moffett, 7 June 1897, in Gold, *Hatching Ruin*, 154.

41. SLC to HHR, 10 September 1896, CHHR, 234.

42. Twain, *Autobiography*, 259.

43. SLC to HHR, 26 October 1896, CHHR, 241–242.

44. SLC to HHR, 23 June 1897, CHHR, 286–287, 289.

45. SLC to HHR, 10–11 November 1897 and 29 December 1897, CHHR, 303, 310.

46. SLC to HHR, 6 August 1897, and SLC to HHR, 10–11 November 1897, CHHR, 296–298, 303; CHHR, 320–321, 193.

47. SLC to HRR, 19 August 1898, CHHR, 357.

48. SLC to HHR, 7 March 1898, CHHR, 325.

49. HHR to SLC, 10 April 1896, CHHR, 203.

50. Kaplan, *Singular Mark Twain*, 565.

"Avoid My Example"

50. Mark Twain, "Business," http://www.search-engine-lists .com/marktwain/business.html.

Chapter Eleven   **Back in the Saddle**

1. Twain, *Autobiography*, 263–264.

2. SLC to HRR, 10 July 1898, CHHR, 352.

3. SLC to HHR, 26 September, 2 November, and 6–7 November 1898, CHHR, 365–366, 371, 374.

4. SLC to HRR, 8–13 December 1898, CHHR, 380.

5. CHRR, 384 and 386; and SLC to HRR, 24 January 1899, CHHR, 385.

6. CHHR, 392.

7. SLC to HRR, 10 May and 6 June 1899, CHHR, 395, 398.

8. SLC to HHR, 3 September 1899, CHHR, 409.

9. SLC to HRR, 3 September and 17 November 1899, CHRR, 409, 415.

10. SLC to HRR, 19 February 1899, CHRR, 389.

11. Clemens spoke with Amelia Levetus on 15 March 1898, CHHR, 332.

12. SLC to HRR, 17–20 March 1898, CHHR, 327–331.

13. SLC to HHR, 24 March 1998, Letters, vol. IV.

14. CHRR, 344.

15. SLC to HRR, 11 March 1900, CHHR, 436; and Kaplan, *Singular Mark Twain*, 576.

16. Kaplan, *Singular Mark Twain*, 576–577.

17. Ibid., 576.

18. SLC to HRR, 8–9 April 1900, CHRR, 440.

19. Ibid., 438–441.

20. Kaplan, *Singular Mark Twain*, 576.

21. SLC to Margaret Carnegie, 28 May 1900, quoted in Peter Krass, *Carnegie* (New York: John Wiley & Sons, 2002), 401.

22. Justin Kaplan, *Mr. Clemens and Mark Twain, a Biography* (New York: Simon & Schuster, 1966), 352; SLC to HRR, 22 March 1904, CHRR, 561.
23. Charles Fairchild to SLC, 11 August 1902, CHHR, 492.
24. HHR to SLC, August 5, 1902, CHHR, p. 495.
25. SLC to HHR, 19 June 1901, CHHR, 462-463, 466, 479.
26. Katherine Harrison to SLC, 26 May 1904, CHHR, 568–569; and see CHHR, 606.
27. SLC to HRR, 11 March 1900, CHHR, 436.
28. SLC to HHR, 6 June 1904, CHHR, 569, 451.
29. SLC to Howells, 6 June 1904, in Powers, *Mark Twain: A Life*, 617; SLC to HHR, 7 August 1905, CHHR, 573.
30. *New York Times*, 19 January 1956

How to Live a Long, Successful Life

31. http://www.search-engine-lists.com/marktwain/70th-birthday.html.

INDEX